AF632255

APPRECIATION OF INDIAN ART
IDEALS & IMAGES

APPRECIATION OF INDIAN ART
IDEALS & IMAGES

Editors

C.P. SINHA

&

U.C. DWIVEDI

INDIAN ART HISTORY CONGRESS
GUWAHATI (ASSAM)
in association with
ARYAN BOOKS INTERNATIONAL
NEW DELHI

APPRECIATION OF INDIAN ART : IDEALS & IMAGES

ISBN-81-7305-291-3

© **Indian Art History Congress, Guwahati (Assam)**

No reproduction or translation of this book or part thereof in any form, except brief quotations, should be made without the written permission of the copyright holder and the publishers. The responsibility of the facts stated, opinions expressed and conclusions reached is entirely that of the authors.

First published in **2005** by
INDIAN ART HISTORY CONGRESS
Directorate of Archaeology Campus, G.N. Bordoloi Road,
Guwahati (Assam) - 781 001

in association with

ARYAN BOOKS INTERNATIONAL
Pooja Apartments, 4B, Ansari Road, New Delhi-110 002 (India)
Tel. : 23287589, 23255799; Fax : 91-11-23270385; E-mail : aryanbooks@vsnl.com

Computer Typeset at ABI Prints and Publishing Co., New Delhi
Printed in India at Print Perfect, New Delhi

Preface

We feel happy to introduce the monograph entitled "Appreciation of Indian Art : Ideals and Images" to the world of scholars. Art in India, as in other countries of the world, was principally devoted to the service of religion. It reflects the intimate relationship of ideas and life. Mythology, symbolism and iconography etc. are only vehicles or aids to understand the essence and spirit of Indian art. Each and every symbol and each and every icon in Indian art has a meaning and is expressed with a purpose under a śāstric prescription. As a matter of fact, unless and until we know the inner meaning of the art pieces, the philosophy behind the carving of the image, one can not appreciate the art piece or image in proper perspective.

The articles in this volume are all self explanatory and afford a fairly adequate idea of its contents. The authors have given a lucid exposition of the delicate theme, which is sure to stimulate further fascination on the topic by art lovers and scholars.

C.P. Sinha
U.C. Dwivedi

Contents

List of Illustrations

List of Contributors

Dr. Anand Prakash Srivastava
Department of History of Art, Banaras Hindu University, Varanasi - 221 005.

Dr. Arvind Mahajan
Patna Museum, Buddha Marg, Patna - 800 001.

Dr. B.L. Malla
Indira Gandhi National Centre for the Arts, Janpath, New Delhi - 110 001.

Dr. Bharti Barua
Head, Dept. of History, Guwahati University, Guwahati (Assam).

Dr. C.P. Sinha
Former Director, K.P. Jayaswal Research Institute, Patna.

Prof. Choodamani Nandagopal
Indira Gandhi National Centre for the Arts, Southern Regional Centre, 109, J.C. Road, Bangalore - 560 002.

Dr. D. Gangadaran
Reader in History, A.P.A. College, Palani, Tamil Nadu.

Prof. D.S. Somashekhar
Professor in History, Tunga Mahavidyalaya, Theerthahalli - 577 432, Shimoga, Karnataka.

Prof. G.C. Pande
Chairman, Indian Institute of Advanced Study, Shimla.

Dr. Gourisankar De
South Habra, P.O. Habra District, 24 Parganas, West Bengal - 743 263

Dr. H.C. Das
Former Superintendent of Museum, Govt.of Orissa, Bhubaneswar.

Dr. Indrani Choudhury
Dept. of History, L.C.B. College, Maligoan, Assam.

Dr. K. Ravikumar
S.G. Lecturer in Indian Culture, Arulmigu Palani Andavar College of Arts & Culture, Palani, Tamil Nadu.

Dr. Kalachand Chowdhury
95, LIC Township, Madhyamgram, Dist. North 24 Parganas - 700 129.

Dr. Kapila Vatsyayan
85, SFS Flats, Gulmohar Enclave, New Delhi - 110 049.

Dr. Kolluru Suryanarayana
Dept. of History & Archaeology, Andhra University, Visakhapatnam - 530 003.

Prof. Krishna Kumari Myneni
Professor, Dept. of History and Archaeology, Andhra University, Visakhapatnam - 530 003.

Dr. M. Venkatesan
Archaeologist & Research Scholar, Virudhungar District Historical Research Centre & Historical Exploration Centre, Rajapalayam - 626 117 (Tamil Nadu).

Prof. Manjusri Rao
Professor & Head, Prachya Niketan, G - 2/123, Gulmohar Colony, Love Homes, Bhopal - 462 016.

Prof. Maruti Nandan Tiwari
Dept. of History of Art, Faculty of Arts, Banaras Hindu University, Varanasi - 221 005.

Dr. Puspa Tiwari
Dept. of Ancient History Culture & Archaeology (CAS), University of Allahabad, Allahabad.

Dr. S.N. Shivarudraswamy
Professor & Head, Dept. of History, P.A. College, Tumkur Dist., Tiptur - 572 202 (Karnataka)

Smt. Sarvamangala. G
Lecturer, Dept of History and Archaeology, Kuvempu University, Shankaragahatta - 577 451, Shimoga - Karnataka.

Dr. Shanti Swaroop Sinha
Dept. of History of Art, Faculty of Arts, Banaras Hindu University, Varanasi - 221 005.

Dr. Shrinivas V. Padigar
Chairman, Dept. of Graduate Studies in Ancient Indian History & Epigraphy, Karnataka University, Dharwad - 580 003.

Appreciation of Indian Art : Theoretical Perspective

G.C. Pande

NATURE OF ART APPRECIATION

The enjoyment of art is the distinterested and critical contemplation of beauty, not the enjoyment of pleasure from the satisfaction of some desire.

Art is first and last a matter of enjoyment, but the enjoyment which art gives is of a unique kind *(vilakṣṇāsvaāda)*. It is quite different from other kinds of enjoyment in life *(alaukika)*. Commonly, enjoyments are based on the sensation of pleasure *(sukha saṁvedanā)*, privately enjoyed *(indrīya vikārātma, svagatāḥ)* resulting from gratification of some desire *(kāmabhogāḥ)*. Although wholly subjective *(bhogatṛṣṇāḥ)*, it is the experience of a real external object, which is endowed with causal efficiency *(artha kriyās amartha vastu)*. The enjoyment of such pleasure diminishes as it is continued and finally ceases. Such is the nature of pleasure in the enjoyment of natural objects and consumer goods.

The enjoyment of art by contrast is not produced by sensation directly but by the apprehension of the form of the object, which is accessible to contemplation *(bhāvanāyogya viṣayatā)*. The enjoyment of art is shareable and communicable *(vaitatyam)*. It is disinterested in the reality of the object as an object which can satisfy some desire. The contemplative enjoyment does not diminish or cease, it continues. Although objective, the enjoyment of art does not depend on the external reality of the causally efficient actual object.

The distinction of aesthetic from the hedonic enjoyment, however, is not absolute, and this leads to some serious confusion. The contemplatable art object is normally embedded in material media and the two appear to constitute a unity. The statue and the image, the coloured surface and the picture, sounds and melody are given virtually as inseparable. Statutes and pictures, thus, acquire market values also and their possession gives pleasures to the collector. Nature and natural beauty appear inseparable. Architectural objects and handicrafts have a clear use-value just as the other forms of art have in diverse social, religious and cultural situations. Besides, there is a grey area between the preparation of goods for hedonic enjoyment and of aesthetic objects. Landscape, gardening, culinary art, preparation of beverages like tea, coffee, cold drink and liquor, making of fashion-wear, etc., provide areas of appreciation in which the aesthetic dimension is not altogether absent. Although the enjoyment of tasting tea is private, the quality of the tea is objectively standardizable and tea drinking can be a social ceremony, its enjoyment is shareable. One may tire of consumption on single occasion but not of consumption as such. In this sense even the pursuit of ephemeral pleasures is endless. The subjectivity of such hedonic appreciation is modified by the fact that the taste for them is cultivated and seeks to be in conformity with some social reference.

One may see from this discussion that although aesthetic and hedonic appreciations are clearly distinguishable when the pleasure in question refers to the pleasure one derives in the course of satisfying a desire, however, pleasant sensations can be objectively judged by connoisseurs without reference to any subjective gratification. Thus, tastes, smells, colours and sounds are capable of being examined by experts with a view to determining which kinds are likely to be given more appreciation by the consumers. From the enjoyment of pleasure and satisfaction of desire *(bhogatṛṣṇā sukham)* to the enjoyment of beauty *(prāsādika rūpa darśanam),* there seems to be an evolutionary difference and emphasizing this factor of continuity has become of critical importance today. In all ages, objects of art, craft and consumption have been produced in different communities and classes in accordance with their own standards of making and judging the products of their efforts. In this complex web of life, distinct aesthetic styles interweave with those of technology and approved pattern of social consumption. Generally, however, a distinction is discernible between the folk and the elite styles of art and culture. Quite often the educated elite has created forms of high culture and art by transforming folk forms. As a result, these two levels of art and culture have traditionally remained in a harmonious balance. Today, however, with the emergence of mass power and the role of the media, aesthetic taste and standard run the great danger of vulgarization. Even while their dissemination is apparently taking place, the distinctiveness of the aesthetic needs to be specially emphasized today so that the process of dissemination of art can be joined to the process of education and refinement.

RELATIVITY OF ART APPRECIATION AND AESTHETIC JUDGEMENT

It is a widespread myth that there is a universal and unique science of aesthetics. When Baumgarten founded aesthetics in its modern form in the 18th century, it was based on the notion that aesthetic value is a distinct and unique value. It was been hoped since then to discover this unique value in all forms of art and to connect this value with the manner of presentation of art objects in different mediums. Such a task faces many problems of great difficulty. There are epistemological problems in determining the nature of aesthetic judgement. There are ontological problems about the nature of art object or of aesthetic value. There are strictly aesthetic problems of connecting the medium, the presentation and the judgement. There is the psychological and social question of taste. All these questions have led to an increasing literature of research in aesthetics. The peculiar difficulty in aesthetic research is that it presupposes, on the one hand, the heritage of philosophical theories, on the other hand it has to take note of aesthetic experience and judgement dependent on the tradition of creativity and criticism in art. It follows that aesthetic theory and aesthetic judgement depend not on rational reflection over what is universally given in nature or in experience, they depend on rational reflection in the light of what is given in culture. Thus, behind Baumgarten's assumption of a unique aesthetic value lies the distinctive ethos of his age. This cultural relativity of aesthetic judgement and theory may be illustrated by a few examples. Kant, the first major modern philosophical voice in aesthetics, seeking to formulate a transcendental epistemology of aesthetic judgement presupposes not only the general principles of transcendental philosophy of critical judgement but also the typical distinction of pleasure, goodness, beauty and sublimity as values. For him, cognitive truth is identical with scientific truth and the defining characteristic of beauty is that its contemplation gives disinterested pleasure. As Cassirrer summarizes, Kant states that his analysis is "to show that taste must be regarded as a critical faculty by which an object is estimated in reference to the free conformity to the law *(Gesetzmassigkeit)* of the imagination". For Kant, taste is the faculty of aesthetic judgement. It judges an object to be beautiful if its contemplation produces disinterested delight. This feeling is further regarded by the subject of judgement as universally valid. Since aesthetic judgement is not a logical cognitive judgement, its feeling of universality is only subjective. This subjective universality depends on premising what Kant calls common sense.

It is true that his great successor Hegel, defining beauty as the absolute shining through the veil of sense, tried to give aesthetics a rational basis. His lectures on the History of Fine Arts tried to show that the actual historical developments of the arts parallel the dialetic of reason. If Hegel was wholly successful in his enterprise, his theory of art would be final. However, even with Hegel's system, art belongs to the realm of the absolute spirit, and thus reason in this sphere must be distinguished from abstract logical reason as well as from objective social reason. What is more, on Hegel's assumption, art necessarily gives place to religion and philosophy in the order of rational development. As is well known, Croce had already pointed out the confusion of contradiction and distinction in Hegelian dialectics when applied outside the realm of logic.

Against Kant, attempt was to relate critical judgement to the idea as operative in self-consciousness and cultural experience. That is to say, that Hegel tried to discover the specific character of rationality embodied in art as a cultural form. It is distinct from abstract logical rationality and it is above what Kant calls understanding *(Verstand). Vernunft* operates synthetically; one is tempted to think a bit as a kind of rational intuition, something that Kant rejected. However, most art critics would accept the idea that critical judgement depends on the simultaneous operation of intuitive comprehension of the whole as well as on rational discrimination. Since this intuition is connected with sensibility, it would easily be continuous with imagination. On the other hand, since the rationality of art forms and judgements is considered by Hegel to be related to historical development also, it would, by implication, appear to function within culturally approved tastes and standards. Even though the rationality of organization in sensuous form is the basis of judgement in art, the historicity of reason here appears to bring in the relativity of tastes. For Hegel, however, the dialectical character of reason enables it to transcend the limitation of its particular epochal forms. Thus, for him romanticism succeeds and supercedes classicism just as classicism must supercede oriental symbolism.

Bosanquet's history of aesthetics rightly points out that aesthetic standards presuppose the existing traditions of art and the world of beauty created by art objects. It is this dependance on historical art experience that makes aesthetics, the philosophy of art, historically variable. The universality sought by classical art is the universality of typical perfection within a type, whereas in modern art expression of individual character becomes the ideal. Thus, classical Greek art of the Hellenic Age as preserved in later copies, seeks to represent this perfection of ideally formed feminine and masculine bodies. What it seeks to represent is the generic character in its perfection. In modern art, on the contrary, the form is expressive of individual character.

The paintings of Rembrandt or the plays of Shakespeare illustrate this. Bosanquet's exposition is brilliant. It still continues the Hegelian notion of art as sensuous form exhibiting reason as the principle of identity in difference. At the same time it makes the role of actual art experience in the formation of aesthetic theory clearer.

ART AS IMAGINATION

It is Croce who most clearly distinguishes the primary imaginative reality of art from its sensuous embodiment in some material medium. What normally goes by the name of art is only the sensuous material embodiment. In the case of Hellenic art, this largely perished but the imaginative reality from which it was derived, was re-embodied in Roman copies. It is true that copies are never the same as the original. But that does not negate the distinction between the primary mental image and the sensuous material statue. It only shows the unique dexterity and skill of the original artist in working on the material medium. It is course not to be denied that quite often the artist fully realizes the image within himself. Also, while he seeks to actualize it in the medium, the driving image in his mind often remain incompletely articulated till it is fully expressed in the medium. The original image or intuition is like a flash, which prompts the artists to explore it by fully expressing it. This expressive urge is often described as creativity. Just as thoughts need words and there is a natural urge to preserve the words through permanent graphic records, similarly, the mental intuition or image is sought to be fully expressed and communicated objectively for its permanence by its embodiment in material medium.

Some may be tempted to say that the image is nothing but the vague intention of the artist, that the real objective art is the articulated medium and the image is only the mental impression of this real material object. Just as in the case of natural beauty, what lies in the natural object may be reproduced in imagination. Nevertheless, it might be argued that the primacy belongs to the natural object and the image is only a copy. But can we really think of art objects as analogous to a natural object? The question is not of the artificiality of the art object because its materiality belongs to nature. The question really is that even natural objects, when they are considered as beautiful objects, cease to be merely natural. They turn into images for the spectator. The sunset seen by the tired workman hurrying to go home, is a mere natural scene but for a painter of landscape it is a spectacle into which the materiality or the causal underpinning of its natural basis does not enter at all. It could be an illusion. An illusion appears as beautiful as a natural object. Indeed it has been competently argued that there is no art without illusion.

This distinction between the idea or ideal form and the actually embodied forms or the forms of natural objects is so firm and clear that it is undeniable. All engineering rests on the primacy of geometrical or abstract forms. The whole of science presupposes the primacy of the abstract and non-sensuous form, which can be apprehended by abstract reason and on the basis of which the sensuous natural world can be understood and controlled. It is on this account that Plato had condemned the common notion of art as the representation of natural forms. Since natural forms copy ideal forms, such representational art will become the copy of a copy and thrice removed from the truth.

The irreproducibility of actual or material objects of visual art may be contrasted with the equally patent reproducibility or creative reproducibility of musical compositions. The same composition may be rendered differently by different musicians. It is the same with theatre. The plays of Shakespeare have been rendered differently by different actors and directors over centuries. The composition of the play remains the same. Their objective or communicable essence remains the same but the rendering of the expression varies. Literary work may be translated into many languages. It is true that the original and the translation rarely have the same quality. Nevertheless, all these examples do show that an art object not only has the material medium but also a form embodied in it, which is always suggestive of an ideal form.

We might at this point summarize some of the general results. Although publicly given as well as found as material object, what makes an object an object of art is that it is an imaginative creation. It is in essence a mental image, intuition or idea, which is evocative, significant and expressive of values. It is an image in a very peculiar and unusual sense. Normally, the word image stands for the representation and reproduction of form. The image is an iconic symbol; it is something, which stands for something else by resembling it in some way. An image may be used as part of a discourse or context and as such may signify some meaning into which the object directly represented may associatively enter. Thus, a picture of the moon in a highly stylized form is a pictogram for moon in the Chinese script, but it can go on to signify many ideas and thus a pictogram becomes an ideogram. Similarly, in art the mental image is not separable from the idea. What is directly represented and what is associatively signified, form one whole and this whole as an intuition, which enters conciousness immediately, brings to the latter a whole complex of ideas and feelings. This evocation of feeling is essential for the aesthetic image; otherwise it would turn into a scientific diagram or picture, which has an ideal meaning but no felt significance.

We have defined art as the embodiment of a mental image in a material medium, provided the mental image is evocative of feeling and at the same time has an ideal significance and provided that its rendering in the medium has a perfectionist quality. Idea has the sense of vision or intuitive apprehension, though it is also used for logically determined concepts. The difference between idea as an intuitive vision and idea as logical conception should be kept in mind but although they have a qualitative distinction, they need not be entitatively different. If a determinative or negative aspect of the concept is emphasized, then such a conceptual idea can only have a subsidiary role in art. If attention is focused on this conceptual aspect, the language of art will turn into the language of logic and cease to be felt or evocative. What is relevant in art is not a logical system of concepts but rather the idea as a compelling vision, and intuitively apprehended *idee* force.

The notion of image as copy needs some further clarification. What is it that the mental image imitates? That art is some kind of imitation, is an idea, which has been widely current since Aristotle and Bharata. Thus, the image of Buddha copies some actual human figure. Do images of God resemble the actual forms of God? Does the actor who enacts the role of Rāma resemble Rāma in any sense? Bhaṭṭa Nāyaka in his critique of the imitationism of Śrī Śaṅkuka has given us a devastating critique. It is clear that the so-called image, imitation or copy has no original to fall back upon. It is not even the representation of an idea because an idea subsists intellectually not imaginatively. An idea is abstract while an image is concrete. The concrete structure, of course, is governed by abstract regularities, but the mathematical sense of correspondence or imaging is hardly relevant to art where wholly regular mathematical forms and curves are inadequate. What then can be the meaning of an image? The material art object certainly produces an image on the mind of the spectator and the culturally competent spectator connects the image with an ideal signification. The immediacy of the image and its experiential association with the significance gives it an evocative character. The image is not a copy but an expressive symbol, which may utilize images in the ordinary sense as elements in its structure. The Buddha image, e.g. utilizes an idealized human figure within the context of a mendicant *yogī* attaining enlightenment and poised in meditation or moved by compassion. It is a picture of the historical figure of Śākya Gautama.Whether the *bimba* was heavenly received at Śrāvastī or copied the *nirmāṇakāya,* it was certainly not a portrait.

It has to be remembered that imagination has commonly been regarded as a fanciful creation of images, a faculty which, if pushed to the extreme, becomes hallucinatory and is seen in its full power in dreams. In this sense imagination is basically synthetic reproduction, the faculty of *kalpanā* or making on the basis of refashioned memory fragments.

TWO MEANINGS OF ART

It had been mentioned before that the aesthetics or the science of art appreciation uses the word art in a wide and all-inclusive sense even though many museologists and art historians in India use it in the narrow sense of the visual art alone. The *Nātyaśātra* of Bharata deals with all the performing arts and of these dance and drama have a pronounced visual aspect also. The *Śilpaśātras* include generally architecture, painting and sculpture but in the Purāṇas such as *Agni Purāṇa* and *Viṣṇudharmottara Purāṇa,* the continuity of these art forms with the performing and literary arts is recognized. The word *kalā* has been used in the ancient tradition in an even more inclusive sense so as to include minor arts and crafts also. In Vedic literature *śilpa* refers equally to artefacts and musical structure. Both are brought under a common definition *'Ātmakṛtirvaiśilpam'*. *Śilpa* is the creativity of the self. *Kavi* and *karu* both had the sense of poet or maker, as also in Greek. Making, creating or fashioning of form or *rūpa,* sensible or intelligible, is the essential hallmark of art. Art would thus include not only the visual arts but also the performing literary arts.

In traditional usage, *śilpa* signifies the visual arts including architecture but is also used widely to denote all kinds of useful arts as well. The sharp distinction between the useful and the arts is a relatively modern distinction, which was canonized by the new science of aesthetics founded by Baumgarten. That there is a distinct aesthetic value distinguishable from all other values, that beauty is a thing apart and yet the common pursuit of all the different arts, is the basic assumption of this modern aesthetics. That beauty may subsist along with functional use is amply proved not only by architecture alone but also by the decorative arts. Imagine an architectural monument or a decorative piece which has no use at all. However, beautiful in appearance, it will appear to be toy-like and that will seriously detract from its value. Not merely this, but even in sculpture and painting the objects normally have some functional value. They may decorate a building or a city, or they may be objects of reverence, or may commemorate some event, or celebrate some ideal, they generally have some representation or significance, some symbolic aspects. If we turn to the performing arts—and it is necessary to consider art in its broadest sense to discuss any theoretical issues in aesthetics—we find that drama is never a meaningless charade of actors coming and going. Even after leaving behind its origin in myths and legends, it has been a representation of human reality in its most significant aspect. The greatest of dramatists has advised the actors through Prince Hamlet that the perpetual function of art is to put the mirror unto nature. Here aesthetic value is inseparable from the profoundest cognitive value of self-knowledge. Music has often been regarded as the purest, the most subjective, the highest of the arts. 'All arts are said to aspire unto the condition of music'. Music seems to be without any representation or meaning and thus to ideally exhibit the purely aesthetic dimension of value. However, music has always had as pronounced a social function as architecture. It is used in devotion, in festivities, in war, in entertainment. It is undeniable that music does not merely give an immediate pleasure to the ears but profoundly affects the human heart. It can rouse one to action, it can be gay, it can be sad, and it can appear to be infinitely significant without actually saying anything. Susan Langer has congently argued that music is capable of suggestively representing the rhythm of life.

We turn to the literary arts like poetry or fiction; their connection with the whole human life hardly needs to be argued. Vyāsa, Vālmīki, Shakespeare entertained and enlightened at the same time. They are essential to liberal education as well as to the formation of aesthetic taste.

From this brief review it would appear that although the different arts differ in their specific media and technique, they agree not only in the fact that they often serve a social function but, over and above, they have an intimate connection with it; they pursue a common aesthetic value. Since the immediate presentations of the objects of different kinds of arts have generic differences, this common value can only be some psychic state or its content, a feeling or a felt truth.

ART OBJECT AS *RŪPA*

What a visual art presents is a *rūpa.* The presentation in drama and dance is *rūpa* along with movement and rhythm. Music presents rhythmic and tonal structures of musical sound, *śruti* and *svara.* The rhythmic pattern of notes is also *rūpa* in the sense of the perpetual form in which elements are combined in specific determinate ways to form a coherent whole. This pattern, although diachronic, has to be perceived as a whole. This diachronicity of the pattern or form of what is immediately presented, is common to the performing and literary arts. Actions, sounds and words are all spread in time. Consequently their presentations are not a simultaneous whole, such as we find in the purely visual arts, which presents spatial structures or structures distributed in space. Nevertheless, despite this difference in the role of space and time in different arts, they all have in common the fact that what they present has to be intuited as a whole. Not only this, what they present is not exhausted by its immediacy. Shapes, colour, musical sounds are in themselves immediate and momentary, sensory, with a distinct qualia of their own. Nevertheless, the sensory effects in their immediacy or separation are only the tangential points from which the curve of the art object is constructed. The mere musicality of a note in terms of its timbre, pitch or duration, or the mere hue and tone of a colour or mere geometrical elements of a spatial form do not constitute an intuitable integral whole, that is *rūpa* in the proper sense. What is presented immediately in arts is only a surface, which intimates a pattern or significance. The presentation of *rūpa* is not merely form but sign *(nimitta lakṣaṇa)*. It is not necessary that the significance should be clearly verbalisable or lend itself to conceptual explications, as is the case in the cognitive and theoretical contexts. It may be recalled that Croce had emphasized that art has the peculiarity of appearing to say without saying anything. In this sense it is close to nature. We have to decipher its message like the riddle of the sphinx (*Nājāne nakshatron se kaun/nimantran detā mujhko maun)*. The significance of art is not conceptualizable as a logical sentence. It is signified ultimately through the power of suggestion or *dhvani*. In fact, even in literary arts what the words say literally is rarely the ultimate meaning of the literary piece. Its real meaning is often revealed metaphorically *(Lakṣā, Rūpaka)* or through indirect suggestions emanating from the associations of words and meanings with emotional states *(vyanjanā* or *dhvani)*. The apprehension of *rūpa* is neither purely sensory nor purely intellectual. It has the immediacy-characteristic of sense perception, but also the intelligibility of a pattern such as is the characteristic of the cognitive apprehensions of symbols. More than this it has the moving immediacy of feeling. It has been described as 'perspicuous and poignant' but these adjectives only describe obvious and self-evident characteristics of the experience of an art object. They do not indicate how these characteristics arise in the experience of an art object because these characteristics are of the experience rather than of the object.

In the Indian tradition, *rūpa* has been a word of high antiquity, going back to the Vedas. Thus, Indra is said to acquire many *rūpa* by his mysterious power or *māyā*. Agni entering the world assumes different forms or *rūpa*. *Śilpa* is what has an appropriate *rūpa, pratirupa*. In *Nātyaśāstras* dramatic forms are *rūpa*. The authenticating form impressed in the coins is also *rūpa*. The diverse forms which the same word acquires in different grammatical formations are also *rūpa*. *Rūpa* does have a sense of form, which manifests something more than itself. It is a significant form though the significance may be implicit and contextual. In *Śilpasāstras, rūpa* is one of the six *aṅgas* and has the sense of distinctive form or character through which diffferent types of objects may be recognized or represented. Quite often *rūpa* in *rūpa bhedah* has been taken to mean the form belonging to the object to be represented. In that case *rūpa* becomes resemblance, representation or imitation. This interpretation cannot really be sustained because resemblance or *sādṛśya* has been mentioned as a separate *aṅga*. What is more, do gods have actual forms? The *devatā* is *nirākāra* or formless by nature. The forms attributed to the gods are only imaginative *(kalpanā āropa)* symbols (*taṭastha lakṣaṇa, vyañjaka)* which are aids in worship and meditation. *Rūpa* is not *svarūpa* or inherent essence but appearance or another *ābhāsa* or *pratibhāsa*. So the Buddha icon is called a *bimba,* which is the same as *pratibimba*. Even where the *rūpa* is representative of actual objects with their own form, the Indian sculptural tradition insists on realistic representation only with respect to animal life. This fact was noted and highlighted by Coomaraswamy but wholly misconstrued by Western scholars like Marshall. Marshall thought that the realistic representation of animals in *Aśokan* sculpture was based on the model of Greek art. On the other hand the figures of gods or human beings are generally idealized or conceptualized. The element of *sādṛśya* emphasizes the fact that the symbolic imaginative aspect of representation should not become so abstract and fantastic as to make the presentation *unintelligible or incredible*.

Rūpa is the perpetual or immediately intuitable aspect of the art object. Why is it appreciated? The reasons have been diversely mentioned as the excellence or flawlessness of the representation or its decorativeness or its effectiveness in communicating some valuable meaning or its evocativeness. We have already argued that representation is not a necessary or major elements in *rūpa*. Quite often *rūpa* appearing to be an icon is really a symbol and in many arts, such as music, not iconic at all. The image of the Buddha is recognized by its signs *(lakṣaṇas),* not by any resemblance to someone never seen by the spectators. Perhaps it may be said that the image has to appear real, natural and alive, without being really so just as characters in story appear real without being historical. Coomaraswamy had emphasized how *cetanā* or vibrant vitality has to be evident in the images. The question however arises: Does the appearance of reality by itself lead to appreciation? It can lead to the appreciation of skillfulness in the representation observing a robot or a puppet. One may admire the skill of the maker but it is not a sufficient reason for aesthetic appreciation for such objects. The theatre uses *āhārya* or stage properties to heighten the sense of reality. But it also uses to produce hypnotic suggestibility. The fact is that the camera and the screen have at once achieved totally illusory effects but therby have shown the hollowness of the naturalistic hypothesis. The illusion of life must appear an illusion to enter art; otherwise, it would merely by a scene out of life perceived in the ordinary way. Life, doubtless, may be amusing, entertaining or moving, but unless is perceived as a spectacle without personal involvement, these features of entertainment, etc., will not be perceived. The humorous person acts like a witty author or enacts a role, thereby, transforming a bit of life. What is undeniable is that in the process of the appreciation of art object, a certain sense of illusion must be mentioned so that what is vividly apprehended in art can for the time being keep the attention of the spectator from wandering into natural reality of the world as well as of his own private life. *Rūpa* must be apprehended as a part of a self-sufficient world, not as an object placed within the natural world. To borrow a phenomenological term, the art object has to be *'bracketed'*. The picture, though framed, on the wall has to be seen in the picture-space. It is the frames, which are part of the wall space. Each picture provides the spectator a door from which he enters a new space and world. In actual life, one is an actor, however casual or accidental. In art, one is a spectator and distanced from the object. If the realistic representation of life does not betray its status as representation, the reaction in the spectator would be similar to those of the actor in life. If the representation is not sufficiently life like, it would make 'willing suspension of disbelief' impossible. Even the most realistic or naturalistic representation in fictional literature on screen or portraiture is already understood as something different from the natural reality by the very fact of being a representation. The representation of life or nature *eo ipso* idealizes it and it is in this element of idealization that the originality and characteristic style of the artist enters. No two portraits are alike, nor even two snapshots. Similarly, some gifted people move through life viewing it as as aesthetic pageant like some *'jīvan mukta'* or liberated devotee seeing the *līlā* of God in life and history. In fact, everywhere, sometime or the other, one is able to glimpse this aesthetic moment. The awareness of natural beauty, romantic love or human compassion or the humorous aspects of things are accessible to most people, sometime or the other. For the moment, the transformation of the outlook transfigures the world. Art and nature are thus neither absolutely identified nor absolutely apart. When the art object, whether an image or a song or a dance or a ritual role are apprehended, within an actual social setting, what they serve to achieve is to transform the perception of the social occasion itself. Just as moonlight transforms objects of experience, similarly when we see the bridegroom in the attire of a prince on horseback with musicians, it helps us to forget the routine reality of the event. What art does is to transform nature into an ideal imaginative world. The film of drab familiarity, which covers things in everyday experience appears to be taken away for a moment.

RŪPA AND *RASA*

Aesthetic experience has a unique flavour or *rasa*. If *rūpa* is where the appreciation of art begins, *rasa* is where it culminates. *Rasa* has been defined as *samvid viśrānti* or repose in consciousness, *camatkāra* or the enjoyment of an original revelation or *cidāvaraṇabhaṅga,* i.e. the dropping of the veil from consciousness or as *bhagnāvaraṇacit,* i.e. the consciousness freed from its veil. It has to be remembered that the Upanisads describe ultimate consciousness as *rasa* or *ānanda.* Aesthetic *Rasa* however, is distinct from *rasa* in this metaphysical sense by virtue of being mediated by the felt experience of the art object (*bhāvopādhika)* it is the self-realization not of the self in its transcendent purity but through the *upādhi* or accident of *bhāva; bhāva* requires the presence of *vibhāva. Rūpa* is the *vibhāva*, which evokes *rasa* though *bhāva.* That is why the *Śilpa Saḍaṅga* after mentioning *rupabhedāḥ* or imaginative forms and *'pramāṇāni'* that is canonial proportions and measurements, goes on to mention *bhāva lāvanya yojanam.* The construction of *bhāva* and *lāvanya*—feeling and loveliness in the object—the reflection of its appropriateness to the *bhāva.*

It may be remarked that *bhāva,* commonly signifies an emotional mental emotional state *(vikāra),* which may be transient *(vyabhicāri* or *sañcāṛi)* or permanent (*sthāyī).* In aesthetic experience however, what causes the mental state is not real, the reactions also are, to borrow I.A. Richards phrase, only 'imaginal'. *Lāvanya* has been defined as the shimmering luminosity within the pearl, which is the analogue to what gleams through the limbs of the body as a whole. It is the indefinable beauty of the whole. It is not an innate feature of the external object. Beauty is not a natural quality of things but a quality protected within the phenomenon of aesthetic experience. To the eyes of the highly cultured but utilitarian Governor General, the Taj Mahal was nothing more than a waste of limestone. So many local rajas and zamindars implemented this idea by taking away the marble of the Amaravati stūpa. Loveliness lies in the eyes of the beholder.

It needs to be emphasized that the imaginative art object, that is, the images and ultimately the mental images, which constitute the art objects and are the starting point of aesthetic experience, have a multiple role. Very often the image has a symbolic connection with some idea or context. In this role, it is able to suggest socially held ideals to the spectator. The image of the Varāha at Udaigiri thus suggests a familiar Puranic myth and through the myth, the ideas of liberating the country from its submergence in *Śaka* rule. The *lakṣaṇas* of the Buddha image identify the Buddha and its particular pose. The many arms or faces of the deities not only identify them but symbolically convey their power and cosmic significance.

The process of art appreciation thus begins with the apprehension of *rūpa* and culminates in the apprehension of *rasa*. One might say that there is expressiveness or *vyañjakatva* in *rūpa,* which leads to *rasa*. Sometimes *rūpa* is directly expressive of a mental state, which leads immediately to *rasa*. This is, for example, the case in music, where the apprehension of the rhythmic note pattern modifies the state of the perceiving mind and that state is felt to be highly delectable *(rañjaka)*. In dance, the pattern of movement may also have a symbolic meaning and that meaning may be expressive of a mood or feeling. In drama, this happens on a larger scale. The acting on the stage directly enacts a story which in turn is expressive of a succession of feelings. Through these feelings, *rasa* is apprehended. Nicoll thus rightly renders *rasa* as total impression. So the classical theory of *rasa* as laid down by Bharata says that *'vibhāva anubhāva vyabhicārī saṁyogāt rasa niṣpattiḥ'*, i.e. *rasa* is manifested through the combination of *'vibhāva, anubhāva* and *vyabhicārī bhāva'*. Here the *vibhāva* is the object, which excites the feeling, *anubhāva* is the bodily expression of an emotional reaction, *vyabhicārī* is a transient feeling. It is through the spectacle of all these that the spectator attains the experience of *rasa*.

It has been argued by some critics that the theory of *rasa* is essentially a theory, which applies to drama or literature. It is true that the theory was first formulated in the context of drama but it was extended to literature and the other arts as well. In the case of music, the *svarayojanā* with its characteristic *lakṣaṇa* takes the place of *vibhāva* and while they heighten, intensify or arouse or melt states of the mind, which may not be definable in terms of specific emotions. These states of *śruti*, etc., manifest *mādhurya, ojas, prāsāda vikāsa*, etc., and these directly evoke *rasa*.

The observation of architectural forms of *vāstu rūpa,* similarly, affects the mind. The *vāstu* , may in its different parts or as a whole produce the sense of spaciousness or of constriction, of aspiring height or of squat strength, of ornamentation or simplicity. In the classical Hindu architecture, two kinds of movements are invariably present. One is from the exterior to the inner centre of *sanctum sanctorum*. This is the counterpart of the mystical movement of *'pratyāhāra'*. The second movement is the upward movement of aspiration, assent, and exultation. This is visually suggested by the *'śikhara'*. The ornamental forms and sculptures on the temple surfaces and columns on the walls not only serve the ornamental purpose but also represent the cosmos as a mythical design. The cosmos, person and the *'vāstu puruṣa'*, are all projections and emanations of the *puruṣa* in the heart, the light and the heart. The *vāstu* is something with which the spectator identifies himself. It represents his abode and location. The mind is the abode of the spirit, the body of the mind, the house of the body. Where the spirit is universal, the house is the cosmos. The temple is a representation of the essential form linking the individual to the cosmic person.

What kind of *rasa* is the temple connected with? The answer must be in terms of the *rasa,* which despite some variation, has to be that of devotion or is appropriate to the worship or contemplation of the deity. In non-mythic terms, it would be a particular mode of self-realization, in which man seeks to move to the centre of his Being and hoping to attain to its highest level. He notices the magic world and hopes to cross beyond it. *Mamevaye prapadyante, mayametam tarantite,* i.e. those who take refuge in me alone, they are able to cross this world of *māyā.* The glitter of the temple is the *Māyā;* the icon in the *garbhagṛha* is the lord. It follows with some variations therefore that the basic *rasa* would be the *rasa* of devotion or *bhakti.*

Vāstu means a dwelling, which forms an inseparable unity with its indwellers. *Vāstu* represents reality as the natural abode of the spirit. Empirical self-consciousness assumes this form—'I am an individual part of the social structure' *(varṇāsramādyabhimāna);* 'I am the dweller and user of the mind and the body' *(dehādyabhimāna).* Both these empirical identifications are fundamentally false. To realize its falsity, however, requires surrender through devotion to the Lord who is the innermost dweller and controller *(antaryāmi).* The temple and the temple worship are thus intended to help take man beyond the world of illusion, 'to the still point of the turning wheel'.

If we turn to the Buddhist cave temples, this would be clearer. Their primary purpose was meditation in the penumbra of the *Caitya* hall faintly illuminated from the *caitya gavākṣa.* Meditation in the cave, one might say, is the monumental expression of the standard mystical prescription. Stillness, silence, detachment are here a prelude to dynamic tranquility or *śānta rasa (nirvānam śāntam).* Architecture had many other forms, preserved and lost. Of secular architecture of ancient times, very little survives except as ruins of old cities and monuments. The *Śilpaśāstra* give an elaborate *nagara māpana* but the city was not just simply a subject of utilitarian planning. It was also a symbol. The city seen in the mirror *(dārpaṇadṛśyamāna nagarī),* the dream city, phantom city *(gāndharva nagara),* etc., were familiar images from literature. However, since ancient cities and secular architecture can only be reconstructed from archaeological evidence, they can hardly be discussed in the present context except as ideas of structural organizations. Ruined examples of *vāstu* and *nagara* illustrate the power of the form or idea, which govern them and which may be generally reconstructed with the help of archaeology and *Śilpaśāstra.*

The visual arts of sculpture and painting perfect the notion of *rūpa* as an immediate presentation in which the constituent elements are intuited as elements of a structural whole. Colours, diverse in use and tones, lines and planes, rhythm and volume are here combined by the judicious use of the principles of design and composition, perspective and modelling. The resultant patterns of coloured shapes have an inevitably representational character or at least the suggestion of a representation. But what is represented is ultimately the whole world, *trilokyasyānukṛti* (the representation of the three worlds). *Bāṇa* also noted that the paintings seem to show the whole world. The world *(bhuvana, tribhuvana, loka, triloka)* is not simply a name for the myriad objects of experience and imagination taken together. Their represented form is always a centred world. It is the world seen from a point of view. Cosmology, mythology, theology provide the perspective from which the artists and spectators saw the world. Mukul De once told me that perspective for us does not mean geometrical perspective. It is the way in which we look at things and want them to be seen. It is amusing to recall an incident related with Marco Polo's visit to the Emperor Kubla Khan's court. It is said that Marco Polo showed some Italian paintings, which attempted realistic representation and geometric perspective. After being repeatedly asked for their reaction, the chief painter of the court briefly remarked that it was like peeping out of the window. Man is the centre of the experienced world and God is the centre of the real world. The major surviving forms of visual arts are religious and their religious perspective relates man to God, the empirical centre to the transcendental centre. This is the fundamental ideological perspective within which is structured the visual art serving religious themes and purposes in the Indian tradition. The plastic forms are often governed by iconographic descriptions and idiom in their representations of real as well as mythical figures. A continuously progressive stream of research work is being devoted to the explication of iconographic aspect of their representation in visual arts. Several scholars like Gopinath Rao or J.N. Banerjea have tried to systematize the iconography of this plastic art utilizing both the *Śilpaśāstras* as well as the actual practice. It is necessary in this connection to sound a note of caution. The icons of the deities were made in accordance with fixed prescription, which has use in meditation and worship. In this sense Coomarswamy's observation that the mental image in meditation is the guiding model for the visual representation of deity is of fundamental importance. It is the *manomaya bimba* that lies behind the *manomaya rūpa*. The *manomaya bimba* in turn is regulated by *lakṣaṇas* and *pramāṇas*. The *lakṣaṇas* are science and symbols of the idea of the deity. Ideally this is the ultimate source of iconography, of mental image as well as the physical image. As Coomarswamy had explained, the meditation and contemplation (*bhāvanā)* of the seed idea *(bījamantra)* is perfected when the form of the deity is vividly apprehended as a luminous presence. The language of science and proportions helps to transfer this mental image to the material medium.

The idea in the context is the determination of deity in thought. The ultimate or transcendental reality, in itself beyond form and character, is also *eo ipso* beyond speech and thought to become the object of meditation and worship. The ultimate Real has to be limited by thought through the superimposition of qualities and characteristics. For example, it is thought of as a person and the person has an exalted human persona. The transcendent deity is thus incarnate in the mind and heart of the devotee. If Buddha, Rāma and Krisṇa were apotheosized, that is only the obverse of the coin, the reverse being the fact of divine incarnation or descent. The Śākyamuni was contemplated as the universal teacher and saviour. This was explained in Mahāyāna through the concept of *'nirmānakāya'*.

The icons constitute the *upāsya rūpa*. At the same time the Gods and incarnations are woven into a rich tapestry of mythology. The *Śātdanta Jātaka* or the story of Sundarī and Nanda present the Buddha as the savior in these fictitious or legendary contexts. Śiva as the universal consciousness was imaged as light or a pillar of light from which derives the idea of *liṅga* form of Śiva. Śiva is also a figure in the myth of the destruction of various demons and the *tāṇḍava* dance. The point is that the sculptures and painters imaged the Gods not merely in the light of their *dhyāna mantras* but also in the light of *ākhāynas* and *upākhyānas*. This gave them considerable freedom of representation. These representations with which the creativity of the artists is associated, should be kept distinct from the iconography proper of the Gods.

It is well known from literature that portraits and landscapes were in vogue but the perishable nature of painting has taken toll of them except where some statues of kings and saints have been identified. In the *Śakuntalā*, the king has a picture made of the scene where he had encountered Śakuntalā. The poet describes a beautiful landscape, which is redolent with memory. In the *Uttara Rāmacarita*, Rāma views a picture gallery, *citravīthī*, where scenes from his forest exile are painted. They are so vivid that he forgets that these are mere pictures. Surviving sculptures and paintings do contain secular themes and figures. In them we find that social life and attitudes have been imaged. From the sculptures of Bharhut and Sanchi to the paintings at Bagh and Ajanta and the sculptures in early medieval temples, the images of men and women engaged in diverse social activities constitute a vertitable pageant of ancient Indian social life. The images in these visual arts appear like fragmentary scenes from some vast ancient drama. They represent comic scenes as in the sculptured story of the monkeys who tried to act as barber to the *Yakṣa*. There are heroic scenes as in the portrayal of the Kalinga war in Ajanta. Devotional scenes are common. In Amaravati they are ecstatic. The scenes of dance and singing are a common tableau. Above all, the artists love to create the images of lovely women and as is well known, erotic scenes are not uncommon. What needs to be specially noted is that the images of men and women in Indian art encompass the whole of the human life and yet intimate what lies beyond. The art of the Gupta age reached an inimitable synthesis of sensuous form and the spiritual ideas, thus intimating the fundamental insight of Indian culture, that divinity is immanent as well as transcendent. It is worth recalling that the originally monastic rules of the Buddhist order did not favour the decoration of the monasteries with paintings. This extreme asceticism was however, gradually relaxed. It is the cave monasteries and temples of Ajanta, which stand as the climatic achievement of Buddhist art.

It has already been mentioned before that the image, which constitutes the object of art is the concrete objective expression of the felt ideals. The image has an innate symbolic and suggestive aspect and the appreciation of the image is not a simple matter of instinctive liking or disliking. *Rūpa* is the suggestive *(vyañjaka) vibhāva* of *rasa* or aesthetic enjoyment.

A few basic facts in this context will bear repetition at the end. Aesthetic appreciation is, at once, a distinct kind of enjoyment as well as a critical judgement. The judgement belongs to sympathetic experts or connoisseurs (*sahṛdaya parīkṣaka).* This enjoyment is not the enjoyment of emotional subjectivity, nor is critical judgement a kind of objective, cognitive judgement. The techniques of manipulating the medium do not exhaust or regulate creativity. Creativity uses or invents a technique which it finds appropriate. There is no universal repertoire of the arts. That is why no one can be taught to be a good or great artist, though a good artist can be helped by acquaintance with the tradition of artists. The cultural relativity of aesthetic judgement is inevitable and consequently the teaching of art can never neglect the history of art. The attempt to disseminate the awareness of art will lapse into ideology and vulgarization if it neglects a simultaneous cultural education of the audience. Art appreciation is a matter of particular judgement, which assesses the adequacy *(sāmarthya)* and appropriateness (*aucitya)* of the image to the felt ideal that it evokes and invokes. The image is really possible. I would like to repeat at the end that the appreciation of art is not like appreciation of a perfume, which is immediate and brooks no questioning nor is it like the appreciation of a scientific drawing. The appreciation of art is always in the context of aesthetic and cultural ideas. These aspire after universality but can never reach it wholly. In this sense, to quote Sainstsbury, 'All criticism lies within the flaming walls of the world of taste'.

NOTES AND REFERENCES

Most of the views expressed in the lecture have been more elaborately argued in my following works—*Mulyamimamsa* (Jaipur, 1973), *Saundarya Darshana Vimarshah* (Varanasi, 1995) *Sahitya Saundarya aur Sanskriti* (Allahabad, 1994).

For references to the history of Western aesthetics, Bernard Bosanquet, *A History of Aesthetic*, London 1956, may be seen.

The reference to Cassirer is from his commentary on the *Critique of Judgement*, especially the Introduction and the section-wise summaries.

For Kant's views see *Critique of Judgement* (Eng. trans.) by J.C. Meredith, Clarendon Press 1964, pp.41-139.

For reference to Hegel see his *Encyclopaedia of Philosophy*, (Eng. trans.) by Gustav Emil Mueller, Philosophical Library, New York 1959.

For Croce, see his *Aesthetic* (Eng. trans.) by Douglas Ainslie, London 1962, especially Chapters I, II, X, XII, XIII.

For Susan Langer's views in a succinct form see her *Philosophy in a New Key*, 1942.

About *Rasa* and *Jivan Mukta* and *Lila* see M. Hiriyanna, *Philosophy of Values;* Introduction to his translation of *Kaṭhopaniṣad.*

For art as imitation see *Nāṭyāśāstra* of Bharata, First Chapter; Artistotle's *Tragedy.* Abhinavagupta explains *Anukṛti* as *Anuvyavasāya.* There have been several comparative studies of Bharata and Aristotle, e.g. Anupa Pande, *The Nāṭyāsāstra Tradition and Ancient Indian Society*, Jodhpur, 1993.

Bhaṭṭanāyaka has been quoted in *Abhinavabhāratī* on *Nāṭyāsāstra*, Chapter VI. Also see Gnoli, *Aesthetic Experience According to Abhinavagupta*, which translates and annotates the *Abhinavabhāratī* on *Rasasūtra.*

For the traditional belief of the origin of the Buddha image see *Divyāvadāna.*

On the Buddhist concept of *Rūpa*, Anupa Pande, *op.cit.*, on the history of Buddha image see S.K. Gupta in *History of Science, Philosophy and Culture in Indian Civilization*, New Delhi 2001, Vol. I, part II, ed. G.C. Pande, New Delhi.

On imagination in art see I.A. Richards, Coleridge on Imagination. He speaks of imaginal action in his *Principles of Literary Criticism.*

The notion of *Śilpa* as *Ātmakṛti* is from the *Aitareya Brāhmaṇa* where *Śilpa* extends from artefacts to *Bṛhatsām.*

Pt. Raj Jagannath in his *Rasagaṅgādhara* discusses the different ways of connecting *Rasa-Bhāva* with *Saṁvit* or *Cit*, whether as *Cidāvaraṇabhanga* or *Bhagnāvaraṇacit.*

On the associative suggestiveness involved in imagination, see my *Mulyamimamsa* Chapter I on *Saundarya Mimamsa.*

The view of Nicoll is referred to his *Theory of Drama.*

On Vastu, see *Vāstopaniṣad*, Stella Kramrisch, *Hindu Temple*, Vols. I & II, Reprint, Delhi, 1976.

For Coomaraswamy's views on contemplation and seed idea reference may be made to his *Figure of Speech or Figure of Thought*, London, 1946.

NOTES AND REFERENCES

Most of the views expressed in this [illegible] have been [illegible] argued to my following [illegible] Aesthetic [illegible] and [illegible] ...

For references to the history of [illegible] see [illegible] History of Aesthetics, London [illegible]

The references to Kant's [illegible] Judgement, especially the [illegible] and the [illegible]

For Kant's views see [illegible] translated by J.C. Meredith, Clarendon Press, 1964, pp. [illegible]

For references to Hegel [illegible] by Gustav Emil Mueller, Philosophical Library, New York [illegible]

For Croce see the Aesthetic [illegible] by Douglas Ainslie, London, 1922, especially Chapters I, II, [illegible]

For Susan Langer's views [illegible] Feeling and Form [illegible] New York, 1942.

[illegible] Keats and [illegible] and [illegible] Philosophy of [illegible] Introduction to [illegible]

For art as imitation [illegible] Aristotle's Tragedy [illegible] there have been several comparative studies [illegible] and Aristotle [illegible] Natyasastra [illegible] Ancient Indian [illegible] 1993.

Bhattanayaka has been quoted [illegible] Chapter VI. Also see Gnoli [illegible] translation and comments [illegible]

For the traditional [illegible] see [illegible]

On the Buddhist concept [illegible] Buddha image see S.K. Gupta [illegible] Culture in Indian Civilization, New Delhi [illegible] New Delhi.

On imagination [illegible] the question, he speaks of [illegible] action in [illegible]

[illegible] extends from [illegible]

[illegible] discusses the different ways of [illegible] or imagination [illegible]

On the associative [illegible] see my [illegible] Chapter I [illegible]

The view of Nicoll [illegible] to his Theory of Drama.

On Vastu see [illegible] Hindu Temple, Vols. I & II. Reprint, Delhi, 1976.

[illegible] and [illegible] reference may be made to his [illegible]

1

Appreciation of Terracotta Art

Gourisankar De

The art of clay is as old as man himself.[1] Specimens of clay art have been discovered from all the centres of ancient civilization—Mesopotamia, Egypt, India, Anatolia, Crete, China and many other places.[2] But in India, earth or clay has a special significance, a profound philosophical meaning. The attitude in life that the Indians are apt to learn from their infancy is the attitude of accepting the philosophy of the impermanent nature of everything. The earth or clay symbolizes the philosophy of the Oriental attitude in life, "the cosmic relationship between creation and destruction that nothing can be held up permanently in the course of dynamic force of nature".[3]

Clay is soft and malleable. But when it undergoes the ordeal of fire, it becomes hard, resistant and permanent as good as stone or metal. Thus clay, after its rebirth through fire, becomes terracotta ('baked earth' or 'fired clay').[4] In spite of the hard competition with new materials in different ages and serious threats, terracotta art has survived from the prehistoric period to the present day.

Terracotta art has often been dubbed as poor man's art.[5] But this is true in case of countries where sharp differentiation exists between the court art and the folk art. In India, clay was given equal importance by the rich and the poor alike.[6] The rich, of course, delighted in figures of stone, metal or ivory.[7] But terracotta also catered to the tastes and needs of the affluent community. The Mauryan royal society and aristocracy of Magadha commissioned special potters (*rājakumbhakāras*) to creat artistic terracotta resembling Hellennistic figurines (pl. 1.1).[8]

Kalidasa talks of a prince playing with a painted terracotta peacock (*chitrita-mrittikā-mayura*) in his *Abhijñānaśākuntalam*.[9] The famous drama of Sudraka is named *Mricchakatika* (The Little Clay Cart). The seventh-century poet Bana writes that Emperor Harsha employed a host of clay modellers on the occasion of Rajyasri's marriage to make terracotta figures of auspicious fruits, trees and aquatic as well as of female figurines holding auspicious fruits for the purpose of decoration.[10]

The urban clay artists of the Indus valley produced fine terracottas.[11] They also devised the mould, the use of which was forgotten in the succeeding ages and was revived in the third century BC.[12]

The main centres of terracotta art are in the North. The art did not flourish in the South for want of fine clay. In the Deccan too, the artists had to work in Kaolin. But except under the Satavahanas the art did not flourish in the Deccan.[13]

Northern India, particularly Ganga valley and Bengal, land of riverine plains, ensured inexhaustible supply of clay. The dearth of stone was more than compensated by clay.[14]

Terracotta plaques and reliefs were made and employed for various purposes.[15] Manteis, private apartments and bed chambers of the *nāgarīkas* were often decorated with plaques of amorous couples, portrait heads, toys, human and animal figurines and beautiful female figurines. Different types of clay figures were made for definite *vratas, puja's* and socio-religious festivities.

The early terracottas were mostly associated with religious ideas. The examples are the mother goddess and the bull of the Indus valley. The Harappans, of course, produced a variety of toys.[16]

True secular objects were handled by Mauryan artists. The evidences are the exquisite statues of boys and dancing girls.[17]

The Śuṅga terracottas represent amorous couples (*mithuna*), a novel motif which became extremely popular in the succeeding periods.[18] Mythological scenes from the epics and the purāṇas occur on plaques and potteries.[19] Moulds came into use, which meant greater accuracy and mass production.[20] The artists seem to have combined in them the social ideology of the upper classes and folk and aboriginal life on the other. Beautiful women appear in diaphanous draperies, heavy jewellery, ornamental headdress, girdles and anklets.[21]

Various types and fashions are represented in the terracottas of the Kuṣāṇa period. This was because of the racial influx that was characteristic of the period.[22] There is also Hellenistic elements in this art.[23] The terracottas are well modelled, smooth and sensuous.[24] The human figurines have almond shaped eyes, flat and heavy nose, broad chest and folds in the garment.[25] The themes displayed are heads of noble men, with tall headgear, characteristic of the Scythian, Kuṣāṇa soldiers, musicians, mother and child, Vasudhārā with her emblem of the fish pair, toy carts, various animals and birds.[26]

The Śuṅga-Kuṣāṇa periods were the heydays of terracotta art. The decline set in from the Gupta period.

Terracotta human figurines are greater in number than those of stone and bronze statuaries.[27] The clay modellers follow some principles advantageous to their material which is different from those followed by the stone-sculptors and bronze-casters.[28]

In India, we have no sculptures of the early historical periods. Reconstruction of some of the forms of those times can be done only from the terracottas.[29] The linear rhythm of early terracottas were to enter sculpture.[30] Many terracotta specimens seldom have replicas in other materials.[31]

The aesthetics of the terracotta is in the primitivist vitality. The simple abstracted forms denote power. The sensuous and warm flesh of the nude goddesses suggests uninhibited acceptance of sexual energies. The toy carts pulled with the string by children are often in the form of lovable bird or animal from whom the young are expected to acquire tenderness from early years. The rattles made in the form of birds, frog, or deities like Kubera were one of the earliest musical instruments.[32]

The terracotta figurines, being essentially the representation of the folk art, display more colours than we find in the case of stone figures.[33] A variety of significant forms and motifs are found in terracotta art.

The study of terracotta art requires the study of its origin, development, characteristics, themes, material, techniques, special qualities, centres of production, literary parallels, comparison with the specimens of other mediums, etc. The present writer has tried to outline the various aspects of terracotta art in general. His special study is based on the specimens collected personally from Chandraketugarh, a noted archaeological site in the North 24-Parganas District (West Bengal). In fact, Chandraketugarh has earned the name of 'terracotta city' from art-lovers of India and distant lands.

The specimens salvaged are (i) seals, (ii) potteries, (iii) rattles, (iv) toy carts, (v) figures and figurines in the round, (vi) terracotta plaques. Probably, the plaques are the most important type. On them are depicted different deities, birds and animals, social scene, narrative themes, erotic life, and various other subjects (*see* pl. 1.1-1.7). The specimens belong to Maurya, Śuṅga, Kuṣāṇa and Gupta period. The terracotta plaques mostly belong to the Śuṅga-Kuṣāṇa period.

In the realm of terracotta art, small is beautiful. Here, the world with its God's and goddesses, *Apsarās* and *Rākṣas*, men and women, fauna and flora, has been reduced to a mini one. Yet perfect proportion has been maintained. To enjoy the composition, charm and details of the plaques-facial expression, body movement, dresses and ornaments, a micro-study is essential.

The picture displayed on plaques are in low relief and two-dimensional. Hence they need to be examined in proper perspective.

There are striking similarities between the terracotta objects of Chandraketugarh with the objects of other sites like Pataliputra, Kausambi, Ahichchhatra, Vaisali, Tamralipta and even distant places like Bhaja. A comparison is must to understand the similarities, parallels, and differences. It also helps to fix the approximate date. A comparison of terracotta art with stone, metal, ivory and wood work is often rewarding. A comparison with folk art or contemporary terracotta art may be of substantial help. Literary parallels may shed important light. An all-India approach to terracotta art may prevent us from following a parochial view.

As evident from Chandraketugarh specimens, the terracotta art is a world by itself passing moods, contemporary tastes, fashions and prejudices which have less scope in sculpture or even in painting, express themselves in the plastic idiom. Whatever the themes, they are presented in vigorous action, playful freedom, and emotional abandon. In fact, quite a different attitude of life and artistic vision are revealed by the deluge of terracotta reliefs. The essential dynamism and rhythm of daily life with its varied associations, not usually recognized by hieratic and high-bred standards, find their joyous and free expression in this inexhaustible inventory of contemporary form and social life, much more complete and variegated than either in sculpture or painting.

Regarding the terracotta works of Chandraketugarh, Enamul Haque writes :

> Scores of plaques depict scenes reminiscent of complex urban culture which reflect intelligent observations. These include court life, music, dance, coquetry, revelry, erotica, men on animals and chariots... some of the delicately executed plaques must have been the products of the high class skilled potters *(rāja-kumbhkāras)* mentioned by Panini and in the Jātakas.[34]

Terracottas represent a very important section in the whole gamut of art objects of the formative period of Indian art. Terracotta art helps to appreciate the directional changes in the form and contents of the artistic creations of India right from the prehistoric period.[35]

NOTES AND REFERENCES

1. H.D. Sankalia and M.K. Dhavalikar, The Terracotta Art of India, *Marg*, Vol. XXIII, December, 1969, No. 1, p.33.
2. Pradosh Das Gupta, *Temple Terracottas of Bengal*, Delhi, p.7.
3. *Ibid*.

4. Paul Bahn (Editor), *Collin's Dictionary of Archaeology*, Glasgow, 1992, p.499.
5. A.L. Basham, *The Wonder that was India*, Bombay, 1963 (First print in India), p.373.
6. H.D. Sankalia and M.K. Dhavalikar, *op.cit., Marg*, p.33.
7. A.L. Basham, *op.cit.*, p.373.
8. F.R. Allchin *et al.*, *The Archaeology of Early Historic South Asia*, Cambridge University Press, 1995, p.272.
9. R.C. Majumdar (General editor), *The Classical Age*, Bombay, p.553.
10. *Ibid.*; Fish, Tortoise Coconut, Plantain etc. Rājyanis Bibāna, *Sanskritic Itihaser Prasange* (in Bengali), D.C. Sircar, Calcutta, 1389 (B.S.), p.216.
11. Stuart Piggott, *Prehistoric India*, Penguin Book, 1961 (reprint), plate 8, Harappa, 1946, Clay Figurines.
12. *Marg, op.cit.*, p.33.
13. *Ibid.*
14. R.C. Majumdar, *op.cit.*, p.553.
15. S.K. Saraswati, *A Survey of Indian Sculpture*, New Delhi, 1975 (Second edition), p.103.
16. *Marg, op.cit.*, p.33, Rama D. Datta, *The Indus Valley Civilization* (The Mother goddess, pp.48-53), New Delhi, 1996, Maurizio Toddel: India (Eng. tr.), Geneva, 1970, p.23.

    Regarding the religious character of bull, Marshall has observed, "The bull, both humped and humpless, is closely associated with Śiva" John Marshall, *Religion of the Indus Valley*, D. Chattopadhyaya (ed.), *Studies in Indian Culture*, Vol. 1, Calcutta, 1992, p.52.

    For Harappan Terracottas, K.C. Jain, *Prehistory and Protohistory of Indian*, New Delhi, pp.149-150.
17. Naseem Akhtar (ed.), *Patna Museum Catalogue (Terracottas and Metal Images)*, Patna, 2001, p.36-Head of a smiling boy, Bulandibagh, Patna, Dancing girl, p.29 and 51.
18. *Marg, op.cit.*, p.33.
19. *Ibid.*, p.34.
20. V.P. Dwivedi, *Indian Ivories*, Delhi, 1976, p.61.
21. V.K. Mathur, *Art and Culture Under the Śuṅgas*, Delhi, 1996, p.80.
22. Suman Mathur, *Art & Culture Under the Kuṣāṇas*, Delhi, 1988, p.100.
23. *Ibid.*
24. *Ibid.*
25. *Ibid.*
26. *Ibid.*, p.101.
27. C.C. Dasgupta, *Origin and Evolution of Indian Clay Sculpture*, University of Calcutta, 1961, p.259.
28. *Ibid.*, p.260.
29. *Marg, op.cit.*, p.2.
30. *Ibid.*
31. C.C. Dasgupta *op.cit.*, p.261.

32. *Marg, op.cit.*, p.2.
33. C.C. Dasgupta, *op.cit.*, p.213.
34. Enamul Haque, *Chandraketugarh*, Dhaka, 2001, p.79.
35. S.P. Gupta, *The Roots of Indian Art*, New Delhi, 1980, p.137.

2

Psycho-analytical and Iconographical Perceptions of Mother and Child

Krishna Kumari Myneni

For the individual and personality development, the first few months of human life, a period of world less oblivion is of root significance. For all later psychological experiences, infancy and childhood are the foundations. The nature of an individual's first relationship with one's own mother, influences profoundly the quality and "dynamics" of social relations throughout the life. The ideals of motherhood, the parental care of the children and the crucial role of this relationship for the development of all subsequent social relations are well recognized and demonstrated in Indian art and literature. The psychological reciprocity between the mothers and infants were well elaborated by Sigmund Freud. While explaining the importance of the mothers to the infants, he described it as "unique, without parallel, established unalterably for a whole life time as the first and strongest love object and as the prototype of all later love relations for both genders".[1] In spite of the significance of the mother-child relations, it remains to be intellectually elusive and relatively unexplored. However, the works of the psychologists, anthropologists and psycho-historians in this direction are preoccupied with the feeding and narturing of the infants to know about the emotional climate and the gestures of mothering and feeding. In this context the appreciation of Hindu art forms would be of great use as they help in the better understanding of mother-infant relations in India as the central dynamic factor in personality formation of the people in Indian culture. This is because a person first learns to relate to the other and begins to develop his capacity to love from the mother-infant relations. Further it is from these relations that an individual originates as a social being and as an adult, all his affiliations and intimacies bear the stamp of one's own particular kind of infancy that was experienced. In this context, an attempt is made here to appreciate the iconography of the relief sculptures of mother and infant with special reference to a stone slab exhibited in the British Museum, London to highlight the mother-infant relationship as reflected in the art forms in the ancient India. It also deals with the stone sculptures of *Saptamātrikās* and few images of *Yoginīs* who were shown with a child on their laps to project the feelings of warmth, intimacy and affection between the mother and child.

Several stone sculptures of mother and child are reported from Central, Northern and Eastern India and are found to be a favourite theme of the artists of Eastern India. The main theme of the sculpture is the female figure reclining either to the right or left with a child by her side, sometimes suckling her breast to the infant surrounded by a number of subordinate figures and a lady pressing her feet. Studies made earlier by the art historian's on these sculptures suggest that such sculptures with Vaiṣṇava affinities come from Central India while the Śaiva type enjoyed great popularity in Eastern India. The identification of the figures of mother and child has long been a subject for debate, especially in the case of the stone sculptures of Bengal. In certain cases the issue was settled through the epigraphic evidence in the proper identification of a mother and child sculpture as Sadyojāta Śiva. The mother and child stone sculptures with certain variations are well discussed and identified from various places such as Dudhai (District Lalitpur, U.P.)[2] Sarya Buzurg (District Deoria, U.P.),[3] Verendi (Bengal),[4] Banswara (Rajasthan),[5] Khajuraho,[6] Gwalior,[7] Dhubela (M.P.),[8] Dinajpur (Burdwan University Museum),[9] Rajshahi District National Museum, Delhi)[10] and Koshan Shahar (District Bogra, Bangladesh).[11] While studying the iconography of these images, scholars have identified them differently as pertaining to various religious sects of Hinduism and non-Hindu religions and accordingly they were referred to as Kṛṣṇa-Devakī,[12] Krṣṇa-Yasodā,[13] Sadyojāta Maheśvara,[14] birth of a *mahāpuruṣa* or an emperor of great magnitude,[15] birth of Mahāviṛa and Skandamātā.[16] N.P. Joshi has explained the reasons for the popularity of the stone sculptures of mother and child with the help of the statements furnished by the *Bhavishyad Purāṇa*.[17] He suggested that perhaps the belief that the worship of such slabs would dispel the fear of attack from outside as stated in *Bhavishyad Purāṇa* and that could be the reason for the occurrence of the stone slabs of mother and child theme in good number in India.

In the present paper an attempt has been made to analyse the iconography of one stone sculpture on a slab depicting the mother in reclining posture with her child lying by her side exhibited in the Indian Art Gallery of British Museum (OA 1872 7-1-107) with the identification as Yasodā feeding Kṛṣṇa. It measures approximately 6' x 4'. The sculptural panel depicts the figure of a mother reclining on her right side on the couch made of serpent coils with a child by her side suckling her breast and her right leg is slightly raised. Above her head, which is slightly elevated, is carved the five-hooded serpent *Śeṣa nāga* shielding her head in the manner of a canopy. The left hand of the mother that runs parallel to her body is broken.The left leg of the mother is slightly bent upwards being cared by a lady attendant who is carved as two handed. The head portion of the female attendant is broken. Above the sculpture are carved in two rows the images of the sages in seated posture, divine beings and flying *gandharvas* while the male attendants are carved to the right side of the slab. Below the bedstead are carved the seated images of the devotees in smaller proportions with their hands folded in *añjali mudrā*. The figure of the mother is adequately decorated with long *hāras* dropping below the breasts, ear ornaments and anklets. The image of the mother demonstrates the heaviness of the body forms with her broad face and very large rounded breasts. This image of the mother nursing the baby gives an idea of the feeding practices which became an almost stereotyped pattern of showing the mother and child in Indian art. The associated figures carved on the top suggest that the child was born with the blessings of the divine beings. The stone slab of the mother and child from British Museum can better be identified as Devakī-Kṛṣṇa instead of Yasodā-Kṛṣṇa as it is now being done and displayed in the signage board at the Museum. The reasoning that the image of the mother represents Yasodā cannot be accepted, as the real mother who gave birth to Kṛṣṇa was Devakī and not Yaśodā who was the wife of Nanda, a landlord. The identification of mother and child slab from British Museum as Devakī-Kṛṣṇa and of its Vaiṣṇavite connection gains further support from the sculptural evidence of similar type of representations of the zoomorphic *Varāha murti* form reported from Badoh in Madhya Pradesh.[18] On the right side of the pedestal of the *Ādi Varāha* form has been carved the images of Devakī feeding Kṛṣṇa who is shown as lying on the *Śeṣa* bed. In the carving of the figures of Devakī-Kṛṣṇa the artist sculptor has very carefully shown the *Śeṣa* hood behind the image of Kṛṣṇa to suggest that Kṛṣṇa is none other than the Supreme God himself. In these cases the mother can be identified as Devakī on the grounds of the textual reference to the birth of Kṛṣṇa in *Bhavishyad Purāṇa* and other texts. According to them Lord Kṛṣṇa should be represented with an image of Devakī on the grounds of the textual reference to the birth of Kṛṣṇa in *Bhavishyad Purāṇa* and other texts. According to them Lord Kṛṣṇa should be represented with an image of Devakī having just delivered the child on the couch.They further describe that the child should be suckling her breast, while Lakṣmī should be massaging her feet and gods witnessing and rejoicing above in the air. A stone sculpture of mother and child with the newborn child on serpent bed with five planets shown on top and the seated figure of elephant headed Gaṇeśa being venerated by a female devotee has been described by C. Sivaramamurti in connection with the explanation of a *mahāpuruṣa* for the newborn child suggested by the exalted position of five planets.[19] In this connection, it is also mentioned that in several Pāla sculptures from Bihar and Bengal, there are all the nine planets shown and that only indicate that the child is born with the blessings of the nine planets favourably disposed to the newborn, with no particular stress or indication as to the future of the child.[20]

Although the mother and child stone sculptures examined above displays the theme of mother as reclining with the child by her side suckling the breast which became stereotyped, they form the primary source material for understanding the feeding activities of the newly born child and his close relations with the mother for the exploration of the dominant personality characteristics within the Hindu culture. For the crucial social interaction, through which an individual starts to separate himself and becomes a person, the infant needs his mother as a whole human being, not merely as a satisfier of hunger and thirst, or to state it more plainly what the infant requires is not a breast but a mother.[21] The significance of the portrayal of feeding the child by the mother should be viewed as a part of the total communication process in which not only the mother's breast but also the quality of her movement, caressing the child and touch affects the quality of the infant's sensory and emotional lease on life. It is rightly pointed out and shown by the anthropologists such as Kardiner, Benedict and Mead that the specific emotional colouring of many of a society's cultural institutions can be directly attributed to the dominant quality or mode of the first relationship, not in the sense of simple causal connection, but in the complementarity's and reciprocal influence between the mother-infant relations and other institutionalized forms of social relations.[22] It may be mentioned that here the breast can be viewed as a symbol for the mother, as feeding symbolized the process of attachment in human development followed by weaning process suggesting the separation of the mother and child, as the child grows. In Indian art, these aspects of nurturing the child by the mother and the childhood activities are very well demonstrated especially in the case of the image forms of Kṛṣṇa as a child (Bāla Kṛṣṇa) with his mother.

The ideal mother is best illustrated in Hindu iconography through the images of *Saptamātrikās,* whose number is usually seven, though eight or more of them can be counted.[23] In the development of the iconography of the Seven Mothers it is observed that each of the mother holds a child in her left arm as it is noticed from a relief sculpture in the Mathura Museum.[24]

In the Gupta sculpture displayed in Gwalior Museum are Seven Mothers each one with a child in their lap.[25] The *Saptamātrikā* relief sculptures from Seraikela in the Singhbhum district now preserved in the Patna Museum represent the mothers with a child on her left lap except Vārāhī, who has a small child seated between her legs.[26] The child seated on the lap of Brahmāṇī is carved very realistically holding a toy in his left hand. The images of Seven Mothers at Jajpur are all four-armed and each except Chāmuṇḍā has a plump potbellied child on the left knee supported by the lower left hand.[27] Likewise, the Markaṇḍeśvara tank at Puri has five *Mātrikā* figures, which are all four-armed supporting a child on their left thighs by their front left hands.

The images of *Yoginīs* are also found to carry a child on their lap being held by their left hand. It is interesting to observe a boar-faced child seated on the left lap of *yoginī* called Umādevī who is shown as parrot-faced goddess.[28] In a *yoginī* temple at Lokhari in Banda district (U.P) is noticed the image of a goddess *Hayagriva* (horse faced) who grazes upwards supporting a similarly horse-necked child on her left knee held by her left hand. She is shown as seated on a human corpse with a skullcap in her hand.[29] Another *Yoginī* image kept in the Indian Museum called *Sri Vasabha* is a bull-faced *yoginī* who supports on her knee a child with an elephant head.[30] The *yoginī* has bull mount and her attendants and worshippers shown below the image include an elephant headed female. Thus the images of *yoginīs* are carved with child being held close to their bodies, where even the child is shown sometimes with different heads as described above.

The preference to the male child in the patriarchal culture of Indian society is very much apparent from the classical literary texts of Hinduism. The Rig Vedic hymns are replete with prayers for sons and grandsons, male offerings, male descendants and male issues and occasionally for wives, but never for daughters. There were no signs of happiness or rejoicing over the birth of a daughter as it was in the case of the birth of a son.[31]The traditional preference for sons is found to be very much intact and the same has been reflected in the realm of art also. In the several images of mother and child described above, it is observed that in all cases they are the male children only. Further it is observed that in all the images the ideal mother is shown as displaying her affection, love and intimacy to the male child. The stone slabs of Devakī-Kṛṣṇa are the best examples of the rejoicing that accompanied the birth of a male child wherein the relief sculpture is beautifully carved with the figures of the several attendants and the divine beings including the image of goddess Lakṣmī who is shown as pressing the feet of Devakī, who just gave birth to Kṛṣṇa. Further it is observed that there is a consistent indication of marked preference for sons in the art forms that closely follows the iconographical and *Agamic* textual descriptions. To understand the idea of parental love bestowed on the male child, the sculptures of Somaskaṇḍa are the excellent examples. They display the theme of parental love on the child who is often shown as seated in the middle of the seated images of Śiva and Pārvatī. In the Pallava stone sculptures and the bronzes of the Chola period, Somaskaṇḍa is a favourite theme of the artists in which the child is shown in between suggesting that the object of love for both on the offspring has been bestowed entirely, which increases a thousand fold though given away in its entirety.[32]

The mother's nearness to the child may be viewed as an intense emotional involvement between the mother and child that plays an important role in an individual's personality formation through unconscious process. This aspect has been studied by Carstairs, who emphasizes the physical closeness between the Hindu mother and her child.[33] It is observed by him that the mother and child are seldom apart in the first two years and the baby is seen astride the mother's hip and the Hindu child has never accustomed to frustration prior to weaning. Like Carstairs, Sudhir Kakar has broadly accepted the Hindu child's prolonged physical contact with the mother.[34] The psychoanalytical approach to study the sculptural data on physical contact between the mother and child in Hindu culture confirms the observational data presented by the psychoanalysts as evidence of sensual over indulgence and of extreme emotional closeness in Hindu infancy. As the behaviour, the personality development, the attitudes of an individual towards women, sensuality, authority, power, non-violence and Hindu view of material world are all based on the childhood experiences, the symbolic representations of the mother-child in the Hindu iconography reveal a pattern which is highly meaningful.

NOTES AND REFERENCES

1. Sigmund Freud., *An Outline of Psycho Analysis*, 1940 (Standard Edition), Vol. 23, p.188; John Boolby, "The Nature of the Child's Tie to His Mother", *International Journal of Psychoanalysis*, 39, 1958, pp.350-73.
2. H.N. Singh, "Mother-Child Sculpture from Dudhai, District Lalitpur, Uttar Pradesh in *Indian Archaeological Heritage (SH. K.V. Soundara Rajan Felicitation Volume)* ed. by C. Margabandhu *etal.*, Vol. II, Delhi, 1991, pp.575-77.
3. *Ibid.*
4. N.K. Bhattasali, *Iconography of Buddhist and Brahmanical Sculptures in the Dacca Museum*, 1929.
5. R.C. Agrawal, "Krishna-Balarama in Rajasthan Sculptures and Epigraphs" *Indian Historical Quarterly*, XXV, pp.343-44.

6. U. Agrawal, *Khajuraho Sculpture and their Significance*, fig. 178, p.81.
7. S.R. Thakore, "Catalogue of Sculpture", *Archaeological Museum*, Gwalior, p.13; A.K. Kumaraswamy, *History of Indian and Indonesian Art*, fig. 178, pp.86, 242.
8. S.K. Dikshit, *A Guide to State Museum, Dhubela*, pls. XII, XIII, pp.28-29.
9. N.P. Joshi, "Purāṇas as Interpreters of Icons", in *Kala: Journal of Indian Art History Congress*, Vol. VII, 2000-2001, ed. by Maruti Nandan Tiwari and Kamal Giri, Delhi, pp.1-15.
10. V.S. Agrawala, *The Heritage of Indian Art*, Delhi, 1984, pl. 70, p.174.
11. *Ibid.*, Also see Susan L. Huntington, *The "Pala-Sena" Schools of Sculpture: Studies in South Asian Culture*, Institute of Asian Archaeology, Leiden, 1984, pl. 248, p.185.
12. R. Awasthi, *Khajuraho ki Deva Pratimayen* (Hindi), 1967, p.115.
13. V.S. Agrawala, *op.cit.*, pl. 70, p.174.
14. R.D. Banerji, *History of Bengal*, p.256; N.K. Bhattasali, *op.cit.*; G. Bhattacharya, "The Munificence of Lady Catuhsma", *Aksayanivi*, New Delhi, 1991, p.317 ff.
15. C. Sivaramamurti, *Expressive Quality of Literary Flavour in Art*, Research Lectures, New Series 6, Dharwar, 1974, pl. XXIV, p.37.
16. Brijesh Krishna, *The Art Under Gurjara Pratiharas*, 1984, pl. 81, p.170.
17. N.P. Joshi, *op.cit.*, p.9; *pujyate Pandavasresta janairutasavasamyutaih para cakrabhayam tatra na Kathapi bhavetpunah-Bhavishya Purāṇa* as cited by Vrataraja.
18. Haripriya Rangarajan, *Varaha Images in Madhya Pradesh: An Iconographical Study*, Delhi 1997, fig. 22, pp.66-67.
19. C. Sivaramamurti, *op.cit.*
20. *Ibid.*
21. Sudhir Kakar, "Mother and Infants", *The Essential Writings of Sudhir Kakar*, Delhi, 2001, p.6.
22. *Ibid.*
23. A. Avalon., Introduction of *Prapañchasaṛa Tantra*, p.35; J.N. Banerjea, *Development of Hindu Iconography*, p.503.
24. V.S. Agrawala, *A Catalogue of the Brahmanical Images in Mathura Art*, no. 552, p.62,
25. C. Sivaramamurti, *The Art of India*, New York, 1977, pp.173-75.
26. Bhagawant Sahai, *Iconography of Minor Hindu and Buddhist Deities*, Delhi, 1975, pp.207-19; *Journal of Oriental Institute*, Vol. XVIII, nos. 1 & 2, figs. 2-8, pp.153-56.
27. *Memoirs of Archaeological Survey of India*, 42, pp.3,18.
28. Vidya Dehejea, *Yoginī Cult and Temple: A Tantric Tradition*, Delhi, 1986, p.146.
29. *Ibid.*, p.159.
30. *Ibid.*, p.168.
31. A.A. Mac Donell, *Vedic Religion*, p.165 quoted in R.M. Das, *Women in Manu and His Seven Commentators*, Varanasi, 1962, p.43.
32. C. Sivaramamurti, *op.cit.*, p.43.
33. Carstairs G. Morris, *The Twice Born: A Study of a Community of High Caste Hindus, Bloomington*, 1967, pp.63-76, 157.

34. Sudhir Kakar, *The Inner World: A Psycho Analytic Study of Childhood and Society in India*, Delhi, 1978, p.193; T.G. Vaidyanathan & Jeffrey J Kripal, ed. *Vishnu on Freudś Desk: A Reader in Psychoanalysis and Hinduism*, Delhi, 1999, pp.185-216.

3

Proper Appellation for Genuine Appreciation

(A Case Study of the Chauri-Bearer Female Figure from Didarganj)

Arvind Mahajan

If a life-size portrait of Sushmita Sen, with a label just mentioning her name, is placed before an art-critic, who is not cognizant of her or India, he may or may not appreciate her beauty and take her as an Indian beauty only. But if just the label is replaced with another one citing 'Miss Universe-Sushmita Sen', the complete outlook of the viewer will be changed and he will appreciate the portait in a better way. Similarly if the portait of Mona-lisa is put before a lay man, who is not versed in the intricacies of the painting, he cannot fully appreciate it and when just a label, titled 'Mona-lisa: The Smiling Beauty', is put there, then even this lay man will be in a better position to enjoy and appreciate this classic work by Leonardo-da-Vinci.

The case of *chaurī-bearer* female figure from Didarganj, Patna (better known as Didarganj *Yakṣī)* is not much different. Till date various nouns like *Yakṣī, Devī, Lakṣmī, Stri-ratna,* etc., have been assigned to it, of which *Yakṣī* is the most popular. But none of the nouns, so far provided, except the *Strī-ratna,* genuinely project this bizarre beauty from the point of view of appreciation.

It is an Indian psychology to take anything bizarre or unparallel as celestial or divine. Anything, which is superhuman but due to certain bindings or characters cannot be classed among the gods, have generally been distinguished as *Yakṣas* and even those, who are alien to Indian physique or appearance have been called in literatures as *Yakṣas*. Apart from that, religion has remained always on forefront and as a guiding force in formulation of Indian art since its inception. That is why Indian art lacks realism and sans human images to be dominated by symbols. Probably the fancy of Kuṣāṇa kings of portraying themselves over their coins or through memorial icons, which have been found at Mathura, earned them the epithet *'Devaputra'*. And possibly these preconditions forced some scholars to designate this figure as *Yakṣī* and compare it with other *Yakṣa* and *Yakṣī* figures.

Scholars have studied it stylistically, religio-culturally, socio-philosophically, i.e. in historical perspective and following are the arguments and pre-conditions to the nouns assigned by different scholars to this female figure.

EARLIER DISCUSSIONS

Pioneer among the advocates of *Yakṣī* are K.P. Jayaswal, V.S. Agrawal, J.N. Banerjea and R.P. Chanda.

V.S. Agrawal[1] accords religious affiliation to this image and compares it with other *Yakṣa Yakṣī* figures, discovered to date, to designate it as *Yakṣī*. Agrawal dates it in the Mauryan period and cites in detail the prevalence the folk cult of *Yakṣa-Yakṣī*.

R.P. Chanda[2] holds that Patna statues (with polish), Didarganj female statue and fragments of the capitals in the Patna Museum are the works of such Indian, or strictly speaking, Magadhan artists who received their early training under foreign masters of the Asokan school and executed these works in the reign of his successor.[3] Chanda identifies this successor with Sampati or Samprati[4]. He concludes, 'The two male statues from Patna in the Indian Museum, one of which shows a fly-whisk and the *chaurī*-bearing Didarganj female statue in the Patna Museum probably represent attendant *Yakṣa* and *Yakṣī* or some other class of superhuman beings attached to *chaitya* trees or sṭupas. This conclusion is suggested by the disposition of the images of the *Yakṣas*, Nāgas, and Devatās on the railing of the *stupa* of Bharhut and on the old railing round the Bodhi-tree at Bodh Gayā.[5]

J.N. Banerjea[6] puts all the statues in round with Mauryan (so-called) lustre (Patna *Yakṣa*s in Indian Museum-Calcutta, Didarganj female figure in Patna Museum, Besnagar figure and the one discovered from Pawaya) in one group. On the basis of the inscription on Pawaya sculpture[7], Banerjea dates them around or slightly earlier to 1st century BC and collectively designates them as *Yakṣa*s and Yakṣiṇīs. He further quotes some Jaina and Buddhist literatures (of much later date) to make his argument impregnable. But the statement of Banerjea, 'there cannot be any doubt that all the above mentioned figures, both male and female, belong to the same category and if we find a clue to the identity of one among them, the others will also be identified with its help',[8] very well reveals his *modus operandi* for the identification of the images in discussion.

Nihar Ranjan Ray[9] calls it Yakṣiṇi and dates as 'Stylistically the figure can perhaps be dated in the second century BC'.[10] But he further declares this irrelevant, so far as the beauty and spirit of this image is concerned, and takes it as the prototype of the later lively Yakṣīs of the Mathura reliefs of the second century AD.[11] But Ray could not deny its aristocratic bearing. Declaring it the prototype of Mathura *Yakṣī* figures, he writes, 'but she is more stately and dignified. A slight stoop forward and a chaste plastic treatment coupled with firm outlines, give it an aristocratic bearing which is not very much unlike that of the Maurya figures crowning the capitals of the monolithic columns'.[12]

S.P. Gupta also calls it *Yakṣī*, but sees in it 'perfect urban sophistification unlike any Bharhut and Sanchi *Yakṣīs* figures and derives an equation- Asokan pillars > Free-standing *Yakṣas* and *Yakṣīs* >Bharhut, Sanchi gateways.[14] Gupta sums up his discussion as, 'the art of the pillars and the art of the free-standing *Yakṣas* appear to have moved hand in hand in the mid to late third century B.C., it is only in the second century BC that the two traditions got separated. Pataliputra was original home of both of them. May be Patna *Yakṣas* were inscribed not when they were actually carved but half a century later....[15] Gupta also could not ascertain the objective of the Didarganj female figure and for the same writes, 'the figure may have adorned the royal palace, the bedroom entrance, the throne hall or some temple, we do not exactly know.[16]

S.K. Saraswati calls this figure *Yakṣī* and presents a brilliant comparative study of similar other figures, hailing from widely distant regions, like Parkham and Baroda near Mathura, Besnagar and Pawaya in Gwaliar, Didarganj and different areas of Patna. He objects to the notion of dating these in Mauryan period for their material and polish. He suggests that this ascription fails to take note of the differences that exist among these two group of sculptures, viz. the sculptural capitals and the *Yakṣa* and *Yakṣiṇi* statues. He further differentiates the *Yakṣa* and *Yakṣinī* statues on the basis of their technique, style and aesthetic expression. He writes, 'The divergences are too tangible to be ignored and become clear when they are placed side by side, particularly the *Yakṣa* figure from Parkham and that of the *Yakṣī* from Didarganj, the former in its massive burliness and flattended treatment without any co-ordination of the parts, and the latter in its smooth, rounded and naturalistic features pleasingly intergrated into a complete, whole and inspired by the fluid naturalism of the mature classical tradition[17].Following a critical analysis of the modelling (only), he places Parkham images of the group in earliest time bracket, i.e. 2nd century BC. Then he puts Patna *Yakṣa* images and Besnagar *Yakṣī*, dating these in 1st century BC. Finally the Didarganj image and Pawaya *Yakṣa* is placed in one group, dated to 1st century AD, reason ascribed to the Didarganj figure is its akinness (I say so-called) to the dainty *Yakṣiṇī* forms on the Mathura jambs[18], calls this figure *Yakṣī* and presents a brilliant comparative study of similar other figures, hailing from widely distant regions, like-Parkham and Baroda near Mathura, Besnagar and Pawaya in Gwalior, Didarganj and different areas of Patna.[20]

Pramod Chandra dates this figure in 3rd century BC,[21] calls it with its popular name *'Yakṣī,*[23] but at the level of concept and motif takes it as 'fertility goddess.'[24] He holds that wide hips and full breasts, physical attributes associated specifically with birth and fertility, are emphasized here and for the same it may be understood loosely as a fertility goddess.

A.K. Coomarswamy, though having a separate and doyen work on *'Yakṣas,*[25] in which he has delineated each and every aspect regarding their cult right from the Vedic period down to the historic age, their physical manifestation *et al.*, even did not bother to make mention of the Didarganj female figure. He could not dare to call this figure *Yakṣiṇī* and preferred to give a safe nomenclature-*'Caurī-bearer'*.[26] C. Sivaramamurti also calls it *Chowrie*-bearer.[27]

Prashant Kumar Jayaswal[28] studies this image in socio-cultural perspective, dates it precisely Aśokan and calls it *'Strīratna'*. He stresses that in post-6th century BC, when the old social and moral values were waning, Asoka carried out a number of social reforms and appointment of *'Ithidhiyak Mahāmātā (Strīdhyaksha Mahāmātya)* was one of these. The sole motto behind appointment of such officers was to inculcate moral values and discipline, without which making of a healthy and wealthy society, he thought, was a distant dream. Jayaswal concludes as, with an objective to propagate the message of an ideal women, which definitely would have been the *Strīratna* (of *chakravartin* concept), Aśoka got installed this image at Didarganj, a place on Pataliputra-Rajgṛha highway.

Karl Khandalavala[29] dates it in Aśokan age and agrees to the nomenclature *'Strīratna'*, suggested to him by Devangana Desai (though pioneer in designating it as *'Strīratna'* is Jayaswal who personally told me that he has suggested this title to Ms. Desai. This is quite evident from the above reference of Jayaswal, published in 1975).

Following the line of Rai Govindachandra,[30] Madhuri Agrawal tries to identify this image with Lakṣmī. She holds that it is not possible to make difference in *Strīratna* and Lakṣmī and this image has all the symbolical traits of later Lakṣmī figures. Possibly such an image would have worked as model for later *chauri*-bearer Lakṣmī figures which appear by the side of Viṣṇu in post-Gupta Viṣṇu images.[31]

REAPPRAISAL

The above citations clearly manifest the dimensions of study by different scholars and their divergence of opinion for antiquity and identification of the Didarganj female figure. For anatomical alikeness and other macro-similarities, this figure and its siblings, of which some are inscribed to designate them *Yakṣa* or *Yakṣī*, have been grouped in one. On the basis of material and lustre a tentative Mauryan date, though with a bit hesitation, has been assigned to these figures by majority of scholars. There was widely in vogue the folk cult of *Yakṣas* and *Yakṣīs* in northern India during the era preceding as well as following the Mauryas and for the same, according to a cultic affiliation, the Didarganj female figure too was designated as *Yakṣī*.

The cult of *Yakṣa* and *Yakṣī* was a folk one and hitherto inscribed *Yakṣī* figures are of folkish nature, but the Didarganj female figure displays an elite gesture. Even the scholars who declare it a *Yakṣī* could not deny its aristocratic bearing[32] and the urban sophistication[33]. Though at macro level all the so-called *Yakṣa* and *Yakṣī* figures may appear same, so far as their stylistic presentation is concerned, but with a minute comparison and micro-analysis of style, all such sculptures may comfortably be differentiated and a plausible chronology too can be given to these.

Lack of naturalism and contoural balance aided with crude presentation places the Basarh lion capital and the Bodh Gaya elephant capital[34] at the remotest end in the series of Mauryan sculptures. The Sarnath lion capital in its naturalism, finest display of craftsmanship and lustre epitomizes the zenith of Mauryan sculptural art and for the same the Didarganj female figure can be grouped with it. The Didarganj figure makes live the standard of feminine beauty in its height, trifold at neck and waist, fully developed breasts, proportionate body *et al.*, whereas naturalism is visible in slight forward bend of the upper portion of body as it appears to be due to the weight of heavy breasts, as well in the slight bend of right knee due to the weight of *chaurī*. The massive body is fully modelled in round, the sides and the back also not excepted. The full and rounded features, including narrow waist and broad hips and gradually tapering down the shapely legs are all kept within the compactness of the whole and within a fluid contour that one may recognize in the rendering of front, back and sides. The Didarganj female figure presents a unique amalgamation of western realism and Indian standards and it may be taken as the earliest female figure which set the standards or served as the model for sculptural represenions of female in later periods.

DATE

It may be pointed out at the outset that the material and polish cannot be regarded as sure and sufficient grounds for assigning these sculptures to one particular period when they differ materially in technical aptitudes as well as in plastic and aesthetic conceptions.

Of these the Didarganj female figure and Lohanipur torso[35] may be declared earliest for their fully rounded form and fluid lines, in the lively and sensitive modelling of the limbs and the almost sensuous touch of the soft, warm flesh, though the Lohanipur torso is a bit archaic in presentation. The figure of *Yakṣa* Manibhadra from Pawaya may also be classed with the Didarganj figure but it will be just next. Though it exhibits a greater sense of modelling, front and back both included, and a well balanced production but in it there appears a conflict between rounded forms and flattened surface, from the point of presentation, which becomes clearly immanent in the sculptures to come.

Then come two Patna statues (now in Indian Museum, Kolkata), almost identical in form and conception, and the *Yakṣiṇī* figure from Besnagar, which show some heaviness in presentation. Their modelling, though appear to be easier and freer, the front exhibits rounded features, including the arms, breasts or chest and belly; but the entire presentation is a bit harsh, specially in linear contour at the sides. The drapery has been given separate volume where it does not cling to the body, but indicated merely by parallel ridges of folds where it does. It may be assumed here that through these sculptures beginning of deterioration in naturalism and three-dimensional treatment can be marked.

Posterior to the above ones are two sculptures from Baroda and Parkham. Of the Baroda sculpture only the upper part remains, while the Parkham specimen is more or less well preserved except for the missing hands and slight abrasions of the surface. These manifest a clear expression of massive portliness and volume, are strictly frontal in treatment and their modelling suffers from inadequate or insufficient technique. The masses appear to be superposed one above the other without any conscious relation among them. The sides and the back have practically no modelling except a slight chamfering. The drapery appears transparent where it clings to the body and has been given flat volume where it is free. The plait in between the two legs is interesting and reminds one of the similar plaits in Bharhut statuary and the sculptures of this group may be considered to belong to the phase of transition of sculptural art from Maurya to Śuṅga.

Thus the extremely flattened treatment of the Parkham *Yakṣa*s with its inane superposition of volume after volume compressed between two surfaces, the front and the back, is allied to or just anterior to the relief statuary on the Bharhut *toraṇas* of the 2nd century B.C. Earlier to these are the portly statues of *Yakṣa*s from Patna, conscientious in rendering of earth-bound weight but with greater roundness of features and better treatment of lines. In the rendering of these colossal statues, no doubt, representatives of old plastic diction one may recognize and can mark alienation of three dimensional depth to two-dimensional treatment. And the earliest among all is the Didarganj female figure for its fully rounded forms, fluid lines and sensitive modelling of the figure from top to toe. Thus in the light of above comparison and discussion, a date contemporaneous to the Sarnath lion capital may be assigned to the Didarganj female figure and it will be 3rd century B.C. during the reign of Aśoka.

OBJECTIVE

The Aśokan sculptures had a definitive objective, i.e. to convey the message of the king. They carry an inherent motif, through which their conceptual background can be deciphered. So far as Didarganj figure is concerned, identifying it as *Yakṣī* figure, majority of scholars have declared its objective to be religious. Some scholars opine that it was meant for decoration in king's apartment or in the royal court. But if it is ascertained that how was this figure installed, the enigma of its objective can be solved. Any sculpture itself tells how was it installed in its full glory.

- The Didarganj figure is carved out in round, so it was installed in such a way that it could be viewed from all the sides.
- It has a mirror like polish or lustre and it compels to infer that like other polished Mauryan sculptures it was not installed inside an apartment or royal court or a chapel of *chaitya,* but in open[36].
- The sculptors do not finish or even leave unhewn the portions of sculpture, which are not visible after installation. For example- in the sculptures of later period, which were to be installed against the wall the back has been left unfinished. Even in those sculptures, whose stele or back slab is cut along the outline of the central figure to give it (the central figure) a three dimensional appearance, the back is unfinished. In the Didarganj figure the feet portion is unfinished and unpolished, which is quite unusual, and hitherto pedestal has been left unhewn. In the Sarnath lion capital even a nail has been intricately carved out and finished, then what was the reason behind leaving the feet of such a beautiful figure unfinished. The reason is simple, as the feet and claws of the Sarnath lion are projecting outward and would have

been visible after installation so they are finished up to the end of the nail. In contrast the feet of the Basarh (Vaishali) lion have been left unfinished because they are invisible in installed position due to its square base. Similar would have been the case with the Didarganj figure, the feet of which too would have been invisible after installation and this was possible only with its installation on a pillar or a high pedestal. The figure has fine carvings and a bizarre expression over the face, and a viewer cannot appreciate or enjoy these intricacies if it was far away from the common visual distance, i.e. on a pillar top. I think it would have been installed on a 7 or 8 feet high pedestal like the figures of leaders today, which are installed in parks or crossroads. Conclusively it can be held that the Didarganj female figure was installed in open, on a 7 or 8 feet high pedestal and at a public place. Moreover Didarganj is the eastern end of Patna and the place was so even in ancient times. This is the entry-point for anything else coming to ancient Pataliputra or present Patna from the east.[37] Now it is obvious that the objective of the Didarganj female figure was definitely not religious and like other Mauryan or Aśokan sculptures its objective too was to convey some message. In the contemporary socio-cultural milieu the only message this figure can convey is that of ideal womanhood.

It is quite evident from the literatures that in post-upanishadic period the position of women in society deteriorated a lot.[38] In post 6th century B.C. when old social and moral values were on decline, Asoka carried out a number of social reforms and appointment of *'Strīdhyaksha Mahāmātya'* was one of these. Perhaps for the first time in the history of mankind, not only in India but in the whole world, women were appointed to such a high post and enjoyed powers equivalent to the other *Mahāmātyas* (ministers). The sole motto behind appointment of such ministers was to inculcate moral values and discipline among women, without which one cannot think of an ideal society. So in all probability, with an objective to propagate the message of 'ideal womanhood' Aśoka got this image installed.

HISTORICAL BACKDROP

Now the question is that when time came to manifest physically 'the ideal women', from where the sculptors got the prescription? Possibly at the level of concept *'bhārya'* of Brahminical literatures and *'strīratna'* of Buddhist literatures, associated as gems or *ratnins* with *chakravartin* or the king of kings, served as the model. The concept of *chakravartin* for the first time appears in the *Bṛhad Devtā*,[39] a post-vedic literature dated in 4th century BC.[40] In Buddhist canons the other treasures are the same as those in the *Bṛhad Devta* except for *strīratna*, *gṛhapati* and *parināyaka* in place of *bhāyrā*, *ratha* and *bhūmi*. These canons are the *Chakvatti sutta*[41] and the *Mahāsihanāda sutta*.[42] The *Digha nikāya* is the first *nikāya* of the *Sutta piṭaka* and the first four *nikāyas* of the *Sutta piṭaka* were compiled before 350 BC.[43]

In historical perspective the race for supremacy among the *Mahājanpadas* heated up with the accession of Ajātśatru to the Magadhan throne. This race concluded with bringing the entire North India under one sceptre during Aśoka. In history Aśoka has got the privilege of becoming the *chakravartin* in real and practical senses, which is evidenced by his undisputed authority over the entire Indian subcontinent and his universal appeal. It is further substantiated by the contemporary writings, including his inscriptions too, in which the king declares himself as *'Devānāmpiyo Priyadasin rājā* and *'Dev(ā)nām piyasa Aśok(a)sa'*.[44] Through these epithets the king declares himself *chakravartin*, as according to the *Mahāsuḍassana sutta*, a *chakravartin* should have four *iddhis* i.e., he should be good looking *(priyadarsi)*; Should be dear to his denizens as well as the gods (*devānām priya)*; free from grief and sorrow *(aśoka)*; and long living.[45] A king can be long living only through his good deeds and Aśoka in his inscriptions hankers that as the sun and the moon shine, his achievements should last.[46]

The literatures dealing with *bhāryā* or *strīratna* give her physical, moral as well as spiritual traits. Physically as well as morally she should be a real gem of women, having a universal appeal. She should be *Jagat kalyāṇī* (benefactor of the world) and her mental stature should be at par to his master, the *chakravartin*. Naturally when the king (Aśoka) would have wanted to propagate the message of 'ideal womanhood' to his women subjects, his choice would have been the figure of *Strīratna*. And when the sculptors were asked to make *strīratna* a reality in stone, they bestowed the standards of feminine beauty in Indian context, delineated in literatures,[47] to the figure. They even did not miss to portray the two inherent qualities of a women, i.e. the motherhood and the service.To portray 'service' the sculptor provided *chaurī* to the figure and 'motherhood' is portrayed by breasts as laden with milk and marked difference in their size. It is a medical truth that the left breast of a new mother happens to be comparatively smaller in size to the right one.

The *chaurī*-bearer figure of *strīratna* set the model for depiction of *strīratna* to come in future. A panel from Jaggayyapeta, belonging to 150 BC,[48] now housed in Govt. Museum, Madras, depicts the *chakravartin* along with his seven jewels and here the *strīratna* is carrying a *chaurī* on her right shoulder. On the reverse of *Aśvamedha* type coin of Samudragupta (AD 350-370), the commemorative coin declaring the *chakravartin* status of the king, the *strīratna* of the king who is *bhāryā* as well, appears holding *chaurī.* In later images, where Lord Viṣṇu appears in full royal gesture and posture, Lakṣmī accompanies him as *strīratna* holding a *chaurī* in her right hand.

CONCLUSION

Thus a proper nomenclature is must for first hand appreciation of any art-creation. It is also helpful in understanding the idealism behind. If the Didarganj image is introduced verbally as *Yakṣī* to a person, who has not seen this figure, he may take it as a robust and tough appearing female figure. He cannot think of the delicacy and charm, which the image possesses. Rather the title *Yakṣī* is not handy in conveying the idealism, which worked at the level of concept in making of this figure. And, if the same figure is introduced as '*strīratna*' to any one who knows or does not know this image, he can better appreciate and enjoy the image and aesthetic therein. This title also conveys instantly the ideals in the backdrop of this image. So *strīratna* is the proper appellation to Didarganj female figure for its appreciation and all purposes.

NOTES AND REFERENCES

1. Vasudev Sharan Agrawala, *Bhartiya Kala* (Hindi), ed. Prithvi Kumar Agrawal, Prithvi Prakashan, Varanasi, 1987 (reprint), pp.122-30.
2. Ram Prasad Chanda, *The Beginings of Art in Eastern India with Special Reference to Sculptures in the Indian Museum, Calcutta, Memoirs of the Archaeological Survey of India,* No. 30, Indological Book Corporation, New Delhi, 1978, reprint.
3. *Ibid.,* p.35.
4. *Ibid.,* pp.35-37.
5. *Ibid.,* p.37.
6. Jitendra Nath Banerjea, *The Development of Hindu Iconography,* University of Calcutta, Calcutta, 1956, pp.97-105.
7. *Gausṭhāyā Mānibhadrabhaktā garbhasukhitāh Bhagvato Mānibhadrasya pratimā pratisṭhāpayamti,* i.e. the image of Bhagvān Manibhadra is being established by the guild of the workshippers of Manibhadra. *Ibid.* p.97.
8. Nihar Ranjan Ray, *Maurya and Post-Maurya Art,* Indian Council of Historical Research, New Delhi, 1975, pp.40-41.
9. *Ibid.,* p.40.
10. *Ibid.*
11. *Ibid.*
12. S.P. Gupta, *Roots of Indian Art,* B.R. Publishing Corporation, Delhi, 1980, p.95.
13. *Ibid.,* p.96.
14. *Ibid.,* p.99.

15. *Ibid.*, p.95.
16. S.K. Saraswati, *A Survey of Indian Sculpture*, Firma K.L. Mukhopadhyay, Calcutta, 1957, pp.52-57.
17. *Ibid.*, p.56.
18. *Ibid.*, p.53.
19. *Ibid.*, pp.54-55.
20. Pramod Chandra, *The Sculpture of India*, 3000 BC, Harvard University Press, London, 1985, p.24.
21. *Ibid.*, p.49.
22. *Ibid.*, pp.24, 49.
23. *Ibid.*, p.49.
24. A.K. Coomarswamy, *Yakshas*, 2 vols., Washington D.C., 1928-31, Munshiram Mahoharlal, New Delhi, 1971 (reprint edn.).
25. A.K. Coomarswamy, *History of Indian and Indonesian Art*, Edward Goldston, London, Leipzig: Karl W. Hiersemann & New York: E. Weyhe, 1927, p.17.
26. C. Sivaramamurti, *The Art of India*, E. Weyhe, New York, 1927, p.17.
27. C. Sivaramamurti, *The Art of India*, Harry N. Abrams, New York, Incorporated, 1977, p.154.
28. Prashant Kumar Jayaswal, *Yakshi aur Strīratna* (Hindi), *Bharat Vani: The Spirit of India Smt. Indira Gandhi Abhinandan Granth*, 4 vols., ed. B.N. Pandey *et al.*, Asia Publishing House, Bombay, 1975, Vol. III, pp.251-45.
29. Karl Khandalavala, Didarganj Chauri-bearer: Another View Point, *Lalit Kala*, ed. Karl Khandalavala, No. 23, Lalit Kala Akademi, New Delhi, pp.12-14.
30. Rai Govindachandra, *Prachin Bharat Mein Laksmi Pratima* (Hindi), Hindi Pracharak Pustakalaya, Varansi, 1965. However, Govindachandra does not refer to the Didarganj figure, though he makes mention of other *Yakṣī* figures of Bharhut and Sanchi to identify them with *Lakṣmī*, pp.10, 24, 114-21.
31. Madhuri Agrawal, *Laksmi Kya Bauddha devi thin? Parishad Patrika*, ed. Hans Kumar Tiwari, Year-16, No. 3, 1976, Rashtra Bhasha Parishad, Patna, pp.27-28.
32. N.R. Ray, *op.cit.*, p.40.
33. S.K. Saraswati, *op.cit.*, p.55.
34. Arvind Mahajan, *Sambodhi : The Facets of Bodh Gaya*, Om Publications, New Delhi, 2002, pp.107-111.
35. Patna Museum Arch. no. 8038.
36. If it was to be installed inside, its sculptor would not venture to lustre it which required great labour (Arvind Mahajan : 'Science and Technique of Lustre Over the Mauryan Stone Artefacts', Paper presented in the National Seminar on Mauryan Art, organized by Patna Museum, Patna in the year 1999). Moreover inside a chamber or hall its bright lustre was meaningless because any surface appears lustrous due to complete reflection of light from the surface and inside any hall or chamber light always remains limited and lesser in comparison to outside. So it was definitely not installed inside a chamber or apartment or hall.

37. Arvind Mahajan, *Pataliputra Nagar ka Prarmbha Evam Vistara, Prajñā Bhāratī,* Vol. X, Year-10, Chief Editor Jagadishwar Pandey, K.P. Jayaswal Research Institute, Patna, 1999, pp.51-56.
38. Arvind Mahajan, *Upanishad Kala Mein Striyon ki Sthiti* (Hindi), *Upanishat-srih,* ed. Urmila Shrivastava, Arya Kanya Degree College, Allahabad, 2001, pp.268-73.
39. *Chakram ratho manir-bhāryā bhumir aśvo gajas-thathā / Etāni saptarathāṇi sarveshām-chakravartinām // (Bṛhad Dev.tā, V.123). Bṛhad Devtā,* An index to the gods of the Ṛig Veda by Śaunaka Āchārya, ed. R.L. Mitra, *Bibliotheca Indica Series,* Asiatic Society of Bengal, Calcutta, 1889, New Series No. 722.
40. M.M. Mehendale, *Language and Literature* (chapter XVI), *The Age of Imperial Unity,* ed. R.C. Majumdar and A.D. Pusalker, Bhartiya Vidya Bhawan, Bombay, 1953 (2nd edn.), p.254.
41. *Chakvatti sutta,* 3.1.2., *Digha nikaya,* Gen. ed. Bhikkhu J. Kashyap, Nalanda, Nav Nalanda Mahavihar, 1958, Vol. III, pp.5, 46.
42. *Mahasihanada Sutta,* 4.6.9, *Digha nikaya, op.cit.,* Vol. II, pp.xviii (intro.) and 134.
43. A.D. Pusalker, *Pali Canon* (Chap.XIX, part-B, Buddhism, section-VI), *The Age of Imperial Unity, op.cit.,* p.408.
44. Maski Rock Inscription of Asoka, *Corpus Inscriptionum Indicarum,* Vol. I, ed. E. Hultzch, Oxford, 1925, p.251.
45. *Mahāsudassana sutta,* 4.9.12, *Dīgha nikāya, op.cit.,* Vol. II, pp.135-36.
46. 7th Pillar edict of Asoka, *Corpus Inscriptionum Indicarum,* Vol. I, *op.cit.*
47. Buddhist literatures follow the preceding Sanskrit literatures in giving details of the *Strīratna.* She has been described as beautiful, 'neither too black nor too fair, neither too tall nor too short, neither too fat nor too thin. Her limbs are warm to touch in winter and cold in summer. They are soft to touch as a scarf from Kalinga *(Kalinga-prāvāra).* The roots of her hair emanate the aroma of sandalwood and her mouth the fragrance of lotus'. cf. Moti Chandra, *Ancient Indian Ivories, Bulletin of the Prince of Wales Museum of Western India,* No. 6, Bombay, 1957-1959, p.25.
48. N.R. Ray, *Maurya and Post-Maurya Art, op.cit.,* pl.69, p.121.

4

Some Landmarks of *Anugraha* Images of Śiva with Special Reference to Rāvaṇānugraha Image

Shanti Swaroop Sinha

Śiva, the god of dissolution (*Vilaya* or *Saṁhāra*) was accorded a venerated position in Vedic-Paurāṇic tradition. He is worshipped in variety of forms under the categories of *Saumya anugraha* and *Saṁhāra* forms.[1] The present paper will deal with some of the distinguishing features of *anugraha* images of Śiva wherein Śiva extends his unceasing compassion and blessings to his worshippers. These worshippers include the devotees like Rāvaṇa and Arjuna as well as the gods like Viṣṇu and Gaṇeśa. Some other forms like Gaṅgādhara and Yamāntaka which are usually taken to be non-*anugraha* forms, have also been included in *anugraha* forms due to the reason that the main theme and the way of representation are suggestive of compassion (*anugraha*) of Śiva. In the Gaṅgādhara form Bhagiratha was blessed with the *anugraha* of Śiva for bringing holy Gaṅgā on the earth, while in Yamāntaka form the main theme was not the award of punishment to Yama but to protect and bless the staunch devotee Mārkaṅdeya. Therefore the Yamāntaka image should be called as Mārkaṅdeyānugraha.[2]

On the basis of available ancient sculptures and the literary texts, it may be presumed that the iconographic features of *anugraha* images were crystalized during the Gupta and early medieval period. The earliest works dealing with different *anugraha* forms were the *Rāmāyaṇa*,[3] the *Mahābhārata*,[4] the works of Kālidāsa[5] (*Raghuvaṁśa, Kumārasaṁbhava* and *Meghaduta*) and Māgha[6] *(Śiśupālabadha)* and also the Purāṇas.

The rendering of Rāvaṇānugraha and Arjunānugraha images started in Gupta period while other forms find usual expression during 7th century AD onwards.[7] The main *anugraha* images of Śiva, in order of popularity, were Rāvaṇānugraha, Arjunānugraha, Chaṇḍeśānugraha, Viṣṇuānugraha

(Chakradāna), Nandīśānugraha and Vighneśvarānugraha. Of all the *anugraha* images, Rāvaṇānugraha and Arjunānugraha forms were the most popular ones, the images of which outnumber all other *anugraha* image. The variety in respect of iconographic features of these forms are also enormous. We shall now discuss in detail some distinguishing features of Rāvaṇānugraha images.

The most graphic representation of Rāvaṇānugraha image in narrative style (Kathātmaka style) are found mainly from Ellora (Kailāśa temple), Bhubaneśvara (Paraśurāmeśvara temple, Satrughneśvara temple) and Paṭṭaḍakal (Virupākṣa temple). In such examples mostly the figure of Rāvaṇa is shown comparatively bigger in dimension than the figures of Śiva and Pārvatī who are sitting at the top of Kailāśa mountain (pl. 4.2). While probing into it, it appears that there could have been two reasons. First is special respect for Rāvaṇa in the region of Deccan and South India. The second reason could be special perspective of the artists, wherein artist has visualized the whole episode with different composition. The artist in such cases has visualized the episode by viewing the whole scene from the ground level and by putting himself in the centre. Due to this perspective the figure of Rāvaṇa automatically becomes bigger and Kailāśa mountain above becomes smaller and finally the figures of Śiva and Pārvatī at the top are shown more smaller (pl. 4.1).[8] This perspective is very realistic as well as the rare feature of Rāvaṇānugraha images from Bhubaneśvara, Ellorā, Kānchīpuram, Mahābalīpuram, Paṭṭaḍakal and Gaṅgaikoṇḍacholapuram.

The landmark of Rāvaṇānugraha images from Khajurāho, Hiṅgalājagarh, Karitalāī, Siron-Khurd, Gurgi, Jabalpur, Maṇdasore and several other places in North India is that instead of narration style, Rāvaṇānugraha image is represented in the form of Umā-Maheśvara image.[9] Actually in North India right from 8th-9th century AD, the Rāvaṇānugraha form was fused with Umā-Maheśvara form, wherein like other Umā-Maheśvara images, Śiva and Pārvatī are seated in *aliṅgana-pose* with usual compositional features showing the figures of Brahmā, Viṣṇu,[10] Gaṇeśa, Kārttikeya, Bhriṅgi, Vīrabhadra and also Nandī and *Siṁha vāhanas.* The bottom of the seat or pedestal however contains the figure of Rāvaṇa (having one, three or ten faces), who is engaged in the act of upholding the seat, sometimes shown in the form of rocks symbolically suggesting lifting of Kailāśa mountain.[11] In North Indian examples, the rendering of the figure of Gaṇeśa ridiculing the abortive attempt of Rāvaṇa was very common, which is conspicuous by its absence in South India, where Rāvaṇa enjoyed a respectable position. In some remarkable representations mainly from Siron-Khurd and Bhubaneśvara, the figures of Gaṇeśa and Kārttikeya are also shown. In the Siron-Khurd example, surprisingly Gaṇeśa and Kārttikeya are shown as helping Rāvaṇa in lifting the Kailāśa mountain, which again points towards the mockery of Rāvaṇa when he fails to lift the mountain.[12]

The representation of *Gardabha Mukha*[13] (donkey face) of Rāvaṇa was specially popular in North India. In North Indian sculptural examples one face of Rāvaṇa is very often shown as donkey face (pl. 4.3). which is either in the centre or above the horizontal row of faces. However in South Indian Rāvaṇānugraha images, except for the solitary example at Ellorā (Kailāśa temple), the donkey face is never shown, apparently due to the respectable position enjoyed by Rāvaṇa in South India. This feature of North Indian images is an enigmatic feature which requires explanation.[14] Does the donkey face symbolically suggest the foolishness of Rāvaṇa, when he overestimates his power and tries to lift Kailāśa mountain? May be that there was some deeper meaning and suggestion? Incidentally Rāvaṇa was great scholar, well versed in the Vedas (*Vedajña*). We know through the texts that the Vedas were visualized in personified forms with animal faces. According to *Śrītatvanidhi, Ṛgveda* in personified form is to be shown with donkey face. If donkey face of Rāvaṇa is considered in this context it becomes very pertinent to suggest that Rāvaṇa is *Vedajña* and well versed in *Ṛgveda* and hence shown with donkey face.[15] In Indian art nothing is merely external and without symbolic suggestion the figure of Rāvaṇa with donkey face therefore bears testimony to this deeper meaning of artistic representation.

NOTES AND REFERENCES

1. *Prabandhachintāmani,* pp.102, 104.
2. S.S. Sinha, *Śiva kī Anugraha Murtiyān* (in press).
3. *Rāmāyaṇa* (Uttara Kirātaparva, Chap. 31-41).
4. *Mahābhārata* (Vanaparva, Kirātaparva, Chap. 31-41).
5. *Raghuvaṁśa* (4/80/12,89), *Kumārasambhava* (8/24), *Meghaduta* (1/62).
6. *Śiśupālabadha* (1/50).
7. S.S. Sinha, *op.cit.*
8. *Ibid.*
9. B.N. Sharma, "Rāvaṇa Lifting Mount Kailāśa in Indian Art", *East and West,* Vol. 23, pt. 3-4, 1973, p.335.
10. M.P. Joshi, "Rāvaṇānugraha Murtī from Kumaun", *Journal of Oriental Institute, Baroda,* Vol. 32, pt. 3-4, March-June 1983, pp.301-302.
11. C. Sivaramamurti, *Masterpieces of Indian Art,* New Delhi, 1971.
12. S.D. Trivedi, *Sculpture in Jhansi Museum,* Jhansi, 1983, pp.56-57.
13. C. Sivaramamurti, *Birds and Animals in Indian Sculpture,* New Delhi, 1974, p.261.
14. S.S. Sinha, *op.cit.*
15. *Ibid.*

5

Some Reflections of the Contemporary Culture and Interactions in the Sculptures of Ellora

Anand Prakash Srivastava

The early medieval period was a period of vigorous art activity, which is evidenced by enormous surviving structural and rock-cut temples and sculptural renderings there on. The contributions of the Rāṣṭrakuṭa rulers towards art activity, particularly the rock-cut architecture and sculptures in respect of their monumentality, animation, proportions, free movement and iconographic details have been invaluable. In earlier writings, the study of ancient Indian art was made for the study of the aesthetic features as well as their religious content and philosophical concepts but now the art is considered the product of the entire society and hence it carries detailed and multiple aspects of contemporary society. Therefore the study of art data has become a very forceful tool for the study of the society of the past in its multifarious activities like dance, music, love, sex, education, war, humour and acrobatics. In the present paper an attempt has been made to study the sculptures of Kailāśa temple of Ellora (Aurangabad district-Maharashtra) from that stand point.

The Kailāśa temple is one of the most brilliant creations of Indian artists. It is a gigantic, magnificent and proportionate example of rock-cut architecture with beautiful and huge but lively sculptures. The temple dedicated to Śiva was built in 8th century AD by the Rāṣṭrakuṭa ruler Kṛṣṇa I.[1] As contrary to medieval temples at Khajuraho, Modhera, Konarka, Bhubaneshwar, the Kailāśa temple has very little representations of contemporary day-to-day life, perhaps because a special emphasis of the artist was to depict Śiva in all his magnificence and magnitude. Śiva is represented in *Saumya Anugraha* and *Saṁhārak* forms to project the Mahādeva aspect. The presence of Maheśa and the Naṭeśa or cosmic dance images also bear testimony to this. It was mainly through the images of Śiva and other deities that one gets reflections of the contemporary religions, tradition, customs, dress and ornaments, hairdresses and weapons.[2]

The study reveals that Jaina Purāṇas namely *Adipurāṇa* (of Jinasena) and *Uttarapurāṇa* (of Guṇabhadra), composed during the Rāṣṭrakuṭa period had great impact on the sculptures of the Ellora caves in general and cave 16 (Kailāśa temple) in particular.[3]

The contemporary texts show that special emphasis was given on dance and music in Rāṣṭrakuṭa society for the expression of gaiety and celebrity and the outcome was the most prolific and vibrant representations of the dancing images of Śiva in Kailāśa temple. The variety of dress and ornaments are also suggestive of the tastes of the Rāṣṭrakuṭa people.

The prosperity of Rāṣṭrakuṭa society is so well and forcefully represented through a rare and huge image of Abhiṣeka Lakṣmī (pl. 5.1), Seated cross legged in the lotus pond, She is accompanied by four elephants in place of two usually shown with Abiṣeka Lakṣmī images. The four elephants represent four main directions and also symbolize prosperity. Two elephants are lustrating the goddesses with water vessel shown above. The goddess is provided with a parasol and flying figures of *vidyādharas* and other semi-divine beings. The entire composition suggests the prosperity of the Rāṣṭrakuṭa rulers and thereby the society. The image is carved just infront of the *gopuram* on the ground level of *nandimandapa* in such a position so that the visitor while entering temple faces the image of Abhiṣeka Lakṣmī first.

Sometimes the customs and traditions are also reflected which are still in continuity in a particular region. In *Pāṇīgrahana* (*Kalyānasundara*) images of Śiva and Pārvatī at Ellora and elsewhere, Śiva is shown as holding the palm of Pārvatī in right hand. But surprisingly in one of the Kalyānasundara images in the Kailāśa temple carved in *vithipa* instead of *pāṇīgrahana* posture, the hand of Śiva is shown in the palm of the right hand of Pārvatī. This appears somewhat unusual but it was in conformity with the tradition of Maharashtra prevailing even today. On the occasion of marriage in Maharashtra the right hand of groom is placed on the palm of the bride. The information about this tradition of Maharashtra was given by N.P. Joshi of Varanasi.

In the sculptures of Kailāśa temple, we also find bearing of different earlier and contemporary art traditions mainly Pallava and Cālukya which show the process of interactions and broad mindedness of Raṣṭrakuṭa artists, as rightly pointed out by M.N.P. Tiwari and Kamal Giri.[4] The two sculptures in particular show such features. One is the Mahiṣamardinī image carved near the *gopuram* (inside) of Kailāśa temple while the other is an episode from the *Rāmāyana* showing the abduction of Sitā by Rāvaṇa, and consequent fight of Rāvaṇa with Jatāyu, who gave him a forceful resistance. The Mahiṣamardinī image shown in narrative style is fighting with Mahiṣāsura shown with buffalo head and human body. This sculpture appears to be the replica of Mahiṣamardinī relief image from Mahabalipuram. On the other hand the episode of Rāvaṇa Jatāyu fight in respect of compositional set up was borrowed from identical representation to be seen on Virupakṣa temple at Paṭṭadakal, a great centre of Cālukyan art.

The rendering of Rāmakathā in continuity in eight panels shown, are above the other in Kailāśa temple, is also interesting. The tradition of precise, representation of the whole of Rāmakathā is preserved in a subsequent work *Rāmkaṛṇāmṛitam* of 14th century AD. This text, belonging to North India, gives a brief description of Rāmakathā just in one verse and hence it is called *Ekślokī Rāmāyaṇa.*

NOTES AND REFERENCES

1. James Fergusson and Burgess, *The Cave Temples of India,* Delhi, 1969, pp.450-51.
2. Maruti Nandan Tiwari, "Jaina Mahapurāna Ki Kalāparak Sāmagrī", *Sanskriti-Sandhāna,* Volume 6, 1993, Varanasi, pp.38; 'Images of Bahubatī in Elloṛa,' *Ellora Caves-Sculptures and Architecture* (Ratan Parimoo), New Delhi, 1988; *Adipurāṇa,* 14. 157-158; *Harivanisapurana* 22. 11-21; 8.233; Vrittanugandhiga-dyam, p.491; *Adipurāṇa,* 14.133; *Uttarapurāṇa* 50.44.
3. Kamad Giri, *Jaina Mahapurāṇa Kalāparak Adhyayan,* Varanasi, 1995.
4. Maruti Nandan Tiwari and Kamal Giri, *Madhyakāleena Bhartiya Murtikala,* Varanasi, 1991, pp.72-73

6

Ideals of Some Śaiva Images

C.P. Sinha

Art in India, as in other countries of the ancient world, was principally devoted to the service of religion. It has not developed in isolation. Indian art is a monumental expression of metaphysical symbolism. It was not an aesthetic luxury of a few individuals but a persistent, conscious and well regulated religion-oriented pursuit of the whole race. It reflects the intimate relationship of ideas and life, natural observations and inner substance and material and spiritual world. K.V. Soundara Rajan[1] has rightly observed that religion in India had been the vehicle and art the Veneer. Indian art is a vehicle for the conveyance of valuable religious ideas. Charles Fabri[2] has pointed out that image of an Indian sculptural history being unveiled before your eyes in this manner, will give a fare glimpse of the beauty and loveliness of this great and original forms of art. Mythology, symbolism, iconography, etc., all are only vehicles or aids to understand the essence and spirit of Indian art. Indian art together with Indian myth and legend by which it is constantly inspired and replenished, suggests rather than depicts inner versions and experiences. Each and every symbol and each and every icon in Indian art has a meaning and is expressed with a purpose under a śāstric prescription. The icons are embodiments of various gods in their particular forms with deep philosophical meaning for the welfare of devotees.

Śiva has been one of the most important and popular deities in India, both in past ages and in present times. In the plastic art he has two forms, aniconic and anthropomorphic. The aniconic form is the *Liṅga* with a variety of types. Phallicism is one of the ancient forms of worship in India and the ancient World. *Liṅga* (or phallus) is the symbol of creation. The various anthropomorphic forms of the deity are Umā-Maheśvara, Ardhanārīśvara, Lakulīsa, Rāvaṇānugraha, Yoga-Dakṣiṇa Murti, Vinādhara-Dakṣiṇa Murti, Vyākhyāna-Dakṣiṇa Murti, Umā-Sahita Murti, Gaṅgādhara Śiva, Sadāśiva,

Liṅgodbhava Murti, Saṁhāra Murti (Tripurāntaka and Andhakāsurvadha Murti) Baṭuka Bhairava and Maheśa Murti, etc.

The Urdhvaretas Śiva is usually shown naked with his phallus erect, symbolizing this form. The *retas* is styled in the language of symbolism as butter[3] The seed (*retas*) is the great power of Śiva, and is further symbolized as the Nandī Bull. V.S. Agrawala[4] has pointed out that the foundation of the physical and Psychical or vital energy is the seed, and therefore, the highest emphasis is laid on *brahmacharya*, or the purity of physical, vital and psychical sheaths in each body represented as urdhvaretas aspect of Śiva, even though he has accomodated Pārvatī or the Female Energy as one half of his total aspect. This philosophical speculation of Vedas later led to the formation of images of Ūrdhva-retas Śiva either standing or seated alone or in Ardhanāriśvara form, or along with Pārvatī in an embracing pose. The Ardhanāriśvara pose of Śiva and the comingling of Viṣṇu and Śiva in the form of Harihara and the mingling of Śiva and Śakti or *Paruṣa* and *Prakriti*, really bridge the gap of mythological as well as archaeological evidence of the past.

Śiva is the best of the yogīs, and as such he is known under the applications Yogendra, Yogeśvara Mahātapaḥ and Mahāyogī, etc.[5] Besides being a *yogī*, Śiva is also known as the lord or protector of animals, pastor of the flock or herd (*Paśupati*), a title which has been attributed to Śiva in the Vedic and subsequent literature very often.[6] Śiva, the *Mahāyogī*, is also Natarāja, the Lord of Dancers. The form of Śiva as Natarāja, Nateśa or Nṛtyeśvara was and still is a curious theme for devotees, religio-philosophic thinkers, artists, painters, poets and writers alike. Hardly any ancient culture of the world has such a popular and powerful master of dance as we have in the form of Śiva Natarāja. The dance of Śiva has cosmic force in it. Dancing is an act of creation. Through his frantic motions, he generates the power of evolution, maintenance and dissolution of the world.

We may mention the philosophical significance of the various forms and attributes of Śiva. The five faces of Mahādeva represent Sadyojāta as earth, Vāmadeva as water, Aghora as light, Tatpurṣa as air and Iṣāna as sky.[7] The three eyes of each face of Śiva represent the sun, the moon and the fire.[8] The *daṇḍa* in the hand of Bhairava is the death itself.[9] The three prongs of the trident represent *sattva, rajas* and *tamas* qualities.[10] The tiger skin of Śiva represent the various *tṛishṇās* (desire).[11] The citron in the hand of Bhairava indicates the seed of the world. These seeds represent the atoms, constituting the world.[12] The moon digit on the head of Śiva is indicative of his divine power.[13] His mount bull is a symbolic form of divine four footed *dharma*,[14] Vāsuki Snake, associated with Śiva represents anger subduing the three world.[15] The colour of Mahādeva is white which represents *Prakriti.*[16]

The images of Umā-Maheśvara form a distinct class of the Uṁāliṅganamurti of Śiva which do not seem to have association with any particular mythology. In such images Umā (or Pārvatī), seated on the left thigh of Śiva, is shown in close embrace of each other. Śiva has four-arms (sometimes two) and is elaborately dressed and ornamented and seated on a high *āsana*. His right leg rests on *vāhana*, the bull. In this form various love sports like *āliṅgana* (embracing), *kuca sparśa* (gently touching the nipple of the breast), *aṅkārohana* (holding spouse in one's lap), *mukha-darṣanam* (looking face to face) and *cibukothānam* (uplifting the face by chin) have been beautifully and tastefully depicted. The love sports like *āliṅana, Kuca-sparśa, aṅkārohana* and *mukha darṣana* have been mentioned in different *silpa* texts and other literary works but *cibukothānam* has no where been clearly and specifically mentioned.

In such form Śiva has been represented or carved like a true *dampati* leading married family life. Śiva's *mithuna* figures are large in number than many of his other forms and the Umā-Maheśvara form outnumbers all other such images.

To sum-up, we can say that unless and until we know the inner meaning of the art piece, the philosophy behind the carving of the image, one cannot appreciate the art piece or image in proper perspective.

NOTES AND REFERENCES

1. K.V. Soundara Rajan, *India's Religious Art, Ideas and Ideals*, p.ii.
2. Charles Fabri, *Discovering Indian Sculptures*, p.v (Introduction).
3. Atharvaveda, XI, 8-29.
4. V.S. Agrawala, *Śiva Mahādeva*, Preface, p.5.
5. Monier-Williams, *Religious Thought and Life in Ancient India*, p.83.
6. Macdonell and Keith, *Vedic Index*, p.35.
7. Visnudharmottara-III 48, 2-3.
8. *Ibid.*, III, 48-9.
9. *Ibid.*, III, 48-12.
10. *Ibid.*, III, 48, 14-15.
11. *Ibid.*, III, 48, 18.
12. *Ibid.*, III, 48, 12.
13. *Ibid.*, III, 48, 17.
14. *Ibid.*, III, 48, 18.
15. *Ibid.*, III, 48, 17.
16. *Ibid.*, III, 48, 19.

7

Moving Perspective in Ajanta Murals

Kalachand Chowdhury

At one time in the West perspective was considered the measure of advancement in art, irrespective of the basic identity of a culture. Where art did not comply with the western perspective, it was considered the deficiency of that art. In this scheme, observer's position is fixed, and he looks through a frame, as if from a window, where his body below the waist does not come in interaction with the object represented in the art. The observer stands before a visual pyramid with an elevated planar cross-section producing a homogeneous and mathematical space.

The Western perspective is dependent on two basic assumptions. Here Panofsky's observation may be quoted.

> In order to guarantee a fully rational, that is infinite, unchanging and homogeneous-space, the 'central perspective' makes two tacit but essential assumptions that the planar cross section of the visual pyramid can pass for an adequate reproduction of our optical image. In fact these two premises are rather bold abstraction from reality, if by reality we mean the actual subjective optical impression.[1]

Ajanta style presents a different experience, which is diametrically opposite to that of the western perspective. The Indian artist allows his scene to unfold like a panorama, without any boundary of a frame. Unlike an observer in western perspective, the spectator for Ajanta frescoes does not occupy a fixed position, he moves along with the frescoes from one direction to another.

Ajanta frescoes were predominantly meant for the pilgrims or *śramaṇas* who passed before the frescoes in a *parikramā,* i.e. circumambulation. A long established practice in Buddhism is to keep the principal deity on his right while in a *parikramā*. In Ajanta, principal object of worship, such as, Buddha or a *stupa,* in a *chaitya* hall, is kept near the back wall. For the pilgrim to keep it to his right he has to enter the cave from the left side. Ultimately, he always keeps frescoes on the wall to his left, both while entering or leaving of the cave.

Apart from this, Ajanta frescoes have some more extraordinary characteristics, in contrast with the western perspective, which are briefly given below :-

(a) An objective in Western perspective recedes from the stationary observer towards a horizon. However, in Ajanta murals it comes forward to the spectator, who is in a *parikramā* and there is no horizon or any sky in the painting. Further there is no background in Ajanta painting, in the true sense, what comes forward comes uncreated to the created.

(b) In the Western perspective the lines converge from the observer's eye towards a distant point on an imaginary line called the horizon; but the lines of Ajanta painting converge from the object towards spectator's eye, thus reversing the diagonals.

(c) Western perspective takes in only that much of what we see. In the Ajanta painting, artists brings out what we know.

(d) These two opposite characteristics of looking at the things in its trail brings another distinction which is dominance of visuality over tactility in one and dominance of tactility over visuality in the other.

(e) Jeanne Auboyer had written a full length article on perspective in Ajanta murals. Many of the features mentioned above are taken from his observations. Above all he tried to trace a moving receding point on the imaginary horizon. But he did not indicate that the observer also moves along with the moving receding point on the horizon line. The reason for his not doing so, was perhaps, due to the function of the observer, who was not supposed to leave his fixed position. Had he done so, the entire edifice of Western perspective would have collapsed. However, for Ajanta murals there was no observer in ancient India, there was only a slowly moving spectator who was supposed to follow the narrative panel so as to come to it's conclusion. As a result there was no fixed position for the observer in ancient India but there was a fixed path for the moving spectator. Further, he was not supposed to take the murals piece by piece, he took them at a time in its totality. It must be remembered that the story in the murals was already known to him and as such it was not difficult to take it in its entirety.

(f) Now in Eastern perspective there was no distance between the spectator and the spectacle since they were sharing a common ground. As indicated earlier, converging lines from the frescoes make a stage around the spectator which plays out all the sentiments and powerful urge for sacrifice, gift or *Nirvāṇa* and ultimately purges him of impurities, if any, in this consciousness. In a way, functionally, this process is not very different from catharsis in the spectator of Greek tragedy.

We must not forget that in 200 BC, when the frescoes on the left wall of Cave 10 of Ajanta was painted, the writing as such (we do not mean here monumental writing) was not in existence in the society. In that sense, it was predominantly an oral culture which had its own distinguishable characteristics. Few of these characteristics as propounded by Walter. J. Ong are as follows.

(a) It is additive rather than subordinative.
(b) It is aggregative rather than analytic.
(c) Overflowing or redundant.
(d) Empathetic and participatory rather than objectively distanced.

Painting on the left wall of Cave 10 flows in a horizontal band which is astonishingly simple and different from the paintings of the fifth and the sixth century, where the entire wall is covered with painting. Earlier painting was not segmented as frequently as it was done in the later paintings. Concentration in composition was comparatively sparse and relaxed. Long almond-shaped eyes and noses of the figures in the earlier paintings show that they had nothing to hide in their eyes nor anything more to reveal.

In the fifth century writing was well established in cities and towns of India. The vestiges of oral culture was not totally eliminated and its lingering presence was discernible in the paintings of that period.

The three distinguishable effect of writing on painting of the fifth century onward can be mentioned. These features are :-

a) Use of architecture as punctuation mark in the painting.
b) Arrangement of background in subordination to foreground or in depth.
c) Back looping in composition.

Use of architectural break as punctuation mark is a prominent feature in the paintings of the fifth century onward and it has been frequently highlighted by different commentators.

As regards back looping, a representative instance may be cited. Two pavillions painted side by side, in the depiction of *Mahājanaka Jātaka,* presented them as coming forth from two different directions, where spectators were supposed to place themselves in between the two. As a result the spectator had no choice but to turn alternatively towards the one and then towards the other. Back looping is nothing but retrieval of context by glancing back over the text selectively.

The mind concentrates our energies on moving ahead, because what it back loops into lies quiescent outside itself, always piecemeal on the inscribed page.[2]

Depth in Ajanta painting came through the replacement of the vertical disposition of the foreground and background in depiction of buildings, pavillions and gates. In opposition to additive trend, subordination can also be observed in showing the principal personage larger in stature than the others. It is quite possible that it was the path along which artist's technique was to travel in order to differentiate the size of the figures by placing them in the context of distance.

At the end it must be admitted that Ajanta style never stopped at one place. Instances cited are not to be found very frequently. As a result we will have to keep our search going to find number of more minor systems rather than a totalized systematization aiming at establishment of a grand theory.

NOTES AND REFERENCES

1. Panofsky, *Perspective as Symbolic Form,* pp.28-29.
2. Walter J. Ong, *Orality and Literacy,* p.39.

8

Landmarks of Early-Medieval Indian Sculptures

Maruti Nandan Tiwari

Early medieval period (c. 7th to 11th century AD) of Indian art is characterized by predominance of regional features and innovations. In the present paper some non pareil examples of Brahmanical, Buddhist and Jaina images of varying time and space will be discussed with a view to appreciate their landmarks and uniqueness. Of enormous sculptural examples, only a few will be taken up to focus our attention.

We come across a good number of Pāla and Sena Buddhist sculptures, belonging to 8th to 10th century AD, from Eastern India which are beautiful in terms of composition, body, contours and embellishments but what is unique in some of them is that they represent Buddha with *mukuṭa*, necklaces while Buddha after renouncing the world took the path of complete renunciation and austerity. Thus it was an innovation on the part of the artist which has to be examined and explained further. They are taken to represent सम्भोग काया also (pl. 8.1). In other examples carved on the wall of the Sun temple at Modherā (Gujarāt), one finds the *tridhā* (triad) aspect of Surya (rising, noon midday, setting Sun), who has been represented here as having three legs, three arms and three heads. We do not find any textual reference to this form. There is lotus in hands but one hand carries sword. The mount is horse(?) The *Viṣṇudharmottara* however, refers to *Jvara* form of Śiva as having 3 face, 3 arms and 3 legs but there is no mention of attributes.

At a number of places we find several examples showing continuity of action or event in sculptural art, the best of all such examples is the Gajalakṣmī images (Abhiṣeka-Lakṣmī) from Mahabalipuram (Tamil Nadu - 7th century AD) and *Pancha musti-keśaluñchana* of Jaina images at Kumbhariyā (Śāntinātha, and Mahāvira temples, 11th century AD, Gujarat). Other rare example is on the Pārṣvanātha temple of Khajurāho (AD 950-70). The temple besides having the figures of Jaina Tīrthaṅkaras and Jaina *Yakṣis,* does contain the figures of Śiva, Viṣṇu, Brahmā, Balarāma, Rāma and Kāmadeva either alone or even alongwith their Śaktis in *āliṅgana* pose. Thus interactive approach indeed is a rare feature of Indian art. The image showing Rāma-Sītā with Hanumāna (as *Vinaya-murti)* on northern facade is specially to be appreciated.[3]

In Jaina sculptures of Ellorā (Maharashtra, 9th century) and Deogarh (10th-13th century AD) we find that several divine beings like Bāhubali, Bharata and Sarasvatī were accorded an exalted position to make them almost at par with the Jaina Tīrthaṅkara, who were, highest in Jaina worship.[4] Such forms are not visualised in any of the known texts and hence they apparently suggest certain social and value oriented thought process which was intended to underline the immense potentials of humans which, when sustained, nurtured and manifested can elevate him to make him equal to Rāma, Śiva, Buddha and Mahāvira or any other deity worthy of adoration. This is the true spirit in which we can, rather we should, appreciate Indian art.

The placement of the figures on the walls of the temples also sometimes help in identifications. One such example is on the Surya temple (No. II) of Osiāñ (Rajasthan-8th century AD) which does contain on its eastern facade the figure of two-armed Surya (in *sambhaṅga)* in central niche while Revanta (riding horse) and Manu (with *Akshamālā* and *Pustaka* and beard and *Jaṭā-mukuṭa* with two flanking figures-one with manuscript, *Viṣṇudharmottara Purāṇa*-70.1-3) the two sons of Surya, carved in two flanking separate niches, could be identified on the basis of placement.[5] Equally important are the representation of Vaiṣṇava themes in Delvāḍā Jaina temples (Vimala-Vasahī, Luna-Vasahī-12th-13th century AD — Mt. Abu-Rajasthan). In Vimala Vasahī, besides the Kāliyamardana episode (pl. 8.2) and forceful image of Sthauṇa Narasiṁha, the scene of Holī is also carved, wherein Kṛṣṇa is playing Holī with sprinklers made of cow horn *(Kanaka Śriṅgakośa of Harśacharita). Pītāmbaradhārī* Kṛṣṇa is surrounded by the figures of *gopa* and *gopikās* carrying identical sprinklers. The mood of gaiety and festivity is noteworthy.[6] Such representations are distinct examples of religious interactions and mutuality.

We all are familiar with the *Kalyāṇasundara* images which should instead be called *Pārvatī Pariṇaya* because no text does refer to this form as *Kalyāṇasundara*. In one rare example of *Kalyāṇasundara* image (from Etah, U.P., 10th century AD) representing the wedding of Śiva and Pārvatī for the birth of Kārttikeya, surprisingly Kārttikeya (on left) is also shown in the *parikara* along with Gaṇeśa (on right). The image is now preserved in Bharat Kala Bhavan, Varanasi (Acc. No. 175).[7] Possibly the artist has made this unusual presence of Kārttikeya (ridings on peacock and holding *śula*) on his own. Another feature is the presence of Mālini, the close friend (*sakhī*) of Pārvatī who is touching the left leg of Śiva as if making request for the well care of Pārvatī after marriage. This is a remarkable moment of love and which goes in conformity with the *Kumārasambhava* and *Vāmana Purāṇa.*

One very important, imaginative and well-known rock-cut sculpture from Mahabalipuram (7th century AD) depicts the scene of *Gaṅgāvataraṇa* (pl. 8.3) Apart from several other features like superb animal figures, the most striking one, is the suggestion of time (morning) and place (riverbank-Gaṅgā). On the right side of the central cleft of rock showing descent of Gaṅgā, the presence of four human figures in the act of worship and *Surya Praṇāma* (arms raised), carrying the holy water in the pitcher and one more figure drying his hair or wringing (squeezing) out his wet garment suggests the morning time and place being riverbank (of Gaṅgā).

Another example of innovative rendering of Śarabhesha image could be seen on the northern facade of Sāsa temple at Nagda (Udaipur, Rajasthan, 1093 AD). Here Śiva is not shown as Śarabha. (eight-legged). Instead Śiva with Umā in *āliṅgana*-pose is shown in the form of Uma-Maheśvara who rides on Narasiṁha figure, an incarnatory form of Viṣṇu, to pacify him after Narasiṁha slew the demon Hiraṇyakaśipu but did not return to his normal form.

NOTES AND REFERENCES

1 R. Sen Gupta, "Probable Genesis of the Crowned Buddha Image Type and the Ajanta Figure", *Bhartiya Vidya,* Vol. 18, No. 3-4, 1958, pp.54-55; Sukeshi Gupta, *Bauddha Evam Jaina Dharmon ki Virala Deva Murtiyan* (in Hindi), Unpublished Ph.D. Thesis of History of Art, Banaras Hindu University, Varanasi, pp.73-78.

2. M.N.P. Tiwari, "A Non-pareil Three-faced Deity in Sun Temple at Modherā", *Bulletin of Museums and Archaeology in U.P.,* Nos. 35-36, June-Dec. 1985, pp.31-35.
3. M.N.P. Tiwari, *Elements of Jaina Iconography,* Varanasi, 1983, pp.115-16.
4. M.N.P. Tiwari and S.S. Sinha, *Jaina Kalā Tirth Deogarh,* 2002, pp.70-72.
5. Durga Nandan Tiwari, *Osiañ ke Mandiron ki Deva Murtiyaon,* Varanasi, 1999, pp.177-78.
6. M.N.P. Tiwari and Kamal Giri, "Vaiṣṇava Themes in Delvādā Jaina Temples", *Vajpeya–Prof. K.D. Bajpai Felicitation Volume,* (ed.) Devendra Handa, *et al.*, Delhi, 1987, pp.110-17.
7. M.N.P. Tiwari and Kamal Giri, *Madhya Kālīna Bhāratiya Pratima Lakṣaṇa,* Varanasi, 1997, pp.31-34.

9

Beauty in Indian Art

B.L. Malla

BACKDROP

The thinkers and philosophers have always found themselves preoccupied with questions like—(i) What is the essence of beauty? (ii) What is art? (iii) Can aesthetic values really be defined?—And with many other intrinsic inquiries, to which they have offered a range of answers according to their individual trends of thought and the dictates of their times. The theoretical understanding and evaluation of such inquiries can certainly throw light on the different periods of the history of art and on the ways in which the works of various artists'/scholars of arts are distinct/different from each other. An artist acquainted with the fundamentals of essential inquiry as well as with the trends of the artistic thought in the history of art, could go a long way in paving the path for fresh, new expressions and innovations in this field. An Artist's concept of beauty and aesthetic values are automatically and strongly influenced by his/her way and level of thinking.

Indian artists have given birth to a distinct approach to Truth and Art. This is even true of many Oriental countries with common cultural elements. This phenomenon has prompted many scholars to commonly categorize the thought of Eastern cultures into the genre of "Oriental Thinking", the general essence of which is the spiritual understanding of Truth. But the emergence of what came to be termed as aesthetic and art appreciation during the modern age, in the West, and particularly during the 18th century, was an unprecedented development in the history of art. During this period, the idea of beauty, that was in earlier times simply used as one of the paths of discovering reality, now came to be applied subjectively and took on the external form of human emotion and creative expression. This fresh approach, in turn, gave rise to the emergence of new theories and the development of various styles of art. This new development in the West that gave birth to the emergence of an innovative kind of essential inquiry based on aesthetics seems to have resulted in the illusion.

AESTHETICS AND BEAUTY : AN INTERRELATEDNESS

The word 'aesthetic' in its original Greek form *(aisthetikos)* means anything that is connected with perception by senses. Interestingly, to feel or to perceive is more or less the common characteristic of all the Indian philosophies *(darśan)*. Indian *Darśan* is something, which draws its references from the "seen", the real world, whereas philosophy (phil+sophia is assumed) draws its references from assumed contexts. Aesthetics is not an independent system of Indian philosophy. The former is regarded as the kingdom of the heart and the latter as the realm of the head. Indian aesthetics is supernatural and divine, and to some extent super sensuous also. It may not be always justified by logical propositions. The elements of Indian aesthetics find their roots deep down in the mystic esoteric concept of "Two-in-One", and unveil the secret of how does one's own soul should look back at the "Paramount Soul", face to face. But the Indian philosophy is natural, mundane and justifiable by logical maxims. It is to convert the pain and suffering into pleasure and peace; the poison into nectar and mundane life into a divine hermitage.

Indian aesthetics is a well-experimented psycho-analytical process of judgement. It is understood today as a science and theory of Beauty and fine arts. Indian logic postulates the perception of (i) the mundane *(laukika)*, or perceptible by sense organs, and (ii) super sensuous *(yaugika)* or realisable introspectively. It assures super sensuous taste in relishing aesthetic beauty and bliss. It is not only concerned with the problem of beauty but also with the question of art and the enjoyment in art.[1] The classification of arts in Indian tradition is based on different aesthetic senses. Amongst the senses that lead to aesthetic experience are vision *(dṛśya)* and hearing *(śravya)*. Architecture, sculpture and painting originate from vision, and music and poetry originate from hearing, and theatre from the two together.

Indian aesthetics has three main streams: (i) literature and poetics (ii) drama and dramaturgy (iii) fine arts and sculpture. But its scope circumscribe almost all the branches and sub-branches of Indian Arts, Crafts, Science, Literature, etc., which entertain our sense organs, satisfy our mind and convey happiness to our soul. All sorts of literature—Prose, Poetry, Criticism, Drama, Dramaturgy, Dance, Music, both vocal and instrumental, Painting and also allied faculties, which convey joy to an aesthetic. It can also be anything, which is sweet, bright, beautiful and true in the phenomenal world, even in dream and imagination, because in ectasy paramount of good and absolute happiness 'Supreme' reigns.

BASIC PRINCIPLES

The Indian theory of aesthetics is deeply rooted in the triple-principle of *satyam* (Truth), *śivam* (Goodness/Auspiciousness) and *sundaram* (Beauty). *Satyam* (Truth) is paired with *ṛtam*[2] (Cosmic Order) in the famous passage of *Ṛgveda* (X.90.1) which says that both of these were born of kindled *tapas*. *Tapas* is the basic effort and form of the manifestation of existence, creation and bliss from the basic cause. This relates to primary analysis of creation where Reality is seen in two forms, viz., *ṛtam*, the kinetic aspect of order and *satyam*, the potential aspect of Truth. Thus *ṛtam* is the framework in which the process of creation, sustenance and dissolution operates. Its most important meanings include Cosmic Order, Truth, Nature *(Dharma)*, Beauty and Continuous Flow. It regulates the cosmos into a systematic whole.

The term 'Beauty' is explained as the philosophy or theory of taste, or of the perception of beautiful in nature and art. Art and Beauty are originally connected with each other and there can be no consideration of Beauty without the consideration of Art. One of its purposes is to define the beautiful and to analyse the attitude of human mind, and this involves very subtle and difficult discussions. Beauty is perceptible in qualities like proportions, symmetry, harmony, balance, rhythm, richness of meaning and conceptual background, etc. Beauty is a value, which underlines formative standards. It is a mark of success. It is something that emerges as a product of reward, but never presupposed. Logically, Beauty is a mark of a successful practical synthesis of the sublime, i.e. the most rational and the particular. Ontologically, it is a realization in a concrete experience of the feeling of affinity between the sublime as the subject and the object.

Truth, Goodness, Beauty, and Happiness are the ends of the human life. Almost all the systems of Indian philosophy—theist, the atheist and the secular carry out the 'divine message' of Truth, Bliss, Beauty and Happiness to the suffering multitude. The 'supreme good' is realized to be the eternal reservoir of the heavenly 'honey', irrespective of faiths, concepts and continents. In the theory of aesthetics, Tagore operates with four concepts, Truth, Beauty, Goodness and Joy. Along with these there are two further terms, 'expression' *(prakāśa)* and 'art' *(śilpa)*. The last two are notions of a different order from the first four, for it is an expression in art that leads us to Truth, Beauty, and Goodness, experienced through joy or delight. There cannot be a consideration of Beauty without the consideration of art. To Sri Aurobindo Ghosh, the Art and Beauty were a part of the process of the human ascent towards an intenser clarity of consciousness. In art lie the deepest life principles. Coomaraswamy reminds us that Beauty is scholasticism, it has to do with cognition, intellection and intelligibility.

Beauty consists in harmony, illumination and shapeliness. There is an individual relation in between Beauty and the beautiful, light and luminosity. Apart from making objects visible, a light brings us something more (glory or Beauty or luminosity). In the same way, a piece of art suggests something more than what is represented by curves of lines, brushes and checkered colours. A man of refined taste *(sahṛdaya)* may enjoy, realize and relish but can have little to express in words. Indian aesthetics attempts to give a verbal shape to that nectarous flow of the aesthetic bliss that waves all over the world.

Beauty is not a fixed notion. It is experienced in various modes and phases and its characteristics is determined on logical, psychological and metaphysical basis. It undergoes evolutionary changes according to the levels of experiences at which we realize it. Actually the success of an artefact consists in how forcefully and vigorously and consciously these values are represented. Aesthetic experience *(Rasawadna* or flavour) and emotional expression of sentiments, is the keynote for the appreciation of Beauty of art, and particularly of dance.

Abhinavagupta equates poetry[3] and drama, since a poetic thought forms a picturesque image on the mental arena, when it is heard or recited. Dance is one of the main factors of dramatic performance. It displays three out of four expressions: the verbal or vocal *(vācika),* the physical *(āṅigika),* the mental *(sāttika)* of a drama, except the extraneous *(āhāraya).*

The fine arts are the media of the union of heaven and earth. Through Art and Beauty, earth comes near to heaven. When the gods descend on earth, they come with music and dance, with colour, with light, with flowers and with incense. The [folk] dances usher in the earth, through their art, something of spirit, the atmosphere of the *Devas* (Gods), A [folk] dancer practices the most dynamic art. He moves and makes others also to move in their turn. He stands vigil on the parapet of Bliss, Knowledge and Beauty. He knows what true cooperation is. Folk dance is the earliest mode of communication between different races, which promotes a feeling of brotherhood. It not only establishes a common culture but also a common language, devoid of any parochialism. Music or dancing is a staircase or *sopans* to unite with the supreme being (or for *nirvāṇa).* There is equal externalisation of mental vision evoked in *Dhyāna* (meditation) with a view to *samādhi.*

The true aim of the artist is not to extract Beauty from nature,[4] but to reveal the life within life, the Noumenon within phenomenon, the Reality within unreality and Soul within matter. When that is revealed, Beauty reveals itself. So all the nature is beautiful for us if only we can realize the divine ideas within it. To express the Truth is the virtue of the artist.

In it he is not bound either by subjective inclinations or by objects or facts in themselves; he is free, what is true is beautiful. What is beautiful is delighting. The freedom of man lies in this delight. To live this life of Truth is, for Tagore, the way of man's being. The works of art thus enables a man to move from quantity to quality, fact to Truth and utility to Beauty.

Beauty is not embodied in the form of matter but it belongs to the spirit and can only be apprehended by spiritual vision. It is subjective and not objective. There is no Beauty in natural phenomena, every object is properly fitted to fulfil its parts in cosmos, yet the Beauty does not lie in the fitness itself but in the divine idea which is impressed upon those human minds which are turned to receive it. Indian artist always insisted upon spiritual Beauty. The spirit is male *(puruṣa)* and considered as the highest type of divine Beauty. It is symbolized by a male figure. The Beauty of the female divinity is regarded as the reflection and counterpart of the male form.

ELEMENTS OF RELISH

There is a universal appeal of relish. Relish is a kind of experience of the all-blissful entity of the 'Universal Soul'. It may be realized at two levels: divine and mundane. Abhinavagupta (10th-11th century AD) feels that the relish of all sorts of aesthetics experience is, more or less, like that of the Quietistic. Lord Śiva is the representative deity of the 'Paramount Relish', who combine in Him; Truth, Beauty and Happiness in an all-blissful harmony of eight or nine kinds of relish, as his eight metamorphic phenomenal forms, such as Earth, Water, Wind, Fire, Sky, Mind, Ego and Intelligence (*aṣṭanāyikās* or *aṣṭaśakhis*). The Quietistic is the meeting point of two kind of relish—the divine and the mundane. But the Quietistic of the mundane state is conditional. In this state, one's own mind temporarily enjoys a Quietistic rest, but it comes back to its original position, as soon as the Quietistic trance breaks. But in other state (divine), the Quietistic relish is in different state of mind, when one's own mind enjoys a unbreakable placidity and looks apparently absorbed in worldly affairs. This is the first step of the divine relish, assessable by a ladder from the level of the mundane Quietistic. The mundane relish is practically the literary aesthetic, open to all, with a literary taste. On the other hand, the divine relish is the subject of devout aesthetics and is equivalent to a self-bequest. It is supra-conscious and blissfully sweetest relish *(ānanda-cinmaya-rasa)*. The Śiva and Śākta thought-currents appreciate only two divine relishes: (i) the Quietude (ii) the Servitude. But the Vaiṣṇava school composes of five varieties of the divine relish: (i) the Quietude (ii) the Servitude (iii) the Friendly (iv) the Foundling (v) the Sweet.

Relish is equally experienced both in picture and dance. Indian aesthetics had indicated different relishes in different colours. Things made of a letter as well as a colour *(varṇas)* have equal importance. One rests on words and other on experience. The *Śilparatna* and the *Manasollāsa* explicitly determine the very sight of a picture which revive a feeling and an emotion *(bhāvacitra, rasacitra)* give due exposure to their respective ideas and relishes.[5]

The concepts of Luminosity preached by Kashmir Śaivism; the doctrine of Beauty and Bliss advocated by Śākta cult, and the maxim of self-conscious Happiness of Bengal Vaiṣṇavism represents three holy (streams) confluences of Indian aesthetics.

Abhinavagupta's philosophy of aesthetics reveals his penetrating insight into principles of artistic beauty and sensibility. He integrated the two concepts in a manner as to bring out the essence of what constitutes 'Beauty'. He uses the term *chamatkāra* (miracle) for it, which has both metaphysical as well as aesthetic relishing or *rasa* in its essential nature. As such *vimarsha* is also called bliss *(Aṅanda).*

NOTION OF *RASA*

Poetry is regarded as the mother of all the creative arts in India. Bharata is perhaps the most complete theoretical statement in the world heritage on the poetic circuit. He has contributed in the field of aesthetic and art activity in his theory of *rasa,* usually translated as sentiment for want of better word. In Sanskrit its *(rasa)* connotations has a wide spectrum including 'taste', 'delight' and 'sap'. But the concept of *rasa* is so inextricably bound with that of *bhāva* (emotion) that it cannot be understood without the another. The great Śaiva thinker, Abhinavagupta, approached the theory of aesthetics from the historical, analytical, psychological, logical and philosophical point of view and discussed the ends of art and the theory of meaning in his text *Abhinava Bharati.* Looking upon a product of dramatic art as a living human body, he like an anatomist analyses it. He analyses experiences into different levels of sense, imagination, emotion, catharsis and transcendency. His analysis begins at the sense-level. But at the level of emotions a person completely forgets himself when he is at high pitch of emotions. It de-individualizes the individual. It raises him to the level of Universal. At this level, emotion is completely freed from all objective references as also from temporal and spatial relations, which are due to limitations of the individual subject. At the higher level of aesthetic experience the duality of the subject and object completely disappears. At this level basic emotions sink into the subconscious and the universalised subject shines in its *Ānanda* aspect. *Ānanda* is nothing but self-experience of self. It is the experience of itself by the self in its absolute university. The *Dhvani-Rasa* school founded by Anandvardhana in the 9th-10th century AD and firmly stabilized by Abhinavagupta has been rightly described as the new school of Indian aesthetic with its emphasis on suggestion, imagination and sensibility. To Abhinavagupta all experiences of different *rasa* leads individual to *śānta rasa* by the beautitude and bliss to realize the fundamental nature of the human spirit.

The theory of *rasa* attempts to analyse the most fundamental aspect of the aesthetic experience. Although the concept of *rasa* has originated in the context of theatre, it relates to other artistic media as well. According to Bharata, drama incorporates into different dimensions, all the other arts—painting, sculpture, architecture, dance, music and poetry.

NOTION OF *BHAVA*

Beauty cannot be shown, it has to be realized by the observer. One has to feel it. A work of art is a statement informed by sentiment *(rasa)*. The origin of *rasa* is from *bhāva*. *Bhāva* (emotion) is a concrete situation and condition for a period of time of some occurrence, and *rasa* is the aesthetic experience of that happening or condition.

The *Nāṭyaśāstra* prescribes the directions for the different forms of gestural renderings of *rasa*,[7] the unity of dramatic work and the details of the spectable etc. It relates to other artistic media as well and provides a deep insight into the psychology of aesthetic experience. It conceives of drama as the perfect synthesis between all arts and integrates in its form poetic text, histrionics, stagecraft, music, dance, painting and even architecture into an organismic whole, with *rasa* as its soul.

In the Indian artistic tradition and aesthetic theory, a very specific theory of emotive significance of colours is found. According to Bharata, the erotic sentiment is represented by a deep green colour, the comic by white; the pathetic by grey; the furious by red; the horrible by black; the odious by blue and the marvellous by the yellow. Since lifestyles influence works of art, the choice of colours for different emotions is revealed in artistic forms of different cultures.

To conclude: There arises few questions: can there be a primitive aesthetic theory? Since we have early legacy of man in the form of prehistoric rock art, can there be any aesthetic interpretation of rock art? Can we have a universal theory of aesthetics? The questions raised are metaphysical in nature. They take us to the higher level of understanding of the ordering of the universe and the nature of man. When viewed at the level of perception and experience, Indian expression of art are held together by an integral vision that makes life an art, part and parcel of a single totality where life functions and creative art are inseparable from myths, rituals, festivals and ceremonies. No dichotomy between the sacred and secular, life and art is found. The human and the divine are in continuum, in a constant movement of interpretation and transformation. Corresponding to this, a man developed temples, which are symbols of the world-mountain, or, analogically, of the universal man *(Puruṣa)* whose body comprehends the universe. The names of the various limbs of the human body from the foot to the crown of the head are applied in Indian architectural texts to the different parts of the temple structure. But the *Vāstu Puruṣa* is lifeless unless the soul resides in it. His real soul being the central image installed on its sanctum being the *garbhagriha* or the house of the womb, built in the universe form of womb. The experience is traditionally justified by the analogy between the dark cave of the heart and the dark space of the shrine where the image appears. Above it rises the high tower, a microcosm of Mount Meru with its vertical thrust leading eye and heart to union with the divine. In the traditional Hindu cosmology the gods are related to the earth by dwelling in the upper reaches of Mount Meru (Sumeru), the central peak and axis of the world. They live in one cosmos with mankind and descend to the foothills when needed. Hindu gods are involved in the living world of a man, though they stand for cosmic laws at a higher level of that world. The deities which are the basic energies of the universe can be approached through the perception of created forms. This necessity has led to the representation of the deity in a thousand variety of thoughts—forms, magic designs, *mantras* and *yantras,* symbols and images. Human ability to construct the images represents the things, which may be regarded as an aspect of his ability to symbolize both at higher (master symbols) and lower (natural symbols) levels.

NOTES AND REFERENCES

1. Indian art is believed to have two streams of expressions from the earliest historical period, i.e. *mārgī* (classical) and the *deśi* (vernacular), both of them forming two banks of the river of the arts. The *mārgī* or monumental tradition, rooted in ancient *śilpa* texts was influenced by the sensibilities of changing patron and environment. Many great schools of hereditary craft-men flourished under the patronage of the royal courts within this tradition. But the arts and skills of village societies operated through the vernacular form of artisan guilds. Fairs, festivals and pilgrimage provided the catalyst, the generating

force for creative expression in rural societies. In fact, the solar and lunar calendar in Indian subcontinent mark the rituals, ceremonies and festivities. These ceremonies and festivals re-evoke the perennial interrelationship of the five primal elements of water, earth, air, fire and ether. In each festival there is the rhythm of creation, consecration, worship and either throwing away, or burning, or immersion.

2. *Ṛta* (Order) and *samkshobha* (Chaos) are mutually antilogous poles; synonymous with negative and positive entrophy, their increase means organization and order in life, disorder and death respectively.
3. The Muse of poetry and art is traditionally appreciated as identical. Yet there is a fundamental difference. In poetry, a poet sings and describes sound and sense picture, but an artist draws sense pictures of various materials in so many styles. They are, in fact, the two sides of a same coin. Śukrācārya has differentiated them on their basic elements. He opines that Learning *(vidyā)* and Art *(kalā)* both are innumerable, yet their number has been counted as thirty-two and sixty-four respectively. Whatsoever is definable by words is Learning; but what every person with an aesthetic taste, even a dumb, can do or explain, is an Art.

   The *Nāṭyaśāstra* is the principal source for all the theories of poetry. Bharata has discussed the various problems relating to poetry. The discussions of poetics were essentially inspired by one fundamental problem: the nature of poetry. The latter thinkers took inspirations from his analysis of these problems. The school of Indian poetics represented by Bhamaha, Vamana, Dandin and Udbhata confine their analysis of aesthetic facts mainly to technical aspects like poetic figure, diction, style and mode of expression, leaving out what actually constitute the essence of poetic experience. These theorists did not go beyond pointing to the togetherness *(sauhitya)* of sound and sense, form and content, but how this fusion results in actual communication of feeling, they could not adequately explain. But with the inception of doctrine of suggestion by Anandavardhana, the ambiguities of analytical thought were removed and some innermost secrets of poetic creativity revealed in an entirely new light.
4. There are three levels of divinity abstracted: (i) spiritual body; (ii) subtle body (emotions and senses hold sway here); (iii) grass or physical body (in phenomenon world).

   All the world religions view the universe as God's artefact. God is The supreme Artist. God's work is the natural world, visible to the human eye. The Upanisadic sages described it as the Cosmic Tree. On the symbolic level, "This tree is the great world mother, the Goddess of Nature who nourishes all life with the milk of her breast". The metaphor of Cosmic Tree shows that the sacred is the proper context of both art and nature. Man is inseparable from nature. Man as a part of nature imitates God's primordial works of art. What he does, as an artist, is "cosmography", a *Kairological* art on which all the arts are hung. Ontologically speaking, there are five *Kairological* moments in human consciousness, namely revelation, expression, identification and tradition. They are mutually interdependent and interrelated and yet each is self-organizing and self-sustaining.

5. The concern for the various problems of aesthetics have continued for more than two thousand years. The *Ṛgveda* and the *Śāmaveda* contain a lot of references to music and prescribes norms for the musical rendition of Vedic hymns. The Vedic poetry manifest a tremendous sensitivity to aesthetic qualities—natural and artistic beauty and aesthetic sentiments and revelators of aesthetic experience. In the *Brāhmana* (the texts interpreting the *Veda)* there are references to *śilpa* included in their domain especially music, poetry and dance. The *Matsya, Agni* and *Viṣṇu Purāṇa* contain a lot of discussion on the different arts.

   One finds mostly treaties devoted to different artistic media rather than works on general problems of Indian aesthetics. The *Nātyaśātra, Saṅgita Darpaṇa* etc. constitute the canons for the evaluation and creation of theatre, music and poetry respectively. The *Purāṇas* contain elaborate instructions for the execution of different artistic techniques. But the problems of aesthetics are discussed in the context of the particular artistic media. This does not imply that there is no speculation on the different concepts of aesthetics. The texts have dealt in the interrelationship between the various arts; the interrelationship between art and reality, unity of work of art; aesthetic experience for the evaluation of different artistic media, etc.

6. The main thrust of Anandvardhana's theory is that aesthetic delight cannot be evoked by propositional statements but by suggestion or the "basic obliquity of poetry". An idea or material image—a distinct subject-is to be called *Vastu Dhvani.* If the suggested sense is imaginative and relates to figure of speech, it is called *Alaṅkāra Dhvani.* If a mood or state of mind or feeling suggested to have *Rasa Dhvani*-the highest category which establishes the supremacy of *rasa* or feeling on elements of form and structure.

7. Bharata analyses the human emotions into eight categories: *śringāra* (erotic), *hāsya* (comic), *karuṇā* (pathetic), *rudra* (furious), *vīra* (heroic), *bhayānaka* (terrible) *bibhats* (odious) and *adbhuta* (marvellous). He has attempted to formulate a semiotics of emotive communication. Abhinavagupta analyses *rasa* as an object with emotions as its constituents: (i) *vibhava* (situation with a focal point); (ii) *anubhava* (mimetic changes); (iii) *vyabhichāribhāva* (transient emotions); (iv) *sthāyibhāva* (basic or persistent emotion).

BIBLIOGRAPHY

Projesh Banerji, 1982, *Aesthetics of Indian Folk Dance,* New Delhi.
A.K. Coomaraswamy, 1985, *Fundamentals of Indian Art,* Jaipur
——, 1995, (revised ed.) *The Transformation of Nature of Art,* New Delhi.
Manomohan Ghosh, 1951, (tr.), *The Nātyaśāstra Ascribed to Bharata Muni,* Calcutta.

S.N. Ghoshal Sastri, 1978, *Elements of Indian Aesthetics,* Vol. I, Varanasi.

——, 1983, *Ibid.,* Vol. II, part I.

Shamala Gupta, 1979, *The Beautiful in Indian Arts,* New Delhi.

Rekha Jhanji 1985, *Aesthetic Communication: The Indian Perspective,* New Delhi.

K. Krishnamoorty (tr.) 1974, *Aṅandavardhanās Dhvanyāloka,* Dharwar.

Malla, B.L., 1990, *Sculptures of Kashmir,* Delhi.

———, 2001, *Trees in Indian Art, Mythology and Folklore,* New Delhi.

———, 2001, "Metaphysis in Indian Art", paper presented in an *International Conference on Metaphysics in the 21st Century,* organized by Delhi University on 15-19th January 2001, at New Delhi.

———, 2001, Aesthetics in Indian Art: The Ordering Principles, paper presented in an International Conference on *The Meaning of Beauty,* organized by The Academy of Art on 7-14th December, 2001 at Tehran (Iran).

J.L. Masson and Patwardhan, 1969, *Santarasa and Abhinavagupta's Philosophy of Aesthetics,* Poona.

K.C. Pandey, 1959, *Comparative Aesthetics,* Vol. 1, Varanasi.

P.K. Roy, 1990, *Beauty Art and Man,* Shimla.

Baidyanath Saraswati, 1999, "The Art of God", in *Invisible Order: Tribute to Haku Shah,* Eberhard Fischer (ed.), New Delhi.

Rabindranath Tagore, 1961, *Art and Aesthetics,* Calcutta.

10

Māheśvarī Trimurti : A Study with Special Reference to Hingalājagarh Sculpture

Manjusri Rao

Hingalājgarh, from where this image of Māheśvarī (pl. 10.1) has been found, is situated in district Mandsaur,[1] the ancient Dashpura or the town of ten *puras* or hamlets mentioned as such in a number of Sanskrit inscriptions[2] which was a flourishing city in the times of the Paramāras, but all the glory, faded away with the passage of time, the magnificient structures built by the artist were ruined and what remained was covered by forests.

The sculptures collected from Hingalājgarh are kept in various museum viz, Bhānpurā, State Archaeology & Museum, Birla Museum, Bhopal.

In the collection of Birla Museum there are 21 sculptures, out of which seven belong to Śākta cult. They are as follows :-

1. Māheśvarī Trimurti?
2. Vaināyikī
3. Simhavāhinī Durgā
4. Chāmuṇḍā
5. Indrāṇī
6. Headless Simhavāhinī
7. Mahiṣavāhinī Yamī.

All the above sculptures furnish ample useful material pertaining to iconography of the *Devī* pantheon and are important from aesthetic and iconographic point of view and are unique in their own way.

Amongst the above mentioned Śākta images, the image with three faces displayed in Devī Gallery of Birla Museum has been identified as Māheśvarī.

A brief survey of literary texts narrating the lakṣanas of Māheśvarī and description of few images preserved in museums would be inevitable for correct identification of this image.

Various literary texts such as *Agni Purāṇa, Aṁśumadbhedāgama, Matsya Purāṇa, Mārkeṇḍeya Purāṇa, Rupamaṇḍana, Śrītattvanidhi,* describe the image of Māheśvarī along with her attributes.[3]

The general description of Sapta Mātṛikās is briefly given in the agamas thus:

Brahmāṇī should be sculptured like Brahmā, Māheśvarī like Māheśvara, Vaiṣṇavī like Viṣṇu, Vārāhī as a short women with an angry face and bearing a plough as her weapon, Indrāṇī like Indra, and Chāmuṇḍā as a terrible women. The last goddess should have her hair in a dishevelled condition, should possess a dark complexion and have four hands, she should wield the *triśula* in one hands and carry a *kapāla* in another. All the *mātṛikās* are to be seated images and should have two of their hands in *Varada* and abhaya poses while the other two hands should carry weapons appropriate to the male counterparts. They are shown seated upon *padmāsana* in the sculptures.[4]

Māheśvarī has four arms, two of which are in the *varada* and the *abhaya* poses respectively, while the remaining two hands carry the *śula* and *akṣamālā*. Her *vāhana* is bull.[5]

In Viṣṇudharmottara this goddess is said to have five faces, each possessing three eyes, and she wears on her crown the crescent moon. Her colour is white and she has six arms, in four of the hands she carries the *śutra, damaru, śula* and *ghaṇṭā,* the two remaining hands being respectively in the *varada* and *abhaya* poses, her head is adorned with the *jaṭāmukuṭa.* Her banner also has the bull for its emblem.[6]

Mārkaṇḍeya purāṇa describes the image of Māheśvarī thus:-

माहेश्वरी वृषारुढा त्रिशूल वर धारिणी ।
महाहिवलया प्राप्ता चन्द्ररेखा विभूषणा ।। [7]

As per the canons of *Aṅśumadbhedāgama* the Māheśvarī image should be shown with four arms and three eyes. She is shown with *śula, abhaya, varada,* rosary, her head is adorned with *jaṭāmukuṭa.*[8]

In the *Purvakaraṇāgama* she is described as having three eyes and with white colour. The hands depict *śula, varada, abhaya* and rosary. Her head is adorned with *jaṭāmukuṭa.*[9]

Rupamaṇḍana has chosen the stanzas of *mātṛikas* from *Matsya Purāṇa.* The description of Māheśvarī is given thus: Māheśvarī be shown with *'Kapāla, śula, khaṭvānga, varada* and her *vāhana* is *vṛiṣbha.*[10]

The Śrītattvanidhi describes her with five heads and ten hands but other śilpa texts mention her with one head and four hands.[11] The *āyudhas* shown in her hands are *khadga, vajra, tṛiśula, paraśu, abhaya mudrā, varada mudrā, pāśa, ghaṇṭa, nāga,* and *aṅkuśa.*[12]

Māheśvarī is adorned with dress, ornaments like the *Kuchabhandha* of snakes and riding on a peacock.[13]

Varāhamihir (6th century AD) while giving the description of the *mātṛikās* says: "The mothers should be made with the forms and congnisances of the individual gods whom they are named after".[14]

In Aparājitaprichhā, she is described as riding on *Vṛiṣabha* and holding *śula, khadga, khatvāṅga, mātulinga* and having matted hair with the decoration of moon. She is described as 'Śvetavarṇā'.[15]

In Devatāmurtiprakaraṇam she is described as follows:-

> She should be shown riding on a bull, should have six arms, five faces, trinetra, matted hair with crescent moon. One of her right hand, should be shown in *Varada-mudrā,* the other two should carry *sutra (akṣaśutra)* and *damaru,* the two left hands should carry *śula* and *ghaṇṭā* and the last left hand should be shown in *abhayamudrā.*[16]

Thus the goddess in Aparājitaprichhā is described as having six arms, in Rupamaṇḍana with four arms and in Devatāmurtiprakaraṇam with six arms, five faces and three eyes.

In sculptural depiction, the goddess is shown either independently or in a group of seven divine mothers. When carved in a group of Saptamātṛikā the icon of Māheśvarī is shown either with two or four hands and her mount *vṛiṣabha* or bull accompanies her.

Sometimes depiction of lion in place of bull is also found. One such example can be seen at National Museum, New Delhi.[17] Māheśvarī images are sometimes shown with a baby. Āyudhas shown in two or four hands are amongst any of the following, *tṛiśula, sarpa, padma, bijapuraka, kamaṇḍalu,* one hand in *abhaya mudrā.* As per the canons of Rupamaṇḍana, the images of Māheśvarī resemble so far the hands and *Vāhana* are concerned but the āyudhas do not tally except for *tṛiśula.*[18]

The independent images of Māheśvarī are either with two or four hands. The image of Mathura Museum, Hingalājgarh, Ladol, Kumbhalgarh, resemble with the description of Rupamaṇḍana.[19]

The image of Māheśvarī, preserved in Mathura Museum is of 9th century AD. Here the bull-faced *Devī* is shown in a unique manner. One of the hands which is damaged might have been shown in *abhaya mudrā.* The upper hands are shown with *ṭṛiśula* and *pāśa* (?) and the lower hands are supporting a playing child. The *Devī* is shown in *lalitāsana* on a *padmapītha.* A *Prabhāmaṇḍala* ornamented with lotus petals is shown behind the head of the *Devī.* She is shown with precious ornaments. The image under description resembles with the prescriptions of Rupamaṇḍana as far as four hands, *tṛisula āyudha* and the mount bull are concerned.[20]

Thus in the image, the four hands, *triśula āyudha* only are depicted as per the canons of Rupamaṇḍana.

The sculpture from Ladol is with four-armed and shown in *tribhaṅga mudrā*. The right hand of the *Devī* is shown in *varada mudrā*, with the upper hands she holds trident and serpent and in one left hand she holds the child in the lap. The *Devī* is bedecked with *jaṭāmukuṭa* and beautiful ornaments. The mount bull is present here as *vāhana* of *Devī*. In front of the bull, a pot full of *modaka* is depicted in front of the sculpture under description resembles with the prescriptions of Rupamaṇḍana so far as the four arms, vehicle bull, *varada mudrā*, trident, are concerned but the variation can be seen in the depiction of two hands where the Devī is shown with child and serpent in place of *khaṭvāṅga* and skull.[21]

The image of Māheśvarī from Kumbhalgarh is preserved in Pratap Museum at Udaipur. Here the *Devī* is shown seated on a high pedestal in *lalitāsana*. The right hand of the *Devī* is shown in *varada mudrā* with an *akṣamālā*. The upper hands are shown with *triśula* and *khaṭvāṅga*. The left hands are damaged. A child is shown in her left lap. She is ornamented with various types of beautiful necklaces, *kuṇḍala, mekhalā*. The mount bull is shown on a *padmapītha*. A pot full of *modaka* is shown in front of the bull as described in earlier image above. There is an inscription on the *padmapītha* which describes the image as Māheśvarī. The inscribed date on the pedestal is Samvat 1515 (AD 1458). The image, contemporary with the author of Sutradhāra Maṇḍana seems to have been carved as per the canons of Rupamaṇḍana.[22]

The three weapons as preserved in this image tallies with the prescription of Rupamaṇḍana but the variation can be seen in the order of holding the āyudhas. The broken left hand of the *Devī* might have been shown with *Kapāla* as described in canons.[23]

Independent images of Māheśvarī are found from different places or India viz; Devangana,[24] Jajpur,[25] Puri, [26] Perukanchi,[27], Bharat Kala Bhavan, Vāranasi.[28] The image of Māheśvarī found in these places are four-handed. The image from Devangana is shown with her mount bull.[29]

R.K. Sharma in his book entitled *The Temple of Chaunsaṭha-Yoginī at Bheraghat* has described an image of Māheśvarī belonging to Kalachuri period. The lower part of the eight armed image below the waist is broken hence no āyudhas can be seen. Māheśvarī is seated on a three-tiered decorated cushion, in *lalitāsana,* with her right leg hanging down and placed on a lotus and the left leg bent across the seat. Remains of the fingers of her left hands, placed on her left knee shows her holding a bunch of pearls. She is shown wearing *Sārī* indicated by wavy hands from waist downwards, *mekhalā* with loops and pendants, *nupura,* rings round the fingers of her legs and *Vanamāḷa* with three skulls.

Below the lotus is a bull couchant with its head upraised, looking at the goddess. The neck and back of this animal are decorated with garlands. There are attendant figures in standing and seated postures flanking the goddess. They are shown with usual dress and ornaments. Inscription on the pedestal reads 'Śrī Māheśvarī'. The images resembles with the description of Rupamaṇḍana and *Viṣṇudharmottra Purāṇa* so far as *vāhana* is concerned. The three tiered decorated cushion, *Vanamālā* with three skulls, couchant bull with neck decoration is quiet unusual.

An interesting torso of Māheśvarī has been procured from Bhānpurā. It has been dated to later Pratihāra period, 10th century AD. She is bedecked with beautiful ornaments, viz., necklaces, *Keyura, Katimekhalā.* Her hairstyle is done in an excellent manner. The third eye has been shown on the forehead.

Another interesting sculpture of the goddesses Māheśvarī has been found from Hingalājgarh. The Devī is shown seated on the *viśvapadma* in *sabyalalitāsana* posture. She is shown with four hands holding *khatvāṅga, triśula* and *Kalaśa* and one of her hands in *abhaya mudrā.* Left part of her face is slightly broken. The transparent cloth and various ornaments on the body of *Devī* show the skill of sculptor. The sculpture can be assigned to 12th century AD.

Another image of Māheśvarī is preserved in the same temple. The image is four-armed, wearing *jatājuṭa, graiveyaka* and *keyura* with *ekāvalī.* Her body from waist downwards is covered with a *Sārī* which is tied at the waist by *mekhalā.* A rope-like plait of *Sārī* is hanging between her two legs downwards. There are three wrinkles below her breasts and two under her neck. A pendant is attached to the lower part of *ekāvalī* and placed gracefully against the left thigh. The image belongs to post-Gupta period. Debala Mitra believes that the image of Matṛikā Māheśvarī, to be identified so by virtue of her *Jaṭāmukuṭa.*[31]

An interesting torso of Māheśvarī belonging to late Pratihāra period has been discovered from Bhanpurā. The *Devī* is bedecked with various ornaments, viz; necklaces, *keyura, mekhalā.* The hair do has been done in a nice manner. The third eye is shown on the forehead.[32]

Another image of Māheśvarī has been found from Hingalājgarh, Distt. Mandsaur. The *Devī* is shown seated on the *viśvapadma* in *Sabyalitāsana* pose. She is four-armed. One of the hands is shown in *abhaya mudrā* while the other three hold *khaṭvānga, triśula and kalaśa.* She is shown with transparent lower garment and various ornaments.

As per the canons of Rupamaṇḍana, the *Devī* should be shown with *kapāla, triśula, khaṭvānga* and *abhaya mudrā*. Here the *Devī* is shown with *kalaśa* and *abhaya mudrā* instead of *kapāla* and *varada mudrā*. The *vāhana* of the *Devī* is not depicted here.

The artists of Hingalājgarh could only make such experiments and the same was one of their characteristics features.[33]

T.V.G. Shastri is of the opinion that the three headed form of the deity represents three fold aspect of the mind-*Guṇa* or nature. The three *Guṇas* are represented as *Parā, Sukṣma* and *Sthula,* the sum total of which forms the nature of the world.

The highest manifestation in the world in '*man*' from whom again the multiplicity of world arises. The human body is esential to understand the yogic energy of *śakti* that leads to liberation. The human being shown below attempts to get the relief from the heavy foot of nature mother.

Devī prior to *Śakti* form, manifests to Śiva in ten different forms-*Daśamahāvidyā*. They are *kriyā śaktis* of *Devī* indicated by twenty arms (most of them are broken).

Śiva, the lord of the eternal world, is elasped in her womb. She represents the image of total peace that follows the dissolution of universe. Her nature as transcendental power of time *(kālī)* is well brought out by those who worked on esoteric symbolism. According to TV.G. Shastri, in this fine tantric sculpture, a unique mode of representing Śiva-Śakti is well displayed. He further observes that it is the sculpture of Śaivite tāntricism, mostly modelled on the images of Naṭarāja Śiva. While Naṭarāja represent active rythem of the universe of life, she represents the passive form after dissolution.This can go well with *Saptamātṛikā* panel and could be identified as Chāmuṇḍī. The presentation of skull is the headdress for Chāmuṇḍī or Kālī. This is typical of medieval sculpture with *chakra* in the raised left hand (the time goddess aspect is clear).[34]

The twenty armed image of goddess Māheśvarī in the collection of Birla Museum is seated in *lalitāsana* on a triple lotus on the *dviratha* pedestal. Three hands on the right side and one on the left side are now extinct. In the right hand she holds a *chakra, pāśa* and *akṣamālā.* The left hand is shown in *vitarka mudrā.*

The central face of the three-faced goddess is flanked by two heads in profile. All the three heads are adorned with nicely carved *jaṭāmukuṭa.* The central head has a skull attached to its *mukuṭa.*

The figure is richly attired with *kuṇḍala, graiveyaka,* beautiful *stanhāra,* armlets, and a decorative thick *Vanamālā.* A finely carved oval *Prabhāvalī* with lotus petals is carved behind her head. Under Māheśvarī lotus-seat lies a naked male figure, the Apasmāra. He supports his raised head with left palm. The rightfoot of the goddess rests on the thigh of the male whose eyes are half open.

The female attendants stand on either side of the deity. They are also bedecked with various ornaments. A big chignon of hair arranged in semi-circular fashion is shown on their heads. They hold *uttarīya* in their hands. On the top corner Vidyādharas are shown holding garlands.[35]

The figure of Māheśvarī does not resemble with any of the texts or known images, so far as number of faces, *āyudhas*, hands, *vāhana* are concerned.

The view of T.V.G. Shastri identifying her with Kālī too does not seem to be proper because images of Kālī are always shown in skelton form, with *muṇḍamālā asthi kuṇḍalas*, protruding teeth, *sarpahāra, sarpakatibandh*, scorpion on belly, a prostrate nude figure (apasmāra puruṣa) etc. Depiction of a prostrate nude figure, *jaṭā-juṭa* on the head, *chakra* are not sufficient base to prove the deity as Māheśvarī.

In view of the above it will be more aappropriate to identify the figure as Sarvatomukhi *Yoginī*.

The worship of *Yoginīs* in the form of a regular cult seems to have come into existence during 8th-10th century AD.

A brief survey of literary texts and description of Māheśvarī images lead us to the following conclusion.

1. Māheśvarī should be shown with one face/five face.
2. The number of hands as described in texts are 2,4,6,10.
3. The āyudhas as seen in the hands could be any from the following:-
   Akṣa, śula, khadga, khaṭvānga, mātuluṅga, kapāla, akṣa-sutra, damaru, ghaṇṭa, vajra, triśula, paraśu, pāśa, nāga, aṅkuśa, kalaśa, sarpa, padma, bijapuraka, kamaṇḍalu, child, rosary, abhaya, varada.
4. The *vāhana* of *Devī* is invariably shown bull except for an example found at National Museum, New Delhi, where she is shown on a lion.
5. The *Devī* is shown seated in *lalitāsana* on three tiered lotus cushion, *padmapītha, Visvapadma* standing in *tribhaṅga mudrā.*
6. In most of the cases hair-style of the *Devī* is done nicely, matted hair is sometimes adorned with *Bālendu*.
7. The goddess is shown with third eye on the forehead.
8. The goddess is bedecked with various ornaments.
9. Her *vāhana* is sometimes decorated with *Vanamālā*, sometimes a *modak-pātra* is kept infront of the *vāhana.*
10. Sometimes the figure is shown with a *Sārī*/ transparent cloth.

NOTES AND REFERENCES

1. *Indore State Gazetter* Vol. 2, p.24.
2. *Cultural History of Madhya Pradesh,* D.R. Patil, p.122.
3. *Śākta Pratimāyen,* R.S. Garg, Puratattva and Samgrahalaya, Madhya Pradesh, Bhopal, 1980, p.5.
4. *Elements of Hindu Iconography,* T.A.G. Rao, Vol. 1, Part II, Motilal Banarasidass, Varanasi, 1985, p.383.
5. *Ibid.,* p.387.
6. *Ibid.,*

   माहेश्वरी वृषारुढा पञ्चवक्त्रा त्रिलोचना।
   शुक्लन्दुमू जटाजूटा शुक्ला सर्व सुख प्रदा॥
   षड्भुजा वरदा दूक्षे सूत्रं डमरुकं तथा।
   शूलधण्टामयं नागे धत्ते महाभुजा॥

   (विष्णुधरमोक्ष पुराण 146-147)
7. *Ibid.,* p.144.
8. *Ibid.,* p.146.

   चतुर्भुजा त्रिनेत्रा च अतिरकृतसमप्रभा।
   शूलागय्करा सत्ये तागे वरदसंगुता॥
   जपमालारागायुक्ता लतामुकुट संगुता॥
   इश्वरेणोपगा हयेषा शिवा माहेश्वरी स्मृता॥

   (अशुंमद्भेदागम सप्तचातारिंश पटले।)
9. *Ibid.,* p.147.

   त्रिनेत्रा शुक्ल वर्णा च शूल पाणिवृषध्वजा।
   वरदागयहस्ता च साक्षगालकरान्विता॥
   जटामुटिनी शम्भोर्भूषणी सा माहेशवरी।

   (पूर्वकारणागगे पटले।)
10. *Rupamaṇḍana,* B. Srivastava (Editor), Motilal Banarsidas, Varanasi, Samvat 2021, V, 64, p.199.

    माहेश्वरी प्रवर्त्तव्या वृषभासनसंरिनाता।
    कपालशूल खट्वाङ्गवरदा च चतुर्भुजा॥
11. *Mother Goddess in Central India,* O.P. Misra, Agam Kala Prakashan, Delhi 1985, p.118; R.S. Garg, *op.cit.,* p.50.
12. B. Srivastava, *op.cit.,* p.141.
13. *The Glorification of Great Goddess* (Devī Māhatmya), V.S. Agrawala, Ramnagar, Varanasi, 1968, 8.15.
14. *Bṛihat Saṁhitā,* 57,58.
15. *Aparājitaprichhā* (Acharya Bhuvandeva) Gaikwad Oriental Series, Baroda, 1950, 223, 31.
16. *Devatāmurti Prakaraṇ Tatha Rupamaṇḍana.* (Sutradhara Mandana, Calcutta Sanskrit Series Calcutta) 1948, 8, 63-65.
17. *Hindu Tathā Jaina Pratimā Vigyāna,* P. Srivastava, Sulabha Prakashan, Lucknow, 1990, p.261, fn.5.

18. *Ibid.*, p.262.
19. *Ibid.*, p.262.
20. *Ibid.*, p.263.
21. *Ibid.*
22. *Ibid.*
23. *Ibid.*
24. *Lalit Kala*, No. 8, p.69, pl. xxix, fig. 3.
25. *Memoir of Archaeological Survey of India*, No. 44, p.2, M.M. Hamid Kuraishi, Ancient Monuments of Bihar and Orissa, p.226-28.
26. *Development of Hindu Iconography*, J.N. Banerjea, Munshiram Manoharlal, New Delhi, Third Edition, 1974, p.506, pl. XLIII, fig. 5.
27. S.T. Baskaran, The Saptamātṛikās of Porukanchi, *Lalit Kala*, No. 17, pl. VI, fig. 6, pp.15-16.
28. S.B. Singh, *op.cit.*, p.168.
29. P. Srivastava, *op.cit.*, p.264.
30. *Temple of Chaunsathn Yoginī at Bheraghat*, R.K. Sharma, Agam Kala Prakashan, Delhi, 1978, p.106, pl.54.
31. *Ibid.*, p.139, pl.83.
32. *Shakta Pratimāyen*, R.S. Garg, Puratattva Evam Samgrahalaya, Ist Edition, p.50.
33. *Ibid.*, p.51.
34. A note was sent to Dr. (Mrs) M. Rao by Dr. T.V.G. Shastri.
35. *Prāchya Pratibhā*, Vol. 3, M. Rao, Birla Institute of Art & Music, Bhopal.

11

Vīrabhadra Temples and Sculptures Under the Vijayanagara Empire

S.N. Shivarudraswamy

With the brutal end of the Hoysala dynasty in the hands of the Sultan of Madurai, the politically peaceful atmosphere disappeared in South India. Incessant raids of the Delhi Sultanate aggravated the atmosphere. This encouraged disgruntled chiefs to rebel. Under such politically turbulent situation, the Vijayanagara empire came to be established in the second quarter of the fourteenth century. The new empire ushered in a new era in all walks of life. In the first place, the Vijayanagara empire set up political stability by arresting the devasting inroads of the Delhi Sultanates and repressed disruptive chiefs as well. Thus the empire developed to a great extent, manifesting martial features. Within a brief time after its establishment, the empire comprised practically the entire peninsular India touching the fringes of Kalinga or the present Orissa. This empire dominated the political arena for over two and a quarter centuries, maintaining its supremacy even against the never ending attacks of the Bahmani kingdom. Secondly, the empire made a great stride in the realms of religion, art and architecture. A large number of temples were constructed throughout the length and breadth of the empire. A national movement was created regarding the construction of the temples during the period. The kings made temples as their media to express their grandeur and majesty. The royal members and people of all groups and categories took active part in it. The Vijayanagara art was extended from its imperial capital towards the different parts of South India. The constructional activities took place on a massive scale never to be found in any other part of India during the time before or after the Vijayanagara empire. It was a marvellous creative period in architecture which was then dominating art. The sculptural programme of the period was also enriched suffusely and largely over the wide imperium. As a result, a material spirit was created everywhere. It was a national policy and necessity to quell the political instability and social insecurity created by the sanguinary Muslim inroads. It was a 'heroic age'. It was not an individual character as was in the European High Middle Ages, but it was national during the Vijayanagara empire. This is well mirrored in their structures and their columns symbolising heroic-patriotic themes. As a result of these developments, worship of warrior gods like Vīrabhadra, Bhairava, Narasiṁha and Hanumāna became necessary and gradually popular. It was customary that the gods were worshipped to achieve success in war and progress in life. Temples dedicated to these gods were located on important strategic points of cities and towns of the period.

In the pre-Vijayanagara period, there were shrines dedicated to god Vīrabhadra, but their number was very meagre. After the establishment of the Vijayanagara empire, large number of temples were constructed for this god. In the capital itself, there were two shrines dedicated to this god. These two temples occupy very important places. The Matanga hill is the highest point in the capital. Atopping this hill, there is a temple for the god. This is next to Virupākṣa temple, the family deity of the Vijayanagara emperors, in importance and sanctity within the capital. From this we can infer that the temple had vital importance in the Vijayanagara city. There is another Vīrabhadra temple onlooking the main road leading from Kamalapura to Virupākṣa temple at Hampi. This has a large worshipping icon of Vīrabhadra and now it is called Mudduvīraṇṇa. This was sculpted in AD 1545 by an officer of Aḷiya Rāmarāya.[1] There are 1200 temples in Hampi and in most of them the worshipping icons have disappeared. It is not possible to know to which god they were dedicated to. Besides these temples, a large number of Vīrabhadra images (Pls. 11.2 & 11.3) both in round and relief could be seen in Hampi.

One of the prominent Vīrabhadra temple could be seen at Nagamangala in southern Karnataka. It appears that it was originally a palace and transformed into the temple in the fifteen century AD. Later in the sixteenth century it was expanded by adding a *mahāraṅgamaṅṭapa* to it.[2]

Prominent temples dedicated to the god Vīrabhadra, located in various places of Karnataka, belonging to the period of Vijayanagara empire have been listed below:

S.No.	Place	District	Date
1.	Havinadu Virapura	Bellary	1532[3]
2.	Bagali	"	16th century[4]
3.	Hampi(Uddāna Vīrabhadra)	"	1545[5]
4.	Hampi (Matanga Hill)	"	15th century[6]

S.No.	Place	District	Date
5.	Hospet	Bellary	1531[7]
6.	Balehalli	Chikamangalur	1368[8]
7.	Balehonnur	"	16th century[9]
8.	Kamasamudra	Chitradurga	16th century[10]
9.	Dummi	"	1530[11]
10.	Ganderi	"	1530[12]
11.	Kaduru	"	1540[13]
12.	Kottadegudda	"	16th century[14]
13.	Keralapura	Hassan	14th century[15]
14.	Ramasagara	Kolar	16th century[16]
15.	Harabikottanur	"	1404[17]
16.	Santhebachahalli	Mandya	14th century[18]
17.	Bellur	"	15th century[19]
18.	Nagamangala	"	15th century[20]
19.	Pura	"	15th century[21]
20.	Haralkote	Mysore	1523[22]
21.	Nagarahole	"	15th century[23]
22.	Mitigre	Shimoga	14th century[24]
23.	Agara	"	1377[25]

If anybody undertakes an extensive fieldwork, some more temples of this deity may come to light. However, these temples testify to the popularity and dominance of the Vīrabhadra cult in Karnataka. These temples usually have a square *garbhagṛha*, an *aṅtrāla* and a *raṅgamaṇḍapa*, surrounded by a *prākāra* wall. Some temples possess *mahāraṅgamaṇḍapa*, *devī-shrine* and shrines for attendant deities. The temples are usually set up on *adhiṣṭhāna* and some temples have *upapītha* in addition to *adhiṣṭhāna*. Walls of the temples are either plain and smoothly dressed or decorated with pilasters, *kumbhapañjaras* and niches. Superstructures on the *garbhagṛha* are fashioned in Dravidian type of architecture.

SCULPTURE AND ICONOGRAPHY

One of the important aspects of Śiva is the disintegration and destruction of the universe. As a cosmic law, everything itself disintegrates creating a boundlers void leads to creation and recreation and finally existance of the universe. In this sense Brahmā and Viṣṇu are also Śiva.[26] The god assumes several forms such as Vīrabhadra, Gajahamurti, Bhikṣātanamurti, Kaṅkālamurti, Bhairava and so on for the ultimate creation of the universe.

As stated above, the representation of these gods reflect the martial nature of the society. Profound worship of these gods became essential during this period.

Vīrabhadra is the embodiment of Śiva's wrath, He is commonly sculpted both in round and relief throughout the Vijayanagara region and period. *Kurmapurāṅa, Varāhapurāṇa* and *Bhāgavatapurāṇa* furnish a backdrop for the rise of Vīrabhadra. *Śrītatvanidhi* and *Kāraṇāgama* contain the description of the image of *Vīrabhadramurti.*[26a] *Śilpa-saṅgraha* and *Śilparatna* enumerate several images of Vīrabhadra.[27]

Generally, the deity stands in *dvibhaṅga* or *samabhaṅga* pose holding an arrow and a bow in the upper hands, a sword and a shield in the front hands. He wears *kirīṭamakuṭa, makarakuṅḍala, yagñopaviṭa, mekhalā* to which a dagger is tied to the right side, a long *ruṇḍamāla* and highly distinctive *sandala*. To his right, he is attended by Dakṣa with a Ram's head who stands in *samabhaṅga* in an *añjalī* pose. This is a very common variety of Vīrabhadra to be found in both Śaiva and Vaiṣṇava temples of the age. A beautiful cult-icon of Vīrabhadra of 1.5 metres in height is in Mārkaṇḍeśvara temple (Pl. 11.4) at Vakhaleri (Kolar Dt.). Being a rare image, it possesses realistic delineation of limbs. Similar forms of Vīrabhadra is noticed in Basavaṇṇa temple at Irugappanahalli, Śiva temple at Timmalapura, in the royal centre at Hampi, etc. In the worshipping icon of Vīrabhadra in Vīrabhadra temple at Santhebachahalli (Mandya Dt.) a change could be seen in the attributes of the god with other usual ornamental details. Here, the god holds *triśula* and *damaru* in the upper hands and a sword and a shield in front hands. To the left of the god is an idol of Bhadrakālī (Pl. 11.1), the spouse of the god. *Kāraṇāgama* suggests that the presence of Bhadrakālī should be to the left side of the god.[28] Vīrabhadra is rarely shown in sitting postures and such an image is depicted in Jambukeśvara temple at Hospet. Here, the god sits in *lalitāsana* on a *bhadrapītha* carrying usual attributes. Vīrabhadra is also depicted as moving rampantly in a sculpture in the royal centre at Hampi with same attributes. The deity is portrayed in an unusual and different posture at Hampi. Carrying usual attributes, he is represented kneeling valiantly towards left. His right knee touches the ground in *vīrāsana* and the shield is held at the waist level. This reminds of the folk-dance of the *Liṅgada-bīra* which is a folk version of Vīrabhadra punishing Dakṣa for his audacity. In another model at the same place and also at Bhoganandi temple at Naṅdī, the god is delineated in a fighting mode. Here, he is depicted as pulling out an arrow from his quiver.

The incarnation of Vīrabhadra is sequentially depicted in three panels in Śiva temple at Timmalapura near Hampi. Dakṣa's sacrifice which led to the rising Vīrabhadra as a result of ill-treatment meted out to Śiva by Dakṣa, is delineated in these panels. In the first panel, Vīrabhadra is shown moving ferociously towards the place of the sacrifice. He wears a long tapering crown, earrings, necklaces. He holds a bow in the upper left hand and draws an arrow with the upper right hand from his quiver. He carries a rapier in the front right hand and mace in the left. In the next panel Vīrabhadra has already cut of the head of Dakṣa. A beheaded person is sitting before sacrificial fire. He is seated cross-legged pouring ghee with a ladle on the sacrificial fire. In the third panels Dakṣa is shown in an *añjalī* pose with a ram's head. Vīrabhadra has here pardoned him for his audacity and granted him life mercifully.

Śilparatna mentions a form of eight armed Vīrabhadra riding on a vampire *(vetāḷaruḍha)* surrounded by his attendants.[29] This is a rare form, depicted in Jambukeśvaran temple at Hospet. Having eight hands, he carries a *triśula*, a *paraśu*, an arrow, a sword in right side hands. *Vīṇadhara-Vīrabhadra*, also a rare and unique icon is found in Jambukeśvara temple Hospet (Pl. 11.5), Markaṇḍeśvara temple at Vakkaleri, etc. Here, the god is shown seated in *sukāsana* wearing usual ornaments. He is showing playing with *Vīṇā* in front hands and carrying *triśuḷa* and *ḍamaru* in upper hands. Vīrabhadra with two hands carrying a sword and a shield is an exceptionally rare sculpture. The icon is housed in the Archaeological Museum at Kamalapura and it is brought from a nearby ruined temple at Hampi. Another very rare sculpture of Vīrabhadra known as *digambara* Vīrabhadra is found in Jambukeśvara temple at Hospet. He wears usual ornaments and attributes but it shown naked. This is a very fine and well-executed sculpture. His face is frowned in anger. The sculptor who made this image has used his genius to express utter frightful nature on the face of his icon.

In the *Sapta-mātṛikā* panels, Vīrabhadra is shown usually at the right end and Gaṅapati at left and flanking seven mother goddesses. Such panels are to be seen in several Vijayanagara temples. Here, Vīrabhadra is depicted as squatting.

The above survey and analysis of the Vīrabhadra temples and sculptures under Vijayanagara empire illustrates clearly the popularity and importance of Vīrabhadra cult in Karnataka.

NOTES AND REFERENCE

1. *ARIE*, 36 & 37, 1889, *SII* VI 266.
2. *EC*, VII (1979), Ng., 9; IV (I ed.), Ng., 4.
3. *SII*, IX pt. ii, 533.
4. S.N. Shivarudraswamy, *Vijayanagara Temples in Karnataka*, 1996, p.238.
5. *SII*, IV, 266.

6. S.N. Shivarudraswamy, *op.cit.*, p.239.
7. *SII*, IX, 539.
8. *MAR*, 1916, p.10.
9. S.N. Shivarudraswamy, *op.cit.*, p.241.
10. *EC*, XI, CI., 46.
11. *Ibid.*, Hk., 15.
12. *Ibid.*, Hk., 20.
13. *Ibid.*, Hk., 71.
14. S.N. Shivarudraswamy, *op.cit.*, p.242.
15. *Ibid.*, p.244.
16. *MAR*, 1941, p.54.
17. *EC*, X Kl., 73.
18. S.N. Shivarudraswamy, *op.cit.*, p.251.
19. *MAR*, 1939, p.35.
20. *EC*, VII (1979), Ng. 8.
21. S.N. Shivarudraswamy, *op.cit.*, p.251.
22. *EC*, IV (1925) Ch.224.
23. *MAR*, 1918, p.25; *EC*, III (1974), Nj. 335.
24. *EC*, VIII, CI., 28.
25. *Ibid.*, Ti. 16.
26. Swami Harshananda, *Hindu Gods and Goddesses*, Hadigs, 1988, p.61.
27. S.K. Ramachandra Rao, *Pratimakosha*, Vol. VI, p.150.
28. *Idem.*
29. S.K. Ramachandra Rao, *op.cit.*, Vol. VI, p.150.

12

Art and Architecture of Muvaraivendran Rock-Cut Cave Temple: A Study

M. Venkatesan & K. Ravikumar

The tradition of rock-cut architecture in India developed during the Mauryan period. In succeeding centuries it spread all over India. The history of architecture and sculpture in South India, the Pallavas and Pandyas apart from a number of small dynasties had been well-established. There are four well-known Pandya rock-cut cave temple in Virudhunagar District, that is Muvaraivendran Thirumalai Kolundisvar Temple (Śiva) Tiruthangal (Viṣṇu) Pudupattai (M) (Śivakasi) and Sevapatti (Śiva, Sattur TK.) In this article the Muvaraivendran Thirumalai Kolundisvarar (Śiva) rock-cut cave temple art and architecture will be discussed.

The Muvaraivendran (in latitude 0936'585N and longitude of 77 44'408E)is a land lying in between Srivilliputhur and Madurai Road (on the Mangammal Salai). It is situated in Srivilliputhur Taluk in Virudhunagar District, Tamil Nadu. It is located at 58 km South-West of Madurai in South Tamil Nadu.

Thirumalai Kolundisvara cave Temple is situated 4 km away from Muvaraivendran in the North-West. The hill is called as Dekshina Kailaya Malai (Mottaimalai). The East-facing temples, measuring 3.9 mts. x 6.7 mts. has a large *maṇḍapa* within a pillared faced and a *garbhagriha*. There are three panel carvings of Subrahmanya, Natarāja and Gaṇeśa in the *ardhamaṇḍapa*.

It has a large *ardhamaṇḍapa* and a shrine behind, facing east. The natural scarp of the rock being vertical. The actual cutting of the baseline of the excavation is raised at a height of 6 ft. from the ground-level in front of the almost vertical and large rock. The shrine's entrance is cut (5 x 2½ ft.) between two inner pilasters, the pilasters thus forming the jambs and the thin beam on the top of the lintel which consists of five steps, each steps with a small landing on the top. In front, a moulded *adhisthāna,* cut the

Jagati rising directly from the floor of the *maṇḍapa* (2½ ft.) over the *Jagati* is a *Tripatta Kumudha,* a *Kantha* with two *Kampa*-courses one above and one below it, with a *Patika*. The cylindrical *liṅga* and its *pitha* in the centre are separate parts and are not known out of the rock. This feature is unknown in the Pallava temple. The shrine wall of the interior as well as the ceiling are plain. The interior of the shrin-chamber measures 8 square ft.

The *ardhamaṇḍapa* itself is 17 ft. 6 inches x 6 ft. 8 inches including width of the pillars. The facade of the *ardhamaṇḍapa* has six massive pillars and 4 pilasters, which have, as usual, their base and top of square type. The pillars of the facade are massive with cubical sadurams at the base and top. The ceiling of the *ardhamaṇḍapa* too shows the supporting *Vajana*-moulding. On the right side of the *ardhamaṇḍapa,* there are three panel carvings of Gaṇeśa, Subrahmanya and Natarāja. These sulptures show evidence of being re-cut, however, the first and third panel still retains vestiges of the original flying Vidyādhara pair in the upper parts of the carvings.

The *mukhamaṇḍapa* have openings with entrance-portico on the other three sides, East, South and North. It is attached to *ardhamaṇḍapa*. The *mukhamaṇḍapa* are not furnished with walls. The roofing is formed with large slabs of granite supported by monolithic pillars. The *naṅdī* is found at the centre of this *maṇḍapa* which is facing the main shrine (East). An inscription engraved on the *peetham* of the steps to cave temple refers to the Pandya king Maravarman Sundara Pandyan I. This *maṇḍapam* architecture seem to belong to the 12th-13th century AD.

Facing the cave temple is a Śiva temple and on the opposite of it is the *Navagraha Maṇḍapa* and a shrine for the Goddess Maragadavalli Amman.

In the absence of any foundation-inscription it is difficult to date the rock-cut cave at Muvaraivendran. It is generally held that the Pandyas in far South took to rock-architecture only after the Pallavas. The later started it some time in the later quarter of the 6th or first quarter of the 7th century AD. In the circumstances, one may easily date the rock-cave temple at Muvaraivendran at least to the middle of the 9th century of the time of Srimara Srivallabha (815-862) although the possibility of an earlier date can by no means be ruled out. It has also some sculptural features, which consist of the re-cut of the panel carving of Gaṇeśa, Subrahmaniya, and Natarāja seems to be on the 12th-13th century of Pandyas. The *Navagraha Maṇḍap* and the shrine for the Maragadavalli were built in the Nayak period.

13

The Eighteen-Step Karuppasamy at Alzharkoil in Tamil Nadu

D. Gangadaran

Among the major temples of Tamil Nadu, Alzharkoil has got a distinctiveness of its own, for the main entrance is always closed. Since the minor or folk deity, the eighteen-step Karuppasamy resides here, hence the place has acquired the name-The "Eighteen-Step Entrance".

The eighteen-step door in Alzharkoil is smeared with sandal paste, *kumkum* and is also decorated with flowers and garlands at the time of *pujās.* In the days of temple festival *(Brahmostva)* during the Tamil month of *Aadi* (July-August), it was opened for the entrance of Chakrathalvar (Viṣṇu's symbol and weapon).[1] After the *Aadi* festival, the significant door step is always locked. The *Sthala puraṇa* says that entrance to the eighteen door step was through the northern gate *(vadavasal)* which is on the northern side.

The eighteen-step Karuppasamy dwells on the door, which is applied with sandal. There is no definite form for this deity and hence the eighteen door-step is considered as the deity and *pujas* are performed. In other places in Madurai region, this deity is depicted in terrific form. He holds a sickle in a right hand and a club in the other with chappals on his feet.

THE TALE OF THE LOCKED DOOR

There is a tale connected with the closing of the entrance of this temple.[2] Once upon a time a group of eighteen tribesmen came from Malabar country to rob this "Spiritual Essence" of the Lord Alzhar. They were experts in the art of black magic and if they applied a black collyrium on the eyes, they became invisible. They entered the sanctum of the deity, extracted its spirtual essence and stored them in huge vessels. In this manner they extracted little by little the spiritual essence of the deity, on the same night the god himself appeared in the dream of the temple-priest and revealed the matter. This news consequently was disclosed to the others of the temple. All put their heads together and designed a master plan to capture the thieves. Accordingly, the next day the servants of the temple performed *pujās* for the deity, offered very hot rice and closed the door outside. The smoke from the hot-rice melted the collyrium which was applied by the thieves in their eyes, and hence became visible again. The servants of the temple cornered the eighteen robbers by opening the door. They were brought out of the temple, beheaded and their heads were buried under the main entrance. Karuppasamy, who came as an escort pleaded, that he should be acquitted, and that he will in future watch the temple from being burgled. Hence he was detained.

CERTAIN INFERENCE

The eighteen people who came to rob in the temple were not Tamils but they were from Malabar but the folk-song says that they hailed from Ayodhya.

The people who came were are not invaders for they were meagre in strength. Besides they came inside to steal very tactfully, which proves the fact that they were mere burglers.

The news that they came to rob the "spiritual essence" is to be analysed. Moreover the race came to rob only after hearing the news from *Siddha* book which narrates the wealth of the temple. Hence, they can be considered only as boot-leggers, who had come to rob not the spiritual essence but the gold jewellery of this temple.

There is yet another version of the story which says that instead of the hot-rice served for the deity, boiled gruel was poured on the floor. Otherwise, there is no other difference in this story.

A short folk-song by name *"Description of Karuppan Origin"* composed by Motaiyakon is being sung by the narrators. By word of mouth it is understood that the author belonged to this century. Though the description is based on the tale prevalent among the folk people.

THE DATE OF THE EVENT

There is no evidence of the installation of the *gopura* door in any inscription. But the inscriptions found on it are belated (AD 1608) and are the inscriptions of Sadasiva Raya (1542-70) of Vijayanagar. Upto AD 1608 this door was frequented by the people. In the *patra* (document) of Vellaijathathar (AD 1709) there is a mention of the 'Eighteen-Step' which bears testimony to the fact that the event might have taken place before AD 1709. Hence this event would have happened between 1698 and 1709. There is no proof as to who was the ruler of Madurai. It is highly probable that the event occured during the reign of Vijayarange Chokkanatha (1706-32) and his queen Meenachi (1732-37). The thieves who came into the temple to burgle were caught, slaughtered and buried under the entrance of the temple. Since this place is polluted hence people do not pass that way. So the main entrance was locked and closed. Since the burglers met with an unnatural death people feared to visit the spot. So minor deity was enshrined there.

KARUPPASAMY AND THE HIGHER CASTE PEOPLE

The higher class people, i.e. Brahmins, who were serving the god Alzhar (Viṣṇu) were compelled to accept the minor-deity Karuppasamy when he was enshrined in Alzharkoil.[3] Hence the Brahmins agreed to offer the food and the garland that was offered to Alzhar during the midnight *pujā*. The Brahmins offer Karuppasamy the excess of thing after the use of Alzhar (god) with a view of regarding Karuppasamy as Alzhar's disciple. Hence the non-Brahmins considered him as a blood-thirsty deity and called him *Kṛṣṇaputhran* or *"son of Kṛṣṇa"*. In order to reduce the enmity between Brahmins and non-Brahmins the relationship between the "Great Tradition" and "Little Tradition" or "Folk Tradition", this mythological story was coined and became popular.

NOTES AND REFERENCES

1. Of the Vaiṣṇava symbols and weapons, the discus or *Chakra* is being worshipped in the Srī Vaiṣṇava temples under the name *Chakra-Perumal.*
2. K.N. Radhakrishna, *Tirumalirunjolaimalai (Alzharkoil) Sthalapurana,* p.211.
3. *Census of India,* 1961, Vol. IX, Part XI-D: Temples of Madras State. VI. Madurai and Ramanathapuram, p.107. The myth told about the Eighteen-Steps under which are said to be buried eighteen magicians from Malabar who came to steal the divinity of this shrine, is given in Whitehead (1921), pp.113-15.

14

The Concept of Kamatopasarga as seen in the Humcha Region

Sarvamangala G. & D.S. Somashekhar

Humcha is a small village situated in Hosanagar *taluq* of Shimoga District, Karnataka. The village is located 27 km south-east of Hosanagar *taluq* and 27 km south west of Shimoga city. Even today Humcha serves as a famous Jaina centre and the place has Digambara Jaina *matha*. According to the inscriptional evidences, the Jaina *matha* here belongs to the Digambara Jaina order and was established centuries back by monks belonging to the *Naṅdī Saṁgha* of Sri Kundakundacharya, between 7th and 10th century when the propagandist activities of the Jaina *acharyas* were at their height.

The ancient Pombulcha or todays Humcha, served as a capital of one of the feudatory rulers of Karnataka by name Santaras. The inscriptions say that the unit they ruled was Santalige-1000, hence they are known as Santaras of Santalige-1000. The localities of the region seem to have associated themselves with Ugravamsa of Uttara Mathura in North India.

The founder of the dynasty was Jinadatta, who is said to have belonged to the Ugra Vamsa, to which family Pārśvanātha, the 23rd Tirthaṅkara is also said to have belonged. (According to Southern Jaina tradition-*Maha Purāṇa and Uttara Purāṇa*).

According to the later inscriptions of the Santara, which gives a beautiful picture regarding the establishment of the kingdom of Jinadatta, Padmāvatī, the *Yakṣī* of Pārśvanātha as per the local tradition and legend blessed Jinadatta with a lion crest *(Mriga Lāñchana)* and monkey flag *(Vānara Dhvaja).*

Though so far Jinadatta's historicity is not yet established, yet he was followed by many important rulers such as Vira Santara, Bhujabala Santara, Vikrama Santara and so on. These rulers and their family members, the rich merchant community and some of the influential section of the society and even the ordinary section of the society engaged themselves in constructional activities of temples, basadis or tanks, etc. But unfortunately though we come across a large number of inscriptional reference, unfortunately only few monuments are still intact in Humcha region. Most of the other monuments have disappeared.

From the surviving temples of the region, there is one temple next to Jaina *matha* within the *matha* complex known as Pārśvanātha *Basadi.* The *basadi* has undergone a lot of renovation from time to time, especially during the Vijayanagara and post Vijayanagara phases. But inside the sanctum, sanctorum and the Navaranga Hall still retains the original features. Inside the *garbhagriha* is seen the image of Pārśvanātha Tīrthaṅkara in *dhyāna mudrā* along with two chowrie bearers on either side.

In the Navaranga Hall are placed the most magnificent Pārśvanātha images, two in number. They are known as *'Kamatopasarga Parśvanatha images'*. On the basis of stylistic grounds these two images can be dated to late 9th century AD and is carved in perfection.

THE THEME OF KAMATOPASARGA

Pārśvanātha according to the Jaina tradition was the 23rd Tīrthaṅkara and he said to have belonged to the *Ugra Vaṁsa.* (Gunbhadracharya *c.* mid 9th century). His *lāñcana* is the snake and even his *Yakṣī* Padmāvathī has *Kukuta Sarpa* as her *lāñcana* (Trisasti Salaka Purusha Chaita AD 1160-70 of Chavundaraya).

Pārśvanātha is a historical person. Some meagre details about him are preserved in early Jaina literature. Pārśavanātha was the son of Asvasena, king of Benaras and his queen was Brāhmī or Vāmā. He lived for thirty-two years as a householder and thereafter performed severe penance and became a *Jina* or *Arhanta.* According to the scholars, he lived in the 8th century BC *(Pārśvanātha Purāṇa of Parsvanatha Pandita* ed. by M. Mariyappa Bhat and Govinda Rao, p. iii).

THE STORY OF KAMATOPASARGA AND ITS ASSOCIATION WITH PĀRŚVANĀTHA

Some Kannada literary works like *Mahā Purāṇa, Uttara Purāṇa* of Gunabhadra, *Trisati Salakā Mahā Purāṇa* of Chavundaraya, *Pārśvanātha Purāṇa* by Parsva Pandita speaks in length the problems created by Kamatha while Pārśvanātha was in deep penance to achieve *Kaivalyajñāna.* But the association of Kamatha and Pārśvanātha is said to have been from the previous births itself (altogether 11 in number).

THE STORY IN BRIEF

Pārśvanātha when he was quite young and still living in the palace, one day went to see the beauty of nature and came to a place where Kamatha, an ascetic was performing meditation, surrounded on all sides by fire called *Panchāgni* under the scratching sun. Pārśvanātha saw a pair of snakes being roasted and stopped the ascetic for his folly. He preached him the doctrine of *Ahiṁsā* being the best of all virtue and that kindness was the root of *Dharma*. (*ibid.*, p. iv). At first, Kamatha did not yield to him. Ultimately Kamatha was convinced by Pārśva's words and thus Pārśvanātha was able to save the lives of the pair of snakes from the piece of burning wood. He preached them *panchamantra*. The pair of snakes died by hearing the *panchamantra* and later on born in the Naga world as Dharanendra *Yakṣa* and Padmāvatī *Yakṣī*.

After many more years Pārśvanātha left the palace and decided to perform meditation to attain *Kaivalya Jñāna* to become a Jina. When Pārśvanātha engaged in deep meditation, at this time the sage who was known as Kamatha in his previous birth was reborn as Shambara in *Jyotir-loka* which existed between the earth and heaven and was moving in the sky along with his wife in his vehicle. As the vehicle approached near the meditating Pārśvanātha, it stopped moving. Wonderstruck Kamatha or Shambara looked down only to find Pārśvanātha performing deep meditation. Immediately Kamatha remembering his past life and decided to abstract Pārśva meditation. He turned into a demon and started inflicting a lot of troubles to distract Pārśva's meditation. He became a demon by name Megamalini and poured heavy rains with thunderbolts continuously for seven days. The water level reached Pārśva almost upto his chin. Then he took a form of wild beast such as a lion, tiger and so on. He started rolling rocks and shot poisonous arrows. But all his efforts went in vain and he could not distract Pārśvanātha from his meditation. It was then the Dharanendra *Yakṣa* and his consort Padmāvatī, who were actually the pair of snakes in their previous birth and who were saved by Pārśvanātha in their previous life came to protect Pārśvanātha from Kamatha's evil deeds.

Dharanendra came and spread his seven hoods and covered Pārśva on top of his head. Whereas Padmāvatī his wife came and held the *Vajrakode* (the diamond studded umbrella) on top of it. Thus these two became the *Yakṣa* and *Yakṣī* of Pārśvanātha Tirthaṅkara. Both of them represent the God's of the world underneath the earth (*Pātāla*). Ultimately Kamatha realizing his bad deeds surrendered to *Jina* along with his wife and prostrated before him and begged to forgive and forget.

Actually the previous births of Kamatha are very vividly described in ancient Kannada literature such as Jinasenacharyas *Poorva Purāṇa* and the *kāvya* written by him which is known as *Pārśvabhudaya. Uttara Purāṇa* of Gunabhadracharya, Vadirajasuri's *Pārśvanātha Charita* and *Pārśvanātha Purāṇa* by Parsva Pandita and so on. The Kamatha's *bhāvāvali* are listed below.

1. Kamatha.
2. Vyada.
3. Kukuta sarpa.
4. Born in a hell.
5. Became a paithon.
6. Born in a hell.
7. Hunter by name Kurangaka.
8. Once again born in the hell by name Tamaprabha.
9. Born as a lion.
10. Then he became a king by name Mahipala (father of Vāmā who in turn became the mother of Pārśva). Mahipala when he turned old took *sanyāsa* and started performing *'Panchāgni'*.
11. Then he was born as Sambhara, the demon.

Pārśvanātha also took different bhāvāvali in his previous life. They are

1. Marubhuti.
2. An elephant.
3. Rashmivega Vidhyadhara.
4. Born as Indra at Achyutakalpa.
5. Born as a son to Vajravijaya of Ashvapura by name Vajranabi and became an. *Chakravarti.*
6. *Chakravarti* later left the kingdom and became a *sanyāsī* by name Vajranabimuni.
7. Born as Ahamindra in heaven.
8. Born as Anada the son of Vajrabahu of Kosala later on renounced the world and went to the forest where he took Jinadikshe to become a *Jina* or *Tirthaṅkara.*
9. Born in heaven (13 ne Swarga).
10. Born as prince Pārśva (the son of Varanasi ruler by name Visvasena and Vāmā or Brahmi).
11. Pārśva the 23rd *Tirthaṅkara.*
    (As mentioned in *Pārśvanātha Purāṇa*).

THE DESCRIPTION OF THE KAMATOPASARGA AS SHOWN IN THE STELLAS AT HUMCHA

The stele measures 60" or 5 feet. Both are almost similar to look at with little or minor variation. The Pārśvanātha is shown in kāyotsarga form and is surrounded by a beautiful *prabhāvalī*. This *prabhāvalī* actually consists of many bas reliefs of Kamotapasarga incidents. The stellas correspond much to the description given in Jaina literature, which denotes that the sculptor who carved this image was very familiar with literary evidence.

Pārśvanātha is shown standing in *kayotsarga* on a double lotus *pitha (Padma Pitha)*. The Dharanendra, i.e. the *Yakṣa* of Pārśvanātha has spread his seven hoods over Pārśva, who is absorbed in deep meditation. The seven hoods form a kind of canopy sheltering against the attacking of Kamatha.

The attacking hosts of Kamatha depicted in the sculpture on the right side are (from top to bottom in descending order), a demon menancingly balancing a big boulder aimed at the Jina Pārśva, a demon shooting an arrow, a leaping lion, a charging bull.

On the left side a demon or monster with a heavy mace on the shoulder, a demon with a dagger in his right hand and a serpent on his left hand, a maddened elephant and a rushing tiger are shown.

Below, it is Dharanendra *Yakṣa* on the right and Padmāvatī *Yakṣī* on the left. Both are in *tribhaṅga* posture, both are shown with many ornaments such as necklaces, bangles, leg ornaments and both are crowned with *kiritamukuṭa*.

Dharanendra *Yakṣa* is shown holding a lotus in his right hand and placing his left hand on his waist. Whereas Padmāvati is holding a canopied club with diamond studded parasol or umbrella *(Vajrakode)*, behind the coils and hoods of the serpent (the *Nāga* king).

Still below on the right at the base is shown the sobered Kamatha in surrendered form, bowing down to Jina Pārśva and is shown begging Pārśva's forgiveness in *añjali mudrā*. On the left opposite to Kamatha is seen his wife half knelt, rising her right hand in praise of *Jina*. Between these two couple are seen two beautiful *nāgas* (half serpent half human form), holding the double lotus *pitha* or pedestal, suggesting that the body of *Jina* was lifted above the hood from water which had inundated him upto his chin.

The same elaborate treatment of the above theme is repeated in the other stella, with minor variation in depicting the details. For example both Kamatha and his wife are shown in *añjali mudrā*.

a) The tail of the serpent starts from right side and the body of the serpent has six bands, where as in the other stella the tails starts from the left side and there are nine coils of the serpent body.

b) The two nāgas lifting and holding the double lotus are not depicted.

c) *Kukutasarpa* is depicted as the lāṅcana, a rare phenomena rarely found elsewhere.

The whole stella thus depicts the most important incident in Pārśvanātha's life and the whole theme is expressed in the art form in a very picturesque manner. The sculpture is very lively and almost looks very close to natural depiction. The sculpture adopted many of the art features of Chalukyas of Badami. The sculptures on the ground of stylistic basis can be assigned to *c.* 9th century AD. Prof. Hampa, feels that these two sculptures must have belonged to the Alupas of Alvakheda. Because before the establishment of the Santara's independent dynasty, the area is said to have been under the control of the Alupas.

Artists of the ancient period knew how to represent different modes of representing Pārśva in sculptures. Here the artist has selected such a beautiful theme and adopted it to their contemporary needs. The way the minute details was depicted, the facial expressions of the *Yakṣa* and *Yakṣī* all speaks of regional depiction.

Thus the whole concept is done in such a magnificient way that any lay person who visits will be able to understand the concept very well. But this concept is not new and is not just confined only to the Jainism. A similar incident is also found in Buddhism. The episode is well known as *Māra parājaya* episode, which is noted in the life of Gautama Buddha. When Gautama was sitting under Macalinda tree or Bodhi tree, all of a sudden huge clouds appeared and started pouring heavy rainfall. But Mucalinda Nāga, the serpent king spread his large hoods over Lord Buddha and protected him from the heavy rains.

Even in Brahmanical mythology Ādiśeṣa supports the earth on his polycephalous head. Lord Viṣṇu, a great *yogī* rest on the coil of Ādiśesa. Thus such of incidents are very common in India.

The sculptural Kamatopasarga commands an artistic appreciation for it's uniqueness. Perhaps the troubles caused by Kamatha to Pārśvanātha are circumstantially meant to give us an idea as to how difficult it is to attain the state of *Jina* through hardest penances being unmindful of the unfavourable situations. In other words it suggests that to become a *Kevalin* it requires an unshakable determination to do uncommon meditation leading to enlightenment.

NOTES AND REFERENCES

1. M. Bhat Mariappa and M. Govinda Rao (ed.), 1954, *Pārśvanātha Purāṇam of Parsva Pandita,* University of Madras, Madras.
2. M.A. Dhaky (1971-72), 'Santara Sculpture', *Journal of the Indian Society of Oriental Art,* Vol. IV, Delhi.
3. B.S. Kulkarni (ed.), 1975, *Trisasti Lakshana Maha Puranam (Chavundaraya Puranam)* (Kannada), Kannada Research Institute, Karnataka University, Dharwar.
4. Hampa Nagarajaiha, 1997, *Santararu-Ondu Adyayana, (Santaras-A Study) (Kannada),* Siddhanta Kirti Granthamala, Hombuja Jaina Matha, Humcha.
5. Hampa Nagarajaiha, 1999, *Jaina Parsva Temples in Karnataka,* Siddhanta Kirti Granthamala, Hombuja Jaina Maths, Humcha.
6. S.V. Parameshware Bhat (ed.), *Kannada Buddha Charite, (Ashvagosha Kaviya Sanskrit Padya Kavyada Sarala Padyanuvada),* Mangalore.

15

Manuscript Painting of Mahāpuruṣa Srimanta Sankardeva (AD 1449-1550)

Bharti Barua

Mahāpuruṣa Srimanta Sankardeva developed the art of manuscript painting in Assam during 15th-16th century AD. Naren Kalita says :

> The genius of performing art is marked by classical fervour, while the latter comprising architecture, sculpture and painting reflected increasing preoccupation with local form as the vehicle of expression of the new social, religious and cultural revolution.[1]

T.C. Rastogi stated that Sankardeva (1449-1568) preached Vaisnavism, absolute faith in Viṣṇu, and his incarnation Kṛṣna basing his teachings on the *Bhāgavata Dharma*. Sankardeva's doctrines were called *Eka-Sarana Dharma*, seeking refuge in the Divinity.[2] Sankardeva has always been associated with the stories of *Rāmāyana, Bhāgavata* and *Kirtana Ghosa*, which is the greatest work dealing with the life of Kṛṣṇa and his beloved devotees. His most important creative art was the *Ankiyanat*, plays based on the stories of the Purāṇas. Sankardeva's Bhakti cult was purely based on Vaiṣṇava religion. His impact was quite deep. According to Rastogi :

> Sankardeva advocated with a religion of extreme ascerticism nor complete renunciation of family life. He adopted the golden mean between the two. He believed that renunciation should be integral, not external. He realized that men and women have to live in the world and pursue their professions. He himself led a family life and married second time after the death of his first wife".[3]

Sankardeva's religion brought a new meaning and depth to social and cultural life. In the socio-cultural history of Assam, for the first time Sankardeva asserted the dignity of man in society independent of the accidents of birth and social rank, and established the spiritual equality of all men. In his religion, Brahmanas, Sudras and men of lower caste enjoyed equal liberty of worship, devotion and prayers. He admitted into his gospel people from all social orders, and among his chief disciples were Brahman, tribals and Muhammadans. "Profundity of thought, unity of outlook and music of diction mark *Namaghosa* as an outstanding work of art,"[4] remarks T.C. Rastogi.

Sankardeva was born at Alipukhuri of Bata Draba in the famous family of a Barabhuyan in Nagoan district in AD 1449. His famous book was *Kirtan Ghosa* and his *Adya Dasam Bhagavata* is also well known. This book contains about 322 miniature paintings with the description of Kṛṣṇa's childhood and his youth. The unique features of the paintings are beautifully and brilliantly endorsed with vegetable colours from various native fruits mixed with special kind of earth, ashes and various kinds of organic colours. Sankardeva attracted his disciples with the illustrated paintings of religious books to popularize the neo-Vaiṣṇava cult not only in his native land but also in the nearby kingdoms like Koch Behar. The king of Koch Behar invited Sankardeva to throw the germ of Vaiṣṇava religion in his kingdom.

Sankardeva with his most trusted disciple, Madhavadeva, established the Vaiṣṇava cult with the thread of national unity. An important difference of Sankardeva's Vaiṣṇavism with that of North Indian Vaiṣṇavism is that in North India, Kṛṣṇa is always worshipped with Rādhā, but in Assam Kṛṣṇa is worshipped alone. Kṛṣṇa receives the sole attention. His most important contributions to Ankiyanat, a different type of dance drama are Patni Prasad, Kalia Daman, Keli Gopal, Rukmini Haran, Parijat Haran and last one is Ram Bijoy Nat. His devotional philosophical books are *Bhakti Pradip, Bhakti Ratnakar, Niminava SidhaSambad* and *Anadipatan*. Translated books are Bhagavat 1st, 2nd, 10 and 11 and 12 Skandha. Books on devotional songs are *Kirtan Ghosa, Gunamala*. His most valuable contribution is *Satriya* dance. He established *Satriya* institution to develop the true Assamese culture through dance, drama and *Abhinoi*. In this institution, the disciples of Sankardeva resided together to do *Nam kirtana* or to sing devotional song with some indigenous instrument as *dhol, khol, tal, bortalka, bor kah,* etc.

In the medieval period Sri Sankardeva introduced the art form of culture which is known as *Satriya* art or *Sankariya* Art. It is also known as *Kamrupiya* Art. Art of 15th-16th century AD was divided into three groups (1) *Satriya Art,* (2) Folk Art or *Darangi Art* and (3) *Gargaya Art,* patronized by Ahom kings. The spiritual and philosophical aspect is found in the *Satriya* art which inspired the devotees with the beautiful descriptive art form to establish the depth of Kṛṣṇa's supreme energy. These miniature (pls. 15.1-15.4) and manuscript paintings were spread out in most of the *Satras* to influence the devotees with 'Kṛṣṇa's Consiousness' and the philosophical concept of Vaiṣṇavism. The material of paintings were mostly Sanchi-bark and *Tula pat* (hand-made cotton or paper). In this connection I want to mention the *"Vrindāvanī Vastra"*, which the king of Koch Behar, Naranarayana asked Sankardeva to weave depicting the whole story of Kṛṣṇa from his childhood to his youth with his playmates and Rādhā at Vrindavan in a cloth. It is unfortunate that no trace of *Vrindāvani Vastra* is found in Assam. The length of the cloth was 180 feet and width was 5½ or 5.6 to 6 feet. But some of the scholars state that it is in Tibet, though with what context it is impossible to say. Dr. Rosemary Crill, curator of British museum of the Indian branch of the Library, came to Assam a few years back to enquire about it and I gave her company to go to most of the famous Majuli Satras to collect information about *Vrindāvani Vastra*. The Satradhikar, chief of the Satras told us that they only knew about it, but have not seen and there is no trace of it.

The religious books were written on Sanchi bark, *Tula Pat,* (Hand-made cotton or paper) and sometimes on *Muga Pat* (special kind of golden silk cloth). Ink used was deep black *Silikha* fruit mixed with ashes, urine of cow and ashes of bora rice (sticky type) which is never damaged by rainwater or eaten by insects but remains for a longer period. The miniature paintings were coloured with green, red, yellow, blue, black earth colour etc. *Geeta-Govinda* was translated in Assamese by Ramanarayana Kaviraj Chakravarty from the original *Geeta-Govinda* by Jayadeva. It was written on Sanchi bark of the size of 41 x 12 cm. It deals with divine sport of Rādhā and Kṛṣṇa as a means of worship and devotion. With the text version the artist called as Khanikar, beautifully painted the mournful moment of Rādhā in separation from Kṛṣṇa. But Kṛṣṇa enjoyed with other women in Braja and Vrindavan and played erotic games with them. This was the composition of the story with marvellous paintings of Rādhā-Kṛṣṇa Lilā. Here the love and devotion came to the forefront with the spread of Vaiṣṇavism. Artist's had to ensure suitable means of expression to give life to the paintings. The book *The Golden Flute*, states that

> The theory of *Alaṅkār, Rasa* and *Dhvani* to the field of painting and sculpture we are at once struck by the community of interest the same moods and feelings actuated the artist to visualize and give affect to his composition, after based on literary counter parts-happy combination *Rasa* and *Alaṅkāra.*

> Colours in Indian Poetics have various roles. According to Bharata dark brown is used to signify *Sringāra* (the erotic), white for *Hāsya* (Joviality), Grey for *Karunā* (Pathos), Red for *Rudra* (fury), fair complexion for *Vīra* (the heroic), black for *Bhayānaka* (terror), indigo or blue for *Vibhatsa* (the odius) and yellow for *Adbhutta* (the marvelous).
>
> —Nātyasāstra, VI, 47-48

It is also significant that the philosophy of colour prescribed for the use of dramatists and poets also served as a guide for painters. It is also stated in *The Golden Flute* that

> The poetical themes actually began to be favoured by painters, but there is very likelihood that this development synchronized with the resurging tide of Vaiṣṇavism in the middle of the 15th century AD. When it replaced the decadent philosophy and cult practices of Buddhist Tantrism and the mystic speculations of the poet-saints by the love of Rādhā and Kṛṣṇa, Rādhā through illicit amours, whether interpreted literally or symbolically, satisfied the aspirations of devotees, who though tired of the sexual aberrations of Tantric worship, still carved for jou-de-vivre sanctified by religion.

Sankardeva and his associates followed this technique to popularize Vaiṣṇavism and he was successful in his sincere effort. The theme of the poetical composition of different book vibrated with meaningful colour of the paintings gave an energy to the devotees to feel the happiness and pleasure by singing the devotional songs of Kṛṣṇa. In most of the cases descriptive analysis was done through the paintings with its colour, the artistic mind of the artist.

Ananda Lahari was composed during Ahom king Swargadeo SivaSingha (AD 1713-AD 1744). The theme of the work is *Śakti* (Power), personified as the mother of Goddess Devī, the first and Supreme principle of the Universe. It is the composition of both soul *(Puruṣa)* and nature *(Prakriti)* of the Sāṅkhya system. Here *Devīs* cosmic power is very distinctly depicted by the poet and artist. The pictorial version is significant as the celebrated work of Indian art in the later period of early 18th century. R.D. Choudhury and Naren Kalita very clearly discuss in the *Manuscript Paintings from Kamarupa Anusandhan Samiti,* about the style and technique of paintings in *Geeta-Govinda* and *Ananda Lahari*. These paintings are called *Satriya* style of painting which was introduced in the religious places of the *Satra,* an institution which was the main centre for propagation of the Bhakti cult propounded by Sri Sankardeva in the middle of the 15th century AD. R.D. Choudhury and Naren Kalita remark that before the changes of the technique in the early part of the 18th century AD "the *Satriya* institution developed a regional school of painting and its conventions. The *Satriya* School is dominated by strictly linear draughtmanship and stiff angularity to define the contours of human figures and simple depiction of certain forms."[5]

The artist of *Geeta-Govinda* followed the same convention as found in *Ananda Lahari*. The love story of Rādhā and Kṛṣṇa depicted with various trees with local flora and fauna, decorated the entire set of paintings. The bees and birds and animal give the gracious look to the pictorial landscape. The artist always in his conventional style followed the local architectural features, viz., standing roofs rested on two slender pillars, decorated with carved capitals. Kadamba tree depicted in the *Geeta-Govinda* is unique which is not found in any painting of *Geeta-Govinda* in Indian Art. Applying the colour in the painting, the artist must have been very concerned with the theme and object of narrated description of the book and according to the depth of the concept of the philosophy, artist reflected the inner meaning through his sense of distributing the colours with his artistic skill. In depicting the figures of male and female persons, the artists had the exotic knowledge to beautify the figures with actual nature and depth of the composition of the theme of the picture. The artist of that period knew the art of Rajasthan, Gujarat even of Orissa. So the turban of the head and the dress of a male person can be compared with the turban and dress design and pattern of the Rajput or Gujarat art style. The figure of a male person drawn in a proportionate posture with charming and attractive way also used to wear various types of ornaments and also a *chaddar* hanging on the shoulder, expressed the dignity of a person.

Female figures are more attractive with nicely decorated hair bun with beautiful white flower, dressed with ornamental design of *Mekhalā-chāddar* (Assamese dress use by women). The women figure is decorated with various types of ornaments made of gold, silver, etc. They used to wear earrings, rings, bangles, necklace, armlets, anklets and wạist covered with beautiful waist ornaments, sometimes hanging upto the thigh with a charming posture. These paintings reflect the Assamese cultural life of women, devotion and peace in mind with charming attitude.

Whatever manuscript painting has been found, all have definite meaning and deep Vaiṣṇavism philosophy. The paintings are composed according to the theme of the prose or verse of the devotional book which are called as *Puthi* in Sankari term or treatises. Actually the legendary stories or the fictions are written to spread knowledge of Vaiṣṇava cult expressed through the media of painting which can attract the people easily by visualizing the beautiful pictures of Kṛṣṇa, Rādhā and also other gods and goddesses. With the help of the artists they expressed the inner beauty and supreme energy of the whole universe through Kṛṣṇa's supreme power with illusion, *Māyā* and sublime beauty. It is the theme of the Assamese version of the *Geeta-Govinda*.

But in *Ananda Lahari* the power of *Śakti* has been personified as the Goddess Devī, the supreme principle of the Universe. Here *Puruṣa* and *Prakiti* of the Sāṅkhya system has been illustrated. It is the Assamese version of original Sanskrit treatise, *Saundarya-Lahari* of Sankaracharya which Ananta

Acharya translated into Assamese during 1720-1722. In the *Manuscript Paintings from Kamarupa Anusandhan Samiti* it is explained as "the cosmos evolves in six stages, which are described anthropomorphically as six *chakras* (circles) in the cosmos conceived as Devīś body". The significant feature of the Assamese treatise is that it is a profusely illustrated in pictorial version and celebrated work of Indian art contributing to the development of Assamese art as the Assam school of painting in the later period. The paintings of this treatise follow the Satriya pictorial convention in the figures of gods, goddesses, even in the trees, birds and animals.

Mahāpuruṣa Srimanta Sankardeva was the pioneer and founder of the *Satriya* institution and *Satriya* art of painting to throw the light of Kṛṣṇa consciousness in 15th and 16th century AD. Later on, his artistic activities were followed by different scholars in different period according to the theme of composition of the valuable treatises.

NOTES AND REFERENCES

1. Naren Kalita, Art in Manuscript Painting of Assam, 2001, p.137, Ed., *Glimpses of the Vaisnava Heritage of Assam* by P. Mahanta, Guwahati.
2. T.C. Rastogi, *Assam Vaisnavaism*, 1994, Omsons Publications, p.5.
3. *Ibid.*, p.85.
4. *Ibid.*
5. R.D. Choudhury and Naren Kalita, 2001, *Manuscript Paintings from Kamarupa Anusadhan Samiti*, p.2.
6. Maurice Diamand, *Indian Miniature Painting*, Bombay.
7. Narayan Sharma, *Purani Asamar Chitrakala* (in Assamese), 1979, Assam.
8. Rajata Nanda Dasgupta, *Miniature Painting of India*.
9. *Geeta-Govinda-Basohli School of Indian Painting*, Forewarded by Dr. Rajendra Prasad, Introduction by R.P.N. Sinha.

16

Images of Sixty-Four *Yoginīs* in Orissa : In Appreciation of their Artistic Excellence

H.C. Das

The cult of sixty-four *Yoginīs* emerged in the early medieval period as an important manifestation of the Śākta principle. In this period the Śakti multiplied herself into many emanations with peculiar iconographic features. In fact, the cult of sixty-four *Yoginīs* and nine Kātyāyanīs are together an expression of the extreme form of Tantricism, which from about 8th century AD was amalgamated with Buddhism, Śaktism and Śaivism, thus enlarging the horizon of art, pantheon, ritual and worship patterns.

The Vedic and post-vedic literature often mention the names of some individual *Yoginīs* but not sixty-four together. The sixty-four *Yoginīs* developed as a cult from about 7th century AD when efflorescence of Śaktism, Tantricism and Śaivism in combination, swayed the religious arcana of India[1] through the process of transformation. *Yoginīs* were multiplied into sixty-four manifestations and together came to be known as sixty-four *Yoginīs*.

It may be noted here that the cult had limited distribution, confined to Orissa, Madhya Pradesh and a part of Uttar Pradesh. So far no *Śilpāśāstra* in regard to the hypatheral architecture of the temple and the iconography of *Yoginīs* have yet been discovered. The circular sixty-four *Yoginī* temple discovered so far are found at Hirapur, Ranipur Jharial (the two temples in Orissa), at Bheraghat, Khajuraho and Sahadol in Madhya Pradesh and at Dudahi and Mitauli in Lalitpur district of Uttar Pradesh.[2] The temple at Hirapur was discovered by K.N. Mohapatra, an eminent historian and an archaeologist of Orissa in 1952 and that Ranipur Jharial temple by J.D. Beglar, a foreign archaeologist.

In regard to the origin of the cult of sixty-four *Yoginīs* and nine Kātyāyanīs we have to depend, as usual, upon the *Mahā Purāṇas* and the

Upa Purāṇas which succinctly record the origin, development and iconography of Hindu gods and goddesses. The *Matsya Purāṇas*[3] records the names of numerous terrific goddesses, who were created to kill Andhaka demon capable of creating innumerable of demons of his stature from the drops of his blood oozing out from his wounds and touching the ground. Many such goddesses are found in the lists of sixty-four *Yoginīs*. According to the *Kālikā Purāṇa*, sixty-four *Yoginīs* and nine Kātāyānīs were created by Durgā and gods to assist her in combat against Mahiṣāsura and his allies.

However, the cult of sixty-four *Yoginīs* and the occult and secret pratices and philosophy were systematized by Matsyendranath (8th-9th century AD) in his famous *Kaulajñānanirnaya*.[4] The secret cult of Matsyendra was practised in the company of women in a circle known as *Yoginī Kaula*. Matsyendra expounded his secret *Yoginī Kaula* in Kamarupa where every women was a *Yoginī* in the company of whom he discovered his new cult. The ultimate aim of *Kaula* is the state in which the mind and sight merged into the objects to be realized. This philosophical trend is reflected in the sculptural representations of Śiva and *Yoginīs* in the circular temple. The image of Śiva, the central figure in the temple echoes the reconciliation of the impassiveness of *Yoga* with the lyricism of sex. In this temple *Kaula Kapalika* practice was in vogue. However, Matsyendra has propounded a kind of monism where *Kula* is ultimately identified with *Akula*-Śiva and such power through the agency of *Yoginīs*.

According to Matsyendra, the *Yoginīs* are sixty-four in number and are classified as *Sahaja, Kulaja* and *Antyeja*. In another classification, they are *Kshetraja, Pithaja, Yogaja* and *Mantraja* based on different principles. The mother goddesses like Brahmāṇī, Māheśvarī, Vaiṣṇavī, Indrāṇī, Kaumārī, etc., are also classified as *Yoginīs*.[5] The *Yoginī Kaula* of Matsyendra also refers to the worship of mystic circles made up of 4, 8, 12 and 64 and more angles at the centre of which there is omnipresent, immovable and unqualified Śiva. The sixty-four *Yoginīs* thus represent the angles encircling Śiva. The circle thus forms a lotus reminding us of the famous tantric *Śrīchakra*.

The nomenclature of sixty-four *Yoginīs* is very perplexing. Different sources have furnished number of *Yoginīs*, but ultimately the number sixty-four is universally accepted.

I have referred to fourteen lists of sixty-four *Yoginīs* found in the *Kālikā Purāṇa, Skāṇḍapurāṇa, Brihad Nandikeśvara Purāṇa, Chaunsathi Yogīnī Nāmāvalī, Chandi Purāṇa* of Sarala Das, *Durgāpujā* (an unoublished palm-leaf manuscript), *Bata Avakasha* of Balaram Das (Oriya) etc[6]. The Bheraghat *Yoginī* temple contains as many as seventynine inscribed images. The lists of sixty-four *Yoginīs* do not consistently conform to the number sixty-four. Except a few names of the *Mātrikās*, the nomenclature varies from list to list. More confusing is the absence of their iconographical features in any list.

Similarly perplexing problem is the hypaethral *Yoginī* temple, the *Śilpāśāstra* of which has not been discovered. Charles Fabri, having not come across any text in regard to the concept of circular structure indicates:

For the two *yoginī* temples possess no *vimanas* or *sikharas* (spires), no *maṇḍapas* or temple chambers, no *garbhagriha* or sanctums no main cult image, such as a *liṅga* or phallus, or a central status of a divinity; no roof at all; the outline of the *yoginī* shrines is fundamentally different from that of any of the contemporary or earlier, or later Orissan temples; their sculptural ornamentation is totally different from Brahmanic and Buddhist structures (for much of the Mahāvihāra of Ratnagiri belongs to this period too); and, in brief, with their circular shape, not covered by any roof, they resemble no Hindu shrine at all. Nor is the remote similarity to the Buddhist stupas, of any validity or interest as the outline is a tenuous identity, for the Buddhist stupa is an entirely solid, closed hemisphere, and not a circular wall, with an open arena within, not covered by any roof at all, as the two *yoginī* temples are.[7]

I do not accept this view that the architecture of circular *yoginī* temple is basically different from Brahmanical and other Hindu shrines. On the other hand, such structures belong to the Hindu Architecture, as the cult itself is a part of Brahmanical pantheon. He sincerely tried to interpret the circular structure (in the absence of any text) in relation to the concepts of *Maṇḍala, Yantra* and *Chakra* which virtually have no beginning nor end. Any of such concept is represented in the circular *Yoginī* temples where the *Yoginīs* form a type of *maṇḍala* as described in the *Samhitas, Matsyapurāṇa, Varāha Purāṇa, Saradā Tilak Tantra, Jñānārnava Tantra, Devī Purāṇa* etc.

In the *Yoginī mandala* represented in the *yoginī* temple, Śiva plays the pivotal role encircled by the *Yoginīs,* the manifestation of the Śaktis. The circular Śiva *liṅga* fixed in Śakti basically represents Śiva and Śakti in one form.

That the male and the female principles are inseparable and are found together in cosmic evolution is the real form of Śiva and Śakti. This idea is represented by the symbols of the *liṅga* and the *yonī* together. In the *Bhāgavata Purāṇa* (second *skanda)* Mahādeva is described by Brahmā as "the *paramabrahma*, the lord of Śakti and Śiva, who are the womb and seed respectively of the universe, who, like a spider, forms it in his sport, through the agency of Śakti and Śiva (who are one with Himself), preserves and reabsorbs it". The *Liṅgapurāṇa* also states that *Pradhāna* (nature) is called the *liṅga* and *Parameśvara* is called the *lingin* (the sustainer of the *liṅga*) and that the pedestal of the *liṅga* is the visible Maheśvara. A more expressive allusion to the generative power of the *liṅga* and the *yonī*, the emblems of the Saiva cult, is found in the *Viṣṇu Purāṇa*, wherein we are told that Brahmā asked Rudra, born of his anger to divide himself, thereupon Rudra divided himself into two, a male and a female portion.

This conception later on must have been exemplified in the form of *yoginī* temple with Śiva as the central figures and *Yoginīs* as various incarnations of Pārvatī in a *maṇḍala*.

In consideration of the facts and interpretations stated above, I may come to a tentative conclusion that the circular architectural design of the *Yoginī* temples is an iconic representation of Śiva and Śakti and it is a part and parcel of Indian architecture[9].

YOGINĪ TEMPLE AT HIRAPUR

The hypaethral temple at Hirapur, the earliest of all, looks like a *Gouripatta* with a projection of 4' in length, 2' 6" in breadth and 5' in height to its east. From the east there is a passage into the temple. The height of the enclosure from the ground level varies from 8' to 9', the length of the outer circumference 90' and the diameter inside is 25'. The entire structure is made of a type of sandstone available in the neighbouring stone quarries, with the foundation of laterite blocks. The measurement of passage is 8' in length and 2' 6" in breadth. The foundations of almost all the temples of Bhubaneswar are constructed of laterite blocks. The middle portion of the enclosure is embellished with a rectangular open *maṇḍapa* known as *Devīmaṇḍapa* (9' 6" x 8') the upper part of which shows recent reconstruction. From the ground level the *maṇḍapa* is 9' high with four doors to the east, south, west and north respectively. The niches in inner enclosure and the *Devīmaṇḍapa* contain the images of *Yoginīs* in chlorite stone and the outer surface contains nine images of Kātyāyanī.

The four images of Bhairava found in the circular *maṇḍapa* echo the beatitude and equipoise smiling in the company of sixty-four counterpart *Yoginīs*. The *pitha* altogether contains eighty images out of which sixty-three are *Yoginīs* (one is missing), nine Kātyāyanīs, four Bhairavas, two dvārapālas and two male figures. Out of the total sixty-three *Yoginī* images, Mahāmāyā, the presiding deity of the *pitha,* is ten-armed; nineteen are four-armed and fortythree are two-armed indicating the predominance of two-armed figures.

YOGINĪ TEMPLE AT RANIPUR-JHARIAL

This *Yoginī* temple is circular in shape, with the inner diameter of 47 feet and devoid of any projected passage like Hirapur. It contains sixty-four niches inside for the sixty-four *Yoginīs*. In the centre of the circular enclosure is seen a *maṇḍapa* that rests on four pillars enshrining an image of three-headed and eight-armed Śiva in *tāndava* dance pose and the images of Gaṇeśa and Pārvatī. The *maṇḍapa* here like that of Hirapur has been reconstructed recently. The temple had originally its opening to the south side which is now closed up and converted into a niche containing a figure of Chāmuṇḍā. Probably on closure of this door, an entrance was made to the east side.

There are 48 images of *Yoginīs* out of the total 64 in the niches of inner circle. The rest are lost. All the images *in situ* are in dancing postures and are eroded badly due to the type of coarse-grained stone used in their making. Hence, it is difficult to identify them. Three of the total 48 images are four-armed and others four-armed, one three-headed and some of them are animal headed (horse, bear, lion, goat, elephant, boar, cow, serpent, buffalo head, etc.).

ARTISTIC IMAGERY

The two extant *Yoginī* temple belong to different dynasties but bear the same artistic tradition. The Hirapur monument is the work of the Bhaumakaras (AD 736-940) while that of Ranipur-Jharial is assigned to the Somavamsis (10th century AD).

Each of the monuments conforms to the art movement of the period, maintaining its tradition in pursuance of the textual description. The *Yoginī* temples and the enshrined sculptures evidently constitute remarkable assay in plastic creations, throbbing with religious symbolism, and have brilliantly illuminated the medieval Hindu art and architecture. The sculptures of *Yoginī* temples may be taken as masterpieces and of exclusively high quality. The images in their jewellery, draperies, coiffures as well as in their postures and gestures far excel other art forms of the time. Of the existing sixty-four *Yoginī* temples, Hirapur temple is not only the oldest but also artistically the best of all and in a good state of preservation.

> With its smaller size, its compact design, admirable proportions, its hard, close-grained stone sculptures neatly arranged in small niches, and the exquisite variety and beauty of many of the poses, it is not only a fascinating monument, it exersises a strange effect on the spectator. The writer of these lines does not hesitate to own that he felt here an almost mystic power in the intensity of the feeling that created this lovely temple, whereas of the much larger and less beautiful temple at Ranipur Jharial he experienced a sense of diffuseness and repetitiveness, a monotony in the sculpture elements that are totally absent at Hirapur. The temple of the sixty-four *Yoginī* Hirapur is a great work of art, an exquisite monument, born out of emotional inspiration. There is an atmosphere here such as pervades the great cave temples of India, or the fine cathedrals of the west; yet the circular temple of Hirapur is hardly bigger than a large room.[12]

The *Yoginī* temple at Hirapur being the work of the Bhaumakara ruler bears necessarily the characteristics of the period. The Bhaumakaras are considered to be the pioneer dynasty in laying the foundation of a big kingdom with sound administrative system and to open a new chapter in the history of art and architecture in Orissa. The *Yoginī* temple at Hirapur erected towards the end of Bhauma rule depicts in full vigour the matured artistic grandeur. Each of the *Yoginī* figures in posture, ornamentation, facial expression and coiffure appears to be different from the other, but at the same time all put together give a coherent effect of superb artistic plasticity. Each fragment of art found expression in these images deserves special attention. So far as the hairstyles of the images in the temples are concerned, each one shows a variety and fashion different from the other and furnishes an interesting subject for study. Of the various patterns of coiffures, mention may be made of hair combed backwards and secured in a roundish bulb or bun with a knot to either side of the head popularly known as *Keśapāsa* style, hair arrangement in the shape of a spiral at the top of the head, coiffure with a top knot and a loose knot on the occiput, hair-dressed in fanshape tiers, hair buns divided into three parts with chains and hair tied in the shape of flames, knotted hair in three or five tiers emitting the shape of halo etc. Ornamentation of the images in the head, ear, neck, arm, wrist, waist and leg are superbly carved out indicating the artistic imagery of the craftmen. However, from bird's eye view it may be concluded that the sixty-four *Yoginī* temple of Hirapur represents a very interesting phase of artistic flourescence of the epoch.

The distinguishing characteristics of Kalingan art are expressed through the cult images and the decorative motifs consisting of erotic figures, decorative female figures of bewildering varieties and other innumerable decorative motifs such as human figures either in individual form or in panels depicting mythological and social scenes, varieties of animals with the exuberance of elephants and floral, architectural and geometrical designs, symmetry and proportions in designing the sculptures with roundness of face, pointed nose, bulging of breasts, sharp facial profiles, swollen cheeks, half-buried eyes, smiling face, profuse ornamentation from leg to head, exquisite workmanship in every inch of the body, leaving no breathing space, compactness and harmony in assimilation of cult images with decorative motifs, proportions in setting component parts in a stone structure, their manifestations of celestial divinities around the presiding cult images in association with human and secular figures, animals and fantastic designs each informative in character symbolising the wholeness in a manner where no other better arrangement can be conceived. These are the peculiarities which can more or less be attributed to Kalingan sculptural art all through the ages. Architecturally the *Yoginī* temples in Orissa are simple but sculpturally they are rich. Most probably the sculptures exhibit their craftmanship, and ingenuity in depiction of the *Yoginī* images leaving the temple barren.[13]

NOTES AND REFERENCES

1. H.C. Das, *Tantricism : A Study of the Yoginī Cult*, 1981, New Delhi, p.3.
2. R.K. Sharma, *The Temples of Chaunsatha Yoginī at Bheraghat*, 1978, Delhi, p.32.
3. *Matsyapurāṇa*, Gurumandal Press, Bombay, ch. 179, pp.154-57.
4. Matsyendranath, Kaulajnanairnaya quoted by V.W. Karambelkar in Indian Historical Quarterly, Vol. XXXI, No. 4, pp.362-74.
5. *Ibid.*, pp.365-66.
6. H.C. Das, *Iconography of Sakta Divinities*, Vol. II, 1997, Delhi, pp.421-34.
7. Charles Fabri, *History of the Art of Orissa*, 1974, Calcutta, p.76.
8. H.C. Das, *op.cit.*, pp.18-19.
9. *Ibid.*
10. K.N. Mahapatra, *Orissa Historical Research Journal*, Vol. II, No. 2, p.24.
11. J.D. Beglar *A.S.I. Report*, Vol. IX, p.60.
12. Charles Fabri, *op.cit.*, p.86.
13. H.C. Das, *op.cit.*, p.58-59.

17

In Appreciation of Indian Art Ideals and Images of Narakāsur Hoard, Kahilipara

Indrani Choudhury

Sculptural art of India occupies the foremost place in the history of art. The artist in India had attained a high degree of excellence at a very early period. The specimens produced were truely marvels of humanity and skill. People find in them intensity of feeling, a revelation of the powers of the unseen. This is a recognized feature of art everywhere the world.

The essential quality of Indian art is its pre-occupation with the spiritual. The approach is not just intellectual but also spiritual.

According to N.P. Joshi, Indian history and culture is a vast ocean, where cultural streams of different land not only met, poured their contents but also carried back a little, or themselves became part and parcel of fathomless collection of water.[1]

The nature of Indian culture is dymamic and has a broad outlook. Religion was the pivot of architecture and sculpture in ancient India. The sculptural art of India received inspiration from the various religious creeds of the land, even those sculptures which were non-religious or secular in appearance found a place on the outer wall of the temples and were accepted as serving the needs of life, religious in aim and inspiration.[2]

The sculptural art in Assam is the domain of Indian art style. It is quite clear that Assam is an integral part of India. The artist of Assam followed the same style and technique as it is referred in the *Śilpaśāstra*. The sculptural activities in Assam began with the expansion of the Gupta empire. The Umachal rock inscription and Nagajari Khanikargaon fragmentary stone inscription of early 5th century AD bear out that Brahmanical religion penetrated into Kamarupa[3] (early Assam).

Most of the idols and images of Narakāsur hoard are of pre-Ahom period. The Narakāsur *pahār* (hill) is situated at a distance of about five miles south of Guwahati. On the southern slope of the hill there is a village called

Kahilipara. The southern slope of the hill is full of huge boulders, scattered throughout. In a hole, caused by the combination of three granite boulders, some of the archeological objects were found in 1964. Soon after P.C. Choudhury first director of Assam State Museum visited that place and found 37 objects of bronze. But in 1967 some articles were missing from that spot. But later R.D. Choudhury former director of the Assam State Museum brought some of the articles to the museum.

These finds consist of a *mukha liṅga,* two *ghaṇṭa* (bells), a snake conch shell, several miniature shells and twenty-two images of various deities. Except a small image of Manasā, which is carved out of a piece of basalt, all the four images are casted in round plates.

The largest image of this group is the icon of Indra (pl. 17.1). It measures 1.1' x 7". Here the deity is seen riding on his *vāhana,* Airavat, facing front. He sits astride on *vāhana.* The deity has two hands, the right hand being held in *varadahasta mudrā,* resting on the right thigh, while the left in the *abhaya mudrā,* resting on the left thigh. He is decked with a *karaṇḍa mukuṭa, kuṇḍalas, hāras, upavita, keyuras, valayas* and *nupuras*. His *paridhāna* consist of a *Kati mekhalā* and *Kati vastra.* He is flanked by two female *chowri* bearers. Both the attendants stand each on a *padma,* so also Airavata. The *aṅkuśa* which was to be placed in one of the hands of the deity is placed on the head of the *vāhana.* Below the *pitha,* male devotee is seen in *añjalī hasta* pose. Behind the deity a round splendid *prabhā* is seen which is arranged on an *ādhara* (frame). Above the *prabhā chatra* is seen.

According to the *Amsumadbhedagama*[4] the image of Indra should be two handed, seated on Airavata and attended by two *chāmara* bearers and his consort. In our image Indrāṇī is not present. Other details of the icon are keeping with the text.

This splendid image is a very rare work of art. Though the *ādhara* and the *prabhā* with the *chhatra* of this image are arranged in the style of sculptures of the Palas, yet to our knowledge, this type of Indra image is not found in Bengal nor in Bihar. On the basis of the style, this splendid work of art should be placed in the 9th century AD if not later.

The second important image of this group is a set of four Viṣṇu images. The description of these four images are given in the chart 1.

Two surya images were also discovered along with these image whose detailed description is provided in the chart 2.

The group includes only one Gaṇeśa image. Here the deity is seated in *mahārājalilā* pose, i.e. putting the right leg vertically and left leg horizontally on *āsana.* The deity has four hands. He holds in the right front hand an unidentified *āyudha* in the right back hand a *dhaturā puspa,* in the left front hand an unidentified *āyudha* and in the left back hand a *triśula.*

CHART 1

Image	*Poses*	*Object in the hands of Viṣṇu Top right (front)*	*Bottom Right*	*Top Left*	*Bottom Left*	*Vehicle*	*Remarks*
1. Viṣṇu	*Sampāda Sthānaka*	*Padma*	*Chakra*	*Śaṅkha*	*Gadā*	Not depicted	The deity is decorated with a *kiritamukuṭa*.
2. Viṣṇu	*Sampāda Sthānaka*	*Padma*	*Chakra*	*Śaṅkha*	*Gadā*	Below the *pitha* the *vāhana* of the deity is depicted	The front hands stretch forward and hold the *āyudha,* while the back hand is down and touch the *āyudha* placed on the *pitha* above the *ādhara,* a round *prabhā* is arranged. Below the *pitha* the *vāhana* of the deity is depicted.
3. Viṣṇu	*Sampāda Sthānaka*	*Padma*	*Chakra*	*Śaṅkha*	*Gadā*	*Vāhana* is not depicted. Both the front hands stretch forward and the back hands touch the *ayudhas.*	
4. Viṣṇu	*Sampāda Sthānaka*	*Padma*	*Chakra*	*Śaṅkha*	*Gadā*	The *pitha* of the deity, the *Ādhāra* and the *āyudhas* of two hands are broken and gone.The *prabhā* is arranged behind the head of the deity.	

CHART 2

Name of the Image	*Measure*	*Posture*	*Hand poses*	*Vahanas*	*Attends*	*Remarks*
Surya	8″ x 5″	*Sampāda Sthānaka attitude*	God holds two *Padma* in both hands	His conventional *ratha* is drawn by seven horses.	To the Right hand of the deity is *Piṅgala* and on the left *Daṇḍa* stands and attends upon the God.	Aruna sits in the middle horse just in front of the deity. Wheel of the *ratha* is not depicted there. There is a *prabhā* behind the head of the deity. The *ādhāra* is not visible.
Surya	——	*Sampāda Sthānaka* attitude	The *padma* of the right hand is broken	Not depicted	The figure of *Daṅda, Piṅgla* and Aruna are not depicted. The *Kativastra* worn by the deity is peculier. Reaching the angles of the deity it spreads outwards over the knees horizontally. Around the thing *khadga-thanadha* is seen. The boots worn by deity are quite clear. Behind the god a round *prabhā* is arranged beautifully.	

The *vāhana* of the deity is exhibited below.

The image of Manasā is the only stone image in the group. It is chiselled in a piece of basalt measuring (3.1/2" x 3"). The deity here is made to sit in *latitāsana* pose. She has two hands, the right hand being held in *varada* pose resting on the knee, while the left holds a *sarpa.* She wears the usual *alankaras* and *vastra.* To the right of the deity a beared male figure is seen seated in *utakatika* pose. This figure may be identified Jaratkaru. To the left is seen a female figure in the same posture. Behind the head of this figure there is three-hooded *sarpa.* This figure may represent a Nagini. Behind the head of the deity there is a canopy of seven-hooded *Sarpa.* This image, stylistically, should be placed in 11th century AD.

There are some images of some deities whose actual identities are not known. Here I discuss one very beautiful image of a female deity. Here the deity is seated cross legged in *Yogāsana* posture. She has eight hands, two front hands being held in *añjalī.* The three right back here as following- (1) raising upwards holding an *akṣamāla* (2) in the *bhumisparsa mudrā* (3) in the Yoga posture resting on the lap. The three left back hands, again are (1) raised upwards holding probably a *padma* on which there is another object *damaru.* (2) resting on the left knee holding an unknown *āyudha* and (3) in the Yoga posture resting on the lap. She is decorated with a *jatāmukuṭa, kuṇḍalas, hāra,* etc. She wears a *kati vastra* looking like a *sārī.* Behind the deity, a *prabhā* and above it *chattra* designs are shown. The *vāhana* of the deity is not shown.

Again another four images casted on four bronze plates have also been discovered from that place. One of these plates contain a high relief of a bust of human figure which is shown to have sprung up from the neck of an upturned buffalo head with horns (pl. 17.2). The head of this bust wears a *mukuṭa* which looks like a cap. Two *kuṇḍalas* are also seen clearly on the ears of it. From its association with a buffalo head, it may be suggested that it is probably the buffalo demon, i.e Mahiṣāsura.

The next plate contains in the same way a figure of a female deity (pl. 17.3). Here the deity stands in *sampāda sthānka* attitude on the back of a buffalo. The deity has four hands. She holds the reins of the *vāhana,* on which she stands with the right front hand, and a *chakra* with the right back hand. With her front left hand she holds a *gadā* while with left backhand she holds a *triśula.* The *mukuṭa* worn by the deity is peculiar. She is decked with all the usual *alankāras* worn by a female deity. The *kati vastra* or *sārī* worn by the deity has some design. A line of letters, which are now obliterated to the left of the deity on the plates, is seen. Letters of this line of writing are now beyond recognition. The identity of this peculiar image is not known.

All these two images are peculiar and such figures are extremely rare. These are very crude in execution and it seems that the sculptors, who executed these images, were ignorant of textual injunction. Such casted figures of deities on plates are not found in Bengal or Bihar. Stylistically, they should belong to a later period. The holes on the borders of these plates indicate that they might have been suspended in some temple walls.

A bell inscription has also been discovered from that place. The bell contains two lines. It is recorded that "Srī Kumāra" who belong to the king of devas and asuras was given this bell for the use of the worship of the deities. The script of the inscription seems to be of eastern variety descending from Kutila type of Brāhmi. According to R.D. Choudhury these letters are similar to those of Hayungthul copperplate inscription of Harjjaravarman (9th century AD).[5]

Images of various other deities were also found like Manasā, Gaṇeśa, Indra, Tārā, a *mukha liṅga* and some other unidentified images. But it is doubtful whether all these images were installed in their temples or not.

It may be mentioned that in the Vedic period Indra was a very important deity. But in the later period his position was lowered and was treated as a *dikapāla* only. Therefore, though the present image of Indra was worshipped as the chief deity in some temple, yet it seems not likely that the other deities centred round him. Because, the importance of Indra has already been reduced. Though Hiuen-tsang mentioned about the existence of Deva temples in Assam, yet we cannot say that all the temples housed Indra as the presiding deity.

All the images, excluding the figures of four plates and the crude female figure, bear the characteristic feature of the eastern school of sculpture. They are similar to the metallic sculpture of Bengal and Bihar. But we cannot say that they were imported into Assam from those states. Because, our images have some regional variations in style and so, the minute details of the images do not resemble those of Bengal and Bihar sculptures.

But it is not known why these were kept hidden under the boulders. Assam in the Ahom period fell victim to many external invasions, particularly from the Muhammedans from the west, by whom most of the Hindu temples were largely destroyed. The legend of the renegade Kalapahar and his atrocities are still prevalent in Assam. Therefore, it is likely that at the time of Muhammedans invasion and the subsequent atrocities to the populace and their faith, the collector kept these images and other associated objects in the hidden place to save them from the iconoclasts, with the hope of recovering them after the panic was over. These splendid sculptures show the artistic handicraft and beauty with the philosophy of different sects in

Assam. From the stylistic point of view these images may be placed in 9th to 10th century AD.

Whatever may be the cause of hiding, such metallic sculptures along with other objects of worship are rarely found.

NOTES AND REFERENCES

1. N.P. Joshi, *Catalogue of Brahmanical Sculpture, State Museum,* Lucknow, 1972, pp.2, 3.
2. R.C. Majumdar (ed.), *The Struggle for Empire,* (3rd ed.), 1979, p.64.
3. M.M. Sarma (ed.), *Inscription of Ancient Assam,* pp.1303-05.
4. Gopinath Rao, *Elements of Hindu Iconography,* Vol. II, pt. II, p.510.
5. *Reading in the History of Assam,* 1984, A note on the Archaeological finds at Narakasura hill, pp.214-15, P.C. Choudhury, Archaeological finds in Narakāsur hill, *Journal of Assam Research Society,* Vol. XVI, 1962.

18

A Rare Sculptural Blend of *Bhāgavata* and Folk Elements in the Amritesvara Temple at Amritapura, Karnataka

D.S. Somashekhar & Sarvamangala G.

One can see many beautiful Hoysala temples in the district of Chikkamagalur—Karnataka. The Amṛiteśvara temple at Amritapura which is 9 km away from Tarikere, the *taluq* headquarters is one such magnificient Hoysala temple. As per the inscriptional evidence, this Śiva temple has been built in AD 1196 by Ballala II, (the grandson of Viṣṇuvardhana) the famous Hoysala ruler, in honour of Amrita Dandanayaka, the commander of the latter who laid down his life in a war against the enemies. This information is derived from a beautiful and high stone inscription (written in Kannada) standing in the temple complex and written by Janna, the famous Jaina poet who was given the title *'Kavi chakravartī'*.

The temple is facing east and on the right side of the temple is found a small shrine known as *Śāradā mandir* and on the left a dilapidated building called *Utsava mandir* is located. The whole temple is enclosed by a *prakara* wall and entrance is provided on three sides, i.e. east, north, and south which are also called locally as Viṣṇudvāra, Brahmadvāra and Maheśadvāra. It is a Śiva *Pañchāyatana* Temple. Śiva is the presiding god along with other deities like the Sun, *Sapta mātrikā* panel, Gaṇapati, Nārāyaṇa, and Kārtikeya.

On plan: The temple consists of a *garbhagriha,* an *antarāla* and a *navaranga.* But soon after the construction of the temple they added one more half-closed pillared hall which was provided with three entrances.

Elevation: The temple is built directly from the ground level and is devoid of any platform or *Jagati.*

Adhisthāna: The *adhisthāna* consists of a series of mouldings and forms a kind of projection and recesses right from the ground level and which is carried upto the superstructure.

Bhittī: The *bhittī* or the wall portion of the temple is decorated with a series of minature shrines and in between these miniature shrines are carved the standing stylistic lions on their two feet and it is further decorated with scroll designs.

Chajjā: The hanging *chajjā* supports a highly decorated superstructure. The superstructure belongs to the Vesara style and once again known for its beautiful decoration. It was provided by a *grivā* and a circular *śikhara,* which is further, surmounted by a *kalaśa* and *stupi.*

Very interestingly on the eastern side of the superstructure is seen the *sukhnasi* projection where there is a symbol of *Sala* striking the tiger which is said to denote the Hoysala *Lāñchana.* Just behind it is also seen the beautiful Natarāja image.

THE ENTRANCE

The half closed pillared *maṇḍapa* can be entered from the entrance and inside the hall, there are altogether 52 lathe turned pillars. The pillars altogether form into 42 bays. These bays support a circular ceiling done in the form of *Kadalikarana* variety. The ceiling is very richly decorated with beautiful carvings. On all the sides of half closed pillared hall there are *sukhāsana* seating arrangements.

NAVARANGA

The *Navaranga* of the temple once again consists of four beautiful pillars in the centre and with a large number of pilasters. The central part of the four pillars is provided with a raised *Nritya Maṇḍapa* platform. The ceiling of the *maṇḍapa* is once again beautifully decorated in a domed variety with *Aṣṭa Dikpāla* panels on the respective directions.

Around the *navaranga,* we come across a few independent sculptures such as Gaṇapati, Shanmukha, Kālabhairava and Saraswatī. Once again they are also done in a typical Hoysala form.

THE GARBHAGRIHA

The *garbhagriha* is square in plan and consists of a *Śiva Liṅga.* As mentioned in the inscription, the *Liṅga* was brought from Gandaki river in Nepal.

THE RAILING

In the front portion of the pillared hall above the basement is built a railing. These are divided into compartments by pilasters and the space between the pilasters is carved with reliefs.

The upper and the lower portion of the railing are ornamented with scroll and floral motifs. The central portion on the railing, which is compartmentalized, is carved with incidents from the epics and other mythologies. The Amriteśvara temple contains the best of the railing sculptures of the Hoysala period. They depict the important incidents from the *Rāmāyana, Mahābhārata* and the *Bhāgavata* besides the graceful female figures and some *mithuna* figures or erotic sculptures.

The *Rāmāyana* panels 71 in number include important incidents from *Rāmāyana* such as *Putrakameshthi Yajña,* Rāma breaking Śiva *dhanuṣa,* Sītā in *Aśokavana* and so on. There are 34 *Mahābhārata* panels which include incidents like Bhima slaying Bakāśura, Bhima shaking a huge tree and dropping the Kaurava brothers, and so on. The depiction of *Bhāgavata* in 24 panels is quite interesting and attractive.

THE SCULPTURES OF *BHĀGAVATA*

It seems the sculptors of the day have carved the figures of *Bhāgavata* story basically according to an epitomising Sanskrit *Śloka* relating to *Bhāgavata*:

> Adav Devaki Devi Garbhajananam, Gopi grihe vardhanam, Maya Putini Jivitapaharanam, Govardhanodharanam, Kamsachedana Kauravadi hananam, Kuntisuta Palanam A tad Bhagavata Purana Khatitam Sri Krishna leelamritam.

As mentioned earlier there are totally 24 figures in the panel relating to the story of *Bhāgavata* like the Court of Kaṁsa, Vāsudeva-Devakī put in the prison, Vāsudeva prostrating before the donkey, preparations of shifting baby Kṛṣṇa from Mathura to Gokula, crossing the river Yamunā, entry into Gokula, handing over the child to Yaśodā, child Kṛṣṇa slaying the demon Shakatāśura, killing Putanā who tried to suckle poison, Yaśodā restricting Kṛṣṇa from going out, slaying the demon Bakāśura, Gandharva *Shāpa vimochana* (Nalakubara and Manigriva), Kṛṣṇa showing the Universe in his mouth to his mother, stealing milk and butter, humbling the Kālia, the troubling serpent, lifting the Govardhana mountain etc. But the last figure of these carvings is the return of Kṛṣṇa from Gokula to Mathura / *(Gokula Nirgamana)* to slay Kaṁsa. There are another four uncarved round stones placed in the same row in the end giving us an impression that the *Bhāgavata* story is incomplete. Anyway, next, the row begins with the story of *Māhābhārata*.

So far as the figures of the *Bhāgavata* story are concerned, the most noteworthy figure is that of Vāsudeva, the father of Lord Kṛṣṇa prostrating before a donkey soon after the birth of Kṛṣṇa as the 8th child *(Aṣṭama Garbha)*.

The sculptors of the day were versed with both *Bhāgavata* (*Sista)* and Folklore (*Janapada).* Here the story of *Bhāgavata* has been interestingly blended with folklore as far as the donkey episode is concerned. The folk story regarding the birth of Lord Kṛṣṇa is thus said.

"BOW BEFORE AN ASS IN EXPEDIENCY"—THE KANNADA PROVERB

Kaṁsa the ruler of Mathura put his sister and brother-in-law (Devakī and Vāsudeva) in the prison as Kaṁsa was told by the *Ashariravani* that he would be killed by the 8th issue of his sister Devakī. Therefore, Kaṁsa placed a donkey near the prison ordering the same to bray after the birth of each child born to Devakī-Vāsudeva, so that he would come to know of the birth of the child and he would kill the child mercilessly and immediately. Thus, Devakī and Vāsudeva lost seven of their children and their pains and grief were beyond description. In the eight pregnancy of Devakī, Lord Kṛṣṇa was born with all the beauty and auspicious symbols as an incarnation. But, now, as per the assigned duty, the donkey was about to bray to signal the birth of a baby. This time, Vāsudeva out of total helpessness prostrated before the donkey and humbly requested the donkey not to bray so that Kaṁsa would not get any clue of the birth of the child and the same could be saved with difficulty from the deadly hands of Kaṁsa. Even an animal like donkey was moved by the prayer of Vāsudeva and it did not bray. It was because of this help of the donkey done to Vāsudeva, the latter was able to save child Kṛṣṇa and shift him to Gokula.

THE DONKEY—VĀSUDEVA SCULPTURAL PANEL

This is the third figure in the panels of *Bhāgavata* story. A midwife is seen with an oil container and there are two helping women standing near Devakī. Two armed soldiers (servants of Kaṁsa) are also seen. The newly born baby (Kṛṣṇa) is sleeping on the cot and Devakī is sitting near the child. Below the cot are placed a drinking water jug and a box. Near the cot is seen a donkey in a braying mood and Vāsudeva is prostrating before the donkey helplessly.

The folk story told in the context of the birth of the Lord Kṛṣṇa indirectly reveals certain interesting aspects relating to life and the Kannada culture.

Even today there is a proverb in Kannada "*Karyavasi Katte Kalu Kattu*" (Bow before an ass in expediency) which means 'mind not to prostrate even before a worthless as a matter of expediency'. The Amriteśvara Temple is 800 years old and the said proverb should have been in use in the region even before the construction of the temple and the same has been adopted by the genius sculptors of the day while depicting the story of *Bhāgavata*. In the original *Bhāgavata* there is no reference to Vāsudeva prostrating before the donkey requesting the same not to bray and help to save the life of Kṛṣṇa. A proverb is said to be 'The wisdom of many and the wit of one'. Vāsudeva by forgetting his position, status, etc., and prostrating before the donkey to persuade the animal not to bray soon after the birth of Lord Kṛṣṇa, reveals that even the strong and mighty at times will have to bend helplessly before the lesser ones or unimportant ones to get the work done. This story elevates even the position of a helping donkey which is generally an animal of neglect. As the donkey is associated with the birth of Lord Kṛṣṇa, it becomes venerable with the attribute of gratefulness. If some one would like to say, in this context that the donkey was unfaithful to Kaṁsa in the end, then the clarification and justification are even the heart of a 'useless' animal like donkey could melt at the helplessly begging attitude of Vāsudeva, but, not the heart of Kaṁsa who had killed seven children. In other words the donkey appears to be more merciful than Kaṁsa, the sovereign.

If we could assume that the donkey represents the watch and ward of Kaṁsa put in charge of the prison, then they are common people who might have been moved by the prayer of Vāsudeva to save the child. The inference is that every person in the society is important whether one is big or small, high or low, mighty or weak. When we hear of the story of Vāsudeva prostrating before the donkey in the context of Lord Kṛṣṇa's birth, it humbles people's ego to have courtesy and humility specially while dealing with others who are termed as "lesser people" by the society. In other words surrendering one's ego before others for a useful cause minus vested interest stands before us as a cultural value.

Anyway, these days some people in our society do not mind prostrating before any thing and any body (let alone donkey) for the sake of power, position and wealth, only to become the laughing stock, whereas the stature of Vāsudeva prostrating before the donkey to save the life of the saviour and the promoter of good appears undiminishingly unique. The sculptors of the day seem to have tried through art to transcend the barriers of classes and heartlessness to build the bridge of humanity and compassion.

It is worth visiting the temple at least once for its artistic grandeur and subtlety having been surrounded by scenic beauty all around. Sir Mirza Ismail, the then Dewan of the Old Mysore state, paid a visit to the temple in the year 1936, and is said to have ordered supporting pillars for the roof to be fixed outside the temple all around for it's preservation. Even today visitors can see fifteen such solid supporting pillars.

NOTES AND REFERENCES

1. *Epigraphia Carnatica*, Vol. VI, Inscriptions in the Kadur District, B. Lewis Rice, Mysore Govt., Central Press, 1901, Bangalore.
2. *Vachana Bhagavata* (Kannada), K. Venkataramappa, Mysore, Printed by Sadgure printers, Ramanuja Road, Mysore.
3. Personal Survey of the Temple by the Authors, Sept. 2002.
4. Collection of Information about the folk tradition.

19

Kimastimālām Kim Kousthambhaṁvā !?

(A Study on the Harihara Images in the Temples of the Kaḷinga-Āndhra Region)

Kolluru Suryanarayana

Kimasthimālām kim kousthambhaṁvā
Parishkṛiyāyām Bahumanyasetvaṁ
Kim Kālakuṭah Kimuvā Yaśodātstanyam
Tava svādu vada probhome[1]

"O! Lord! Which of the two-garland of skulls or Kousthabham to you prefer for adornment? Which of the two-Kālakuṭam or breast milk of Yaśoda, do you prefer for nourishment?-Kindly let me know".

Thus God Hariharanātha was addressed by poet Tikkana, the greatest of Telugu poets that belongs to 13th century AD.

The composite image of Harihara is conceived to transcend the sectarian outlook of the Vaiṣṇavites and Śaivites, and this seems to have come into vogue about very early centuries of the Christian era. The genesis of the conception of god Harihara is to be found in *Śatarudrīya* and *Taittriya Āranyaka,*[2] and the essential oneness of the two deities Hari and Hara was referred to in the *Mahābhārata, Harivaṁśa* and some other Purāṇas.[3] "*Śivāya Viṣṇurupāya, Śivarupāya Viṣṇave, Śivasya Hṛidayam Viṣṇu, Viṣṇuscha hṛidayam Śivah*"-is the idea found in the age old prayer *Sandhyāvandanam.*

Harihara is worshipped in the form of an icon which combined the characteristics of both the gods Hari and Hara. As in the case of *Ardhanārīśvara,* the Harihara form is a syncretic icon; and two vertical halves are combined, the right half is Śiva and the left is Viṣṇu.[4] Different forms of Harihara, i.e. sitting, reclining and aniconic forms are reported; but usually it is a standing icon in *samabhanga* pose. A number of *Āgama* texts described the Harihara form,[5] and in them the icon goes by different names such as Harihara,

Śaṅkaranārāyaṇa, Hari Rudra, Kṛṣṇa Śaṅkara, Rudra Keśava, Īsā Acyuta and Śivanārāyaṇa. All the names are synonymous and in the forms there are rare minor peculiarities; and if the Harihara form has a moustache, it is known as Śaṅkara Nārāyaṇa.[6] According to T.A. Gopinath Rao, in the figure of Harihara, the description of the right half of the Śiva portion is exactly identical with the description given under *Ardhanārīśvara.*[7]

The Harihara cult gained great prominence and wielded tremendous influence all over the country for a considerable time and it has left some indelible marks.[8] Even the Vaiṣṇavite shrine of Lord Venkaṭeśvara at Tirumalai, and the famous Śaivite Liṅgarāja temple at Bhubaneswar are not beyond the influence of the Harihara cult. About the god Veṅkateśvara, J.S. Rukmini states that one of the early *Śrivaiṣṇavas* described the deity as Harihara due to the duplicate nature of the deity and the image is known as Harihara to this day. The right half of the deity is that of Hara and the left half is that of Hari. On the right forearm is to be seen the *bhujaṅgavalaya* which is the characteristic of Śiva.[9] Likewise, in the case of Liṅgarāja temple, K.C. Panigrahi states

> it is now an accepted fact with the priests here that the Liṅgarāja is a combination of both Śiva and Viṣṇu. In other words, he is Harihara and not Hara alone. A natural line that exists in that *Śvayaṁbhuliṅgam'* (Liṅgarāja) is pointed out by them as the line demarcating the Śiva and Viṣṇu portions of the same deity which is invoked as Harihara.[10]

The cult of Harihara developed in the medieval centuries and we have definite literary and epigraphical evidences to show that Harihara temples existed in Āndhra. Tikkana, the great Telugu poet, and the greatest exponent of the Harihara cult stated that he translated *Mahābhārata* into Telugu by sitting in the Hariharanātha temple (which should have existed at that time in Nellore, an ancient city in Andhra). He dedicated his *Āndhra Mahābhāratam* to Hariharanātha and initiated the work with a stanza in praise of the Lord.[11] A nuṃber of Telugu poets of the medieval centuries like Nāchana Somana, Chadalavāḍa Errāpraggaḍa, Koravi Goparāju and Baichirāju Venktanātha also tried to popularise the syncretic spiritualism of the Harihara cult. An epigraph in the Drākshārāma temple (East Godavari district) refers to a separate temple of Harihara.[12]

Kalinga-Andhra region which comprises the areas of the present northern coastal Andhra, preṣerves a number of images of Harihara which testifies to the adornment of the people towards this composite form in a spirit of real tolerance. Judging from the number of images that have been found in the temples of Kalinga-Andhra region, it can be said that in that region that form was a favourite one. Harihara form is, though a syncretic icon, not found usually in the Viṣṇu temples because Vaiṣṇavites consider it as a *'Śivatatvamurti'*. But in the Kalinga-Andhra region, there was a noteworthy tendency towards eclecticism and in the famous Vaiṣṇavite temples of the area like that of Varāha, Lakṣmī, Narasiṁhanātha at Siṁhāchalam and Kurmanātha at Śrikurmam, there are figures of Harihara. This may be stated as a conspicuous feature that testifies to the catholicity of the people of the region.

Though, here and there are exceptions, majority of the icons referred to by scholars in the north Indian context are from various museums; and some scholars doubted that the known images of Harihara do not seem to have been worshipped.[13] But in the context of Kalinga-Āndhra region, all the Harihara icons are from the temples under regular worship. There are all together nine icons of Harihara in the temples of this region, one in the Kurmanātha temple at Śrīkurmam, one in the Varāha Lakṣmī Narasiṁhanātha temple at Siṁhāchalam, two in the Madhukeśvara temple (Pl. 19.1) at Mukhaliṅgam, one in the Someśvara temple (Pl. 19.2) at the same place one in the Nīlakaṇṭheśvara temple at Nārāyaṇapuram, one in the Mallikārjuna temple at the same place, one in the Śiva temple at Jayati, and in the Śiva temple at Śāripalli. As in these icons, the right half corresponds to Śiva and the left half corresponds to Viṣṇu. All the figures except that in the Siṁhāchalam temple, consists of a usual four arms; and the image in the Siṁhāchalam temple consists of only two hands.

In the Kurmanātha temple at Śri'kurmam, the north wall of the temple contains a beautiful figure of Harihara. He is depicted in *samapādasthānaka* pose. Upper right hand carries a *triśula* and lower hand is in the *varada mudrā* whereas the upper left hand holds *gadā* and lower hand has conch. The half third eye and the membrum verile are conspicuously seen. The vehicles, Naṅdī and the Garuḍa are seen in the right and left corners respectively.

On the eastern wall of the *tiruchuṭṭumāla* of the Varāha Lakṣmī Narasiṁhanātha temple at Siṁhāchalam, interestingly there stands on a pedestal a rare icon of two armed Harihara *murti* in the form of Śaṅkara Nārāyaṇa (as he has moustache).[14] The weapons held in these two hands are by no means clearly discernible. His left hand grasps an object which resembles a *damaru* (?) and the right hand carries which resembles a club (*gadā*). Since it is a Vaiṣṇavite shrine due importance is given to Viṣṇu and hence the *gadā* is placed in his right hand. Usually the right hand carries a trident or a snake.

On the north wall of the *Jagamohana* in the Madhukeśvara temple at Mukhaliṅgam, there is an image of Harihara standing in *tribhaṅga* pose.[15] The upper right hand holds a Snake while the lower one shows *varada* with a lotus carved on its upturned palm. The upper left hand carries a club (*gadā)* while the lower one is shown in *kaṭihasta* carrying a conch. On the right half a third eye is carved on the forehead and the membrum verile is shown erect. The right half of the crown worn by the god shows *jaṭāmukuṭa* while the left half has *kiriṭamukuṭa. Jaṭā* is shown falling on the right while the falling locks on the left are coiled. He wears a pearl-stringed *yajñopavīta* and other usual ornaments. Below the pedestal there are carved figures of the bull and the lion. On either side of the bottom are carved the standing figures of the *āyudhapuruṣas.* This presence of *āyudhapuruṣas* shows a stage of elaboration.

In the same temple on the north wall, there is another image of Harihara standing in the same *tribhaṅga* pose.[16] He is also four-armed and his hands carry a rosary and a vase (?) and right a wheel and a conch on the left. The lower left, holding the conch, rests on the right shoulder of a female standing to the left of the god at the bottom. A snake with raised hood emerges from behind the right hand above the right shoulder. The right half wears a *jaṭāmukuṭa* with a crescent moon on it. The third eye is carved on the right side of the forehead. The *urdhva liṅga* is also seen on the right side. The right half of the lower part of the body is scarcely covered except for a garment up to the thighs while the left half is covered with a designed garment up to well below the knee with its folds hanging along the inner side of the left. He wears a beaded necklace, jewelled armlets and wristlets, pearl-stringed *yajñopavīta* and a *kaṭisutra.* At the bottom behind the right leg is carved the bull with its head turned to face front. Garuḍa, the mount of Viṣṇu is conspicuous by its absence. However in its place a female figure is carved in *tribhaṅga* pose. The lower left hand of the figure rests on her shoulder.

On the eastern wall of the sanctum of the Someśvara temple at Mukhaliṅgam, a small niche contains an image of Harihara standing in *dvibhaṅga* pose.[17] The upper right hand carries a trident while the lower one rests on the top of an inverted club. Similar to that of the image in the Madhukeśvara temple this also wears a *jatāmukuṭa* with a crescent moon on the right half and jewelled crown on the left and other usual ornaments including pearl-stringed *yajñopavita.* There is the skin garment on the right side and an ordinary garment on the left closely cover the lower part. On the right the bull stands at the bottom with its head uplifted towards the Lord. Garuḍa, the Viṣṇu's mount stands at the bottom with his head slightly raised to look at the God. Here Garuḍa is represented in human form but has wings on his shoulders. On the top left corner a beautiful lotus has been carved.

The right niche on the west wall of the Nīlakaṅṭheśvara temple at Nārāyaṇapuram contains an image of Harihara . The god is shown standing in *samabhaṅga.* The upper right hand carries a trident while the lower one is broken. The left hands hold a rosary and a *śaṅkha.* The garments and other decoration on both sides resembles the other images of Harihara. Naṅdī and Garuḍa the mounts are carved at the bottom on both sides and Garuḍa is represented in anthropomorphic form.

The right niche on the west wall of the *garbhagriha* of the Mallikārjuna temple at the same place contains another image of Harihara. The upper right hand of the God carries a trident while the lower right is gently placed on the Naṅdī. The upper left hand holds a *śaṅkha* and lower left hand touches the Garuḍa.

The left side niche of the east wall of the Śiva temple at Jayati contains a beautiful figure of Harihara standing in *tribhaṅga* pose. The upper right hand is broken. The lower left hand carries a club. He is fully ornamented. Naṅdi and Garuḍa are seen respectively on the right and left corners.

The left side niche of the east wall of the Sāripalli temple contains another Harihara figure standing in *tribhaṅga* pose. The upper right hand carries a trident while the upper left hand carries a *paraśu*(?). The lower right hand is placed on a dwarf. The lower left hand is placed on the *kaṭi.*

The position of Garuḍa, the mount of Viṣṇu, needs a special attention in this context. According to *Viṣṇudharmottara,* Garuḍa should be stationed on the left side *(Vāmāṅgai Vihaṅgarāh).* The Harihara images at Śrīkurmam and Nārāyaṇapuram have Garuḍas whereas the image of Madhukeśvara has no Garuḍa, and in its place a lion is carved. Another Harihara image in the same Madhukeśvara temple also has no Garuḍa and in its position a female figure is depicted. The Harihara image in the Someśvara temple has the representation of Garuḍa in human form. Here is Garuḍa the half man and half bird. In this form the Vaiṣṇavites call him by the honorific name *Garuḍālwār.* A. Sen opines[18]

> In Indian Art the representation of Garuḍa stands in a separate group which in most cases is not but a winged human figure, the only one to be found in the whole of Indian art.

In almost all the cases except in one context, the Viṣṇu position, i.e. the left side is highly decorated as described in texts like *Śilparatna* as *nānā ratna vibhuṣitam;* and right side decorated with snakes as usual to Śiva, described as *Bhujagendra vibhuṣitam.* In all the images the right eye has a fierce look, and the left eye has a pleasing look *(Dakshinai Vugradṛisṭisyat Vāmaistala netrakam).*

Of all the Harihara images of the Kalinga-Andhra region, the icon in the Someśvara temple in the Mukhaliṅgam is the most beautiful one; and a rare feature is the presence of Harihara images in the Vaiṣṇava temples.

NOTES AND REFERENCES

1. C. Sivaramamurty, *Śatarudrīya Vibhuti of Śivā's Iconography,* p.17.
2. A. Kamala Vasini, *Iconography of Śiva,* p.169.
3. *Harivamsa,* 10666f referred to by Bhagavant Sahai in *Iconography of Minor Hindu and Buddhist Deities,* p.133.
4. T.A. Gopinatha Rao, *Elements of Hindu Iconography,* pp.333-34.
5. Bhagavant Sahai, *Iconography of Minor Hindu and Buddhist Deities,* p.135.
6. F.H. Gravely & T.N. Ramachandram, *Madras Government Museum Bulletin, Hindu Metal Images,* p.12.
7. T.A. Gopinatha Rao, *Elements of Hindu Iconography,* pp.333-34.
8. A.L. Basham, *Wonder that was India,* p.313.
9. Cited by A. Kamala Vasini in *Iconography of Śiva,* p.172.
10. K.C. Panigrahi, *Archaeological Remains of Bhubaneswar,* p.47.
11. Tikkana, *Āndhra Mahā Bhāratam-Virāṭaparvam,* Introduction.
12. *S.I.I.,* Vol. IV.
13. Bhagavant Sahai, *Iconography of Minor Hindu and Buddhist Deities,* p.48; Kalpana Desai, *Vishnu Iconography,* p.56.
14. K. Sundaram, *The Siṁhāchalam Temple,* p.47.
15. B. Masthanaiah, *The Temples of Mukhaliṅgam,* p.63.
16. *Ibid.*
17. *Ibid.,* p.64.
18. A. Sen, *Animal Motifs in Ancient Indian Art,* p.115.

20

Appreciating the Spiritual : Aesthetic Truth of Indian Temple Architecture with Special Reference to Khajuraho Group of Temples

Pushpa Tiwari

Part I	:	Architecture as a Language of Cosmic Principals and Symbology.
Part II	:	Dichotomy of Sensuous and Spiritual.
Part III	:	Spiritual - Aesthetic Truth of Temple Architecture - Vastu-Puruṣa-Ideal and Image of cosmic principles.

Verily, truth is right. Therefore if two people should come disputing, saying, We should trust the one who says, 'I have seen'.

—Bṛhadāranyaka Upaniṣad 5.14.4 [2]

This could be defined as the powers of art and visual medium as accepted in ancient Indian traditions of philosophy. Before we proceed to discuss these pertinent issues, it is imperative to ask what exactly do we mean by the term appreciation of art. Here two important issues are involved, i.e. what is 'appreciation' and what is 'art' and how far two are interrelated and affect each other.

Let us take the problem of appreciation. Appreciation, discussions, evaluation about works of art are either from the point of view of the creator or that of the beholder. What does it require of the person who wishes to appreciate art? Are there objective, universal criteria for art appreciation which could be applied universally, irrespective of time-space dimensions and culture-specificity of art? How the definition of art itself, affects the methodology of appreciation? For example, while appreciating art of modern world, one naturally accepts the division of fine art from that of craft. This very notion of dichotomy between art and craft militates against the traditional world of ancient and medieval times. The problem arises, when there is no universal definition of art itself, then how one could proclaim universal criteria of art appreciation? Answers to these questions are not easy and they require the knowledge of whole gamut of debate centred on the philosophy of language on the one hand, and on the other, having the knowledge of ongoing discussions on the methodological issues, involved in the analysis of socio-cultural and religio-spiritual dimensions of human activities. The terms like Tradition, Modernity, Post-Modernity, Oriental, Occidental, Progressive, Primitive, Classical, Colonial, National, Global, Subaltern, Folk, Elite, Rural, Urban, High and Low Traditions—they all have their own sociological moorings and background in which they were coined to cater to the needs of their contemporary world and in due course of time they have undergone subtle and deliberate changes and transformations of their original meaning.

There are two aspects of any art—physical or material which constitutes the how of art and the other is what of art which reveals the right reason or logic of the composition or in other words the meaning of art. Appreciation of art concerns with both of these aspects. For the study of traditional art "The what of art is far more important than the how; it should, indeed, be the what that determines the how, as form determines shape." (Coomaraswamy, 1956 (1943), Dover Publs., Inc. N.Y., p.10).

In *The Foundation of Indian Culture* Sri Aurobindo has discussed the problems related to appreciation of art in general and Indian art in particular. According to him

> The criticism of art is a vain and dead thing, when it ignores the spirit, aim, essential motive from which a type of artistic creation starts and judges by the external details only in the light of a quite different spirit, aim and motive. A comparative criticism has its use, but the essential understanding must precede it if it is to have any real value.[1]

Speaking in context of appreciation of Indian art in 19th and early 20th century he says:

> To the European mind Indian Art was a thing barbarous, immature, monstrous, an asserted growth from humanity's primitive savagery and incompetent childhood ... In matters of art the western mind was long bound up as in a prison in the Greek and Renaissance tradition modified by a later mentality with only two side rooms of escape, the romantic and the realistic motives, but these were only wings of the same building.... The canons of western artistic creation were held to be the sole valid criteria and everything else was regarded as primitive and half developed or else strange and fantastic and interesting only by its curiosity.[2]

One has only to refer to Hegel's Lectures on Aesthetics where while explaining the Idea or content vis-à-vis form or shape in art he starts :

> that the defects of a work of art are not to be regarded simply as always due, for instance, to individual unskilfulness. Defectiveness of form arises from defectiveness of content. So, for example, the Chinese, Indians and Egyptians in their artistic shapes, their forms of deities, and their idols, never got beyond a formless phase, or one of a vicious and false definiteness of form, and were unable to attain genuine beauty; because their mythological ideas, the content and thought of their works of art, were as yet indeterminate in themselves, or of a vicious determinateness, and did not consist in the content that is absolute in itself ....Christian imagination will be able to represent God only in human form and with man's intellectual expression, because it is herein that God Himself is completely known in Himself as mind.[3]

Hegel's Euro-centric notion of progress and anthropo-Homo-centeric notion of absolute beauty, comes into his way of understanding 'other' arts. This concept of otherness i.e. the vantage point of an outsider in the underlying philosophy of 'Orientalism' which was the major criteria on of art appreciation other than European or Western in 19th and 20th centuries. Last quarter of 20th century has witnessed revolutionary change in the approach to study human cultures. Philosophy of language has raised questions regarding the fixed notion of meaning contained in words/ language and on the issue of objective reality lying beyond the scope and possibility of language itself. Post-structural and Post-modern thinkers are concerned with the deconstruction of any meaning focussed only on meta-narratives and unilinear concept of progression / evolution etc. It has raised serious questions on the classification of art in terms of Primitive, Archaic, Classical, Ethnic, Folk, Romantic, etc.

Earlier it was only the problem of reconciling the dichotomy of Traditional and Modern notions of art which was the main concern of art historians and scholars. Now the very instrument of understanding, i.e. language itself has entered into the debate which emphasizes that everything is a text which has to be deciphered by the reader/viewer either from author's point of view or from his contemporary frame of reference. Author/ creator Text/creation Reader/viewer in this process where lies the meaning? Original meaning is lost forever along with the intention of the author. Text remains as historical/contemporary exhibit. Reader has to break the barrier of his language and specific mode of understanding to decipher the text. This demands hermeneutical approach, i.e. text/art tradition should be evaluated in terms of the criteria of ideals and images, it sets for itself and not from the vantage point of an outsider. In appreciation of the ideals and images of Indian art one has to remember some basic facts. Firstly, in there appreciation of traditional art, form and content or how and what of art cannot be dichotomised. Secondly, there is no scope for the division of fine art from that of craft in traditional philosophy of art. This division is of recent origin, i.e. post industrial/modern/ western origin which distinguishes a work of art from that of craft on the basis of the uniqueness, expressiveness and originality of the former (art) as against the repetitiveness, mechanical process and functionality of the latter (craft). Thus any object to qualify as art must not have been created for achieving certain purpose or aim but for its own sake, for the expression of a genius artist as a masterpiece of his urge of creativity. That is what the philosophy of art for art's sake is all about where form is divorced from the function and intelligible meaning, and unintelligibility of art is propounded as the basic quality of art. Aesthetics becomes the science or philosophy of art which substitutes the study of artefact with that of the artist and his idiosyncrasies to unravel the mysteries of art. This philosophy has to be totally discarded to have any understanding of the ideals and images of Indian art. Thirdly, the notion of novelty and individual freedom has to be properly contextualized so as to understand the concept of man and artist on the one hand and on the other to avoid the misleading generalization by proclaiming that in ancient/ medieval India there were no artists, only artisans existed who were no better than bonded labours or worst zombies.

TRADITIONAL DEFINITION OF ART

Philosophy of art tries to define art as representation, expression, imitation always having formal and metaphorical elements. Whether it is representation, expression or imitation, it always refers to something lying beyond. Art is a language. Symbols constitute the language of art. In this sense 'realism' or 'likeness' is not the primary concern of art. *Ars sine scintia nihil*—Art without science is nothing. In this sense "we cannot call a painting 'art'. As the words 'artefact' and 'artificial' imply, the thing made is a work of art, made by art, but not itself art; the art remains in the artist and is the knowledge by which things are made." (Coomaraswamy, *op.cit.*, p.18). In ancient India or for that matter in any traditional society, the artist was not a special kind of man, but every man a special kind of artist'. Perfection and beauty, functional and symbolic values coincide in art. The purpose of art is always one of effective communication.

> The intelligibility of traditional art does not depend on recognitions, but like that of script, on legibility. The characters in which this art is written are properly called symbols..... Symbols in combination form an iconography or myth. Symbols are the universal language of art; The content of symbols is metaphysical.[4]

For a traditional artist the highest point of creative expression is reached in concretizing an eternal myth. Mircea Eliade points out that creativity for the traditional artist/man emulates the paradigm of cosmic creation, repetition of a primordial act, the transformation of chaos into cosmos by the divine act of creation.[5] In this sense, there seems to exist a complex chain of interrelatedness between history, religion, myth and art. This gives birth to symbols and motifs as a form of language. According to Prof. Negi "Myths and their motifs invariably constitute the leaven of the weltanchauung of a culture and permeate its fabric and identity in the way, matter and form, inform the world of reality.[6]

All ancient civilizations were dominated and governed by religious traditions, characterized by myths and their motifs. Myths are the science of pre-scientific age or in other words they are rationalizations of what pre-scientific cultures cannot understand through other means. According to Zimmer,

> Myths are not the products of individual experience and reactions. They are produced, treasured and controlled by the collective working and thinking of the religious community. They are produced through an anonymous creative process and a collective, intuitive acceptance. In the myths of ancient cultures we are brought the intuitive, collective wisdom of an ageless, anonymous and many sided civilization.[7]

Mircea Eliade has described myths and motifs as systems of micro-macrocosmic correspondences and analogies.[8]

As religion seeks to deal with man's ultimate truth and reality, it is prolific in the production and use of various forms and objects. Therefore it is not surprising that religions have been the inspiring source and fountain head of a large and diverse body of art. The intimate relationship between religions and art gives birth to iconography which is the constant essence of any traditional art. It is in this sense that Coomarswamy declares 'Iconography is art : that art by which the actual forms of things are determined'[9] and that 'Style is the man' i.e. 'human idiosyncracy is the explanation of style and of stylistic sequences'.[10] As nothing can be known or done except in accordance with the mode of the knower and doer, hence style is the manifestation or self-expression in so far it corresponds to the archetype the idea or form. It is beyond doubt that cosmology and divine archetype constitute the content or form of Indian art. Its ideals and images are conceived in cosmic likeness and analogies. Representation of cosmic form and re-enaction of primordial truth are the true ideals of Indian art. According to Sri Aurobindo "Indian architecture, painting, sculpture are not only intimately one in inspiration with the central things in Indian philosophy, religion, Yoga, culture, but a specially intense expression of their significance".[11]

Indian architecture especially demands this kind of understanding of the inner meaning hidden behind its form and a sensitive spiritual self-identification with it.

> These sacred buildings are the signs, the architectural self-expression of an ancient spiritual and religious culture. Ignore the spiritual suggestion, the religious significance, the meaning of the symbols and indications, look only with the rational and secular aesthetic mind, and it is vain to expect that we shall get to any true and disceruing appreciation of this art.[12]

Unless we address ourselves to the spiritual aesthetic truth of Indian architecture, mere knowledge of its technique and physical/material shape will not help us to understand its true meaning or significant form.

Architecture is a language of cosmic principles and symbology in literal sense of the term. 'Form' of the architecture directly corresponds to the function. Through rituals and elaborate purificatory rites, every act of performing architectural canons, starts with a 'depolarization' of the environment which is nothing but the re-inaction of original creation of cosmos out of chaos. Every part of the immediate environment and human body are identified with the Cosmos conceived in human form, i.e. in the metaphor of *Puruṣa*. Even in modern scientific, secular architecture, the orientation of the site/building/layout according to the sun and immediate environmental feature or landscape is nothing but the integration of mindscape/ culture scape with that of landscape. In fact, it is architecture only which still retains its cosmic connectivity in its form, even in this age of modernism/Post-modernism whereas all other art forms have proclaimed their freedom from cosmology and superstition. In ancient India the sacred origin of different arts was emphasized. Contrary to making any claims to novelty, the traditional artists made the opposite claim that nothing novel is rendered by them; rather they are merely mediums/instruments/vehicles of manifesting/expressing/ representing/imitating *Daivī Śilpa* or primordial art forms. The Indian tradition architect is often spoken of as visiting the heavenly region to imitate the divine forms of architecture. Likewise, Indian sculptors, painters, musicians, etc., are said to have received the knowledge of their art from divine source. Art is a revelation not the process of invention. Philosophy of science and philosophy of language both try to address to this problem of revelation vs. invention. Holistic science tries to understand whether the laws of nature, mathematical numerals, etc., are revealed to a scientist or he merely invents them to grasp the reality. It would suffice to say that in Indian world view Art/Architecture does not simply reveal God : it is one of the ways in which God reveals and actualizes himself. Art is the power of creation. This power is divine in nature.

If this is so, then the problem arises regarding the significance and importance we give to the myths of origin of art forms as well as the ritualistic practices undertaken before the commencement of any art. And does the existence of these rituals change the nature of the aesthetic experience?[13]

One can answer this question by stating that the 're-enactment' of the primordial truth/cosmic principles does not mean a mere mechanical repetition devoid of pleasure and fulfillment of creative urge. Consequently, for traditional artist creativity lies not in their novelty but in their transfiguring the eternal into temporal images. They are being original in the sense of turning to the original the primeval. As Jhanji has rightly commented that "the fact that a traditional artist does not experiment with the vagaries of his whims and fancies does not imply that his work is hackneyed and has no ingeniousness about it".[14]

After this brief elaboration of the nature, scope and form of ancient Indian traditional art, let us address to the dichotomy of sensuous vs. spiritual in the modern interpretation of art. This dichotomy has been perpetuated by the term of aesthetics and the way it has been applied in art appreciation. In modern times aesthetics has come to be identified with the sensuous nature of art to the extent that individualism and humanism are supposed to be synonymous with the expression of feelings, emotions in a form that pleases the artist. This demands a complete freedom for the artist, a release from all restraint, from discipline and from concern for convention. Modern theory of art dichotomises the sensuous and spiritual in art forms and asserts that,

> the fact that Indian artists concretized certain eternal myths in their works is not reason enough to categorize Indian art as spiritual.... For, like any other artist the Indian artist was interested in the sensuous pleasure which these myths generated when transformed into lines, colours, sounds or metric compositions and not in their spiritual or moral dimension. If these works also happened to arouse certain spiritual experiences, it is a contingent matter... while creating the work, all he is interested in is the transfiguration of his imagination into a coherent structure. It is only the beholders who violate the autonomy of an art work by imposing moral and spiritual norms on it.[15]

One may recall the famous words of Niharranjan Ray in his pioneer work titled *An Approach to Indian Art* advocating the existence of Indian art for its own sake, for the pleasure of eyes and satisfaction of creative urge than merely a vehicle of religio-spiritual truth:

> it pleads for a more humanistic, social and formal i.e. aesthetic approach to the study of Indian art than a purely religious, symbolical and intellectual one which still remains the dominant approach in Indian art studies... and to provide a

somewhat alternative approach to the study and appreciation of our art and aesthetics, an approach that should be more objective, more closely related to life and actual living and hence more humanistic, not just scholastic and priestly.[16]

This dichotomy of form and function, sensuous and spiritual is the result of extreme individualism and humanism which believes in the autonomy of art only when it exists for its own sake and not as a means to an end.

Here I would like to quote Rabindranath Tagore

> At the root of all creation there is a paradox, a logical contradiction. Its process is in the perpetual reconciliation of two contrary forces... on the one hand, It has been said : The universe has come out of joy. On the other hand, there is the verse which says : God made penance, and with the heat generated there from he created all that there is. The freedom of joy and the restraint of *tapasya,* both are equally true in the creative expression of Brahma. This limitation of the unlimited is personality : God is personal where he creates. He accepts the limits of his own law, and the play goes on, which is this world whose reality is in its relation to the person. Things are distinct not in their essence but in their appearance. This is art, the truth of which is not in substance or logic but in expression. Abstract truth may belong to science and metaphysics, but the world of reality belongs to art.[17]

The power of manifestation inherent in art is being accepted as the essence of art. But manifestation of what this is totally ignored. In fact modern thinkers seem to be more worried for the autonomy of art. Traditional philosophy believes that art reveals the absolute like religion and philosophy does. It is to accept that art expresses the same 'content' as religion and philosophy, but in a different 'form'. It expresses its content in a sensory form, while religion, does so in the form of pictorial imagery and philosophy in the form of conceptual thought. Despite this art maintains its autonomy. Art is an end in itself, not merely a means to some further end. Art, by means of its representations, while remaining within the sensuous sphere, delivers man at the same time from the power of sensuousness. Art has its purpose in itself, in its power of representing the truth in the form of sensuous artistic shape. In this sense art does not simply reveal God, it is one of the ways in which God reveals, and actualizes, himself. In fact the whole question of the dichotomy between sensuous and spiritual in art seems irrelevant in context of ancient Indian art/architecture. In the traditional doctrine of beauty it is distinguished from taste, i.e. liking or disliking. 'Beauty in the master craftsman's atelier is not a final cause of the work to be done, but an inevitable accident'.[18] Beauty is the attractive power of perfection and it has to do with cognition. Modern world view dichotomises spirit and matter and contrast the one with the other in either-or sense of the term whereas in ancient ideals of creativity and art, spirit and matter were never supposed to be mutually exclusive, matter was considered essential for the actualization of spirit. *Sarvam Khalvidam Brahma* makes matter and spirit as two sides of the same coin. Therefore to percieive the sensuous as against the spiritual in art is contradiction in terms and a superficial narrow point of reference to appreciate the ideals and images of Indian art.

This could be substantiated with the inherent spiritual aesthetic truth of temple architecture. In fact the harmony and synthesis of sensuous and spiritual and their complementary is expressed at its best in the formal ideals of temple architecture.

NOTES AND REFERENCES

1. Sri Aurobindo, The *Foundation of Indian Culture*, Sri Aurobindo Ashram, Pondicherry, 1988, p.202.
2. *Ibid.*, p.201.
3. Hegel, *Introductory Lectures on Aesthetics*, Penguin Books, London, 1993, pp.80-81.
4. A.K. Coomaraswamy, *History of Indian and Indonesian Art*, p.78.
5. Mircea Eliade, *The Sacred and the Profane*, tr. R. Willasd Trask, New York, Harcourt Brace & world, Inc. 1959, p.31.
6. (U.P. Arora, *Motifs in Indian Mythologies : Their Greek and Other Parallels*, New Delhi, 1981, Introduction by Prof. Negi, p.vii).
7. H. Zimmer, *Myths and Symbols in Indian Art and Civilization*, N.Y. n.d., pp. 40-41.
8. Mircea Eliade (ed.) *Encyclopedia of Religion and Philosophy.*
9. *Ibid.*, p.41.
10. *Ibid.*, p.39.
11. *Ibid.*, pp. 209-10.
12. *Ibid.*, p.213.
13. Rekha Jhanji, *The sensuous in Art*, Indian Institute of Advanced Study, Shimla and Motilal Banarsidass, Delhi, 1989, p.7.
14. Jhanji, *ibid.*, p.12.
15. *Ibid.*, p.13.
16. Niharranjan Ray, *An Approach to Indian Art*, Panjab University, Chandigarh, 1974, Preface and Proposition, p.18.
17. Rabindranath Tagore, *The Meaning of Art*, Lalit Kala Akademi, New Delhi, 1983, pp.3-4.
18. A.K. Coomarswamy, *op.cit.*, p.76.

21

The Imagery of Female Messengers in Indian Art: An Appraisal

Choodamani Nandagopal

Indian art when viewed in its complete sense has given a significant place to the portrayal of minor characters too. It is quite obvious to expect that the imagery of heroes and heroines are always highlighted and also the characters who are closely associated with the main characters. When we turn our attention to the minor roles, we come across astonishing details in art and literature. One such example is the illustration of the female messengers - the *dutis* or *dutikas.* In our classic literature, sculptural representation and in the art of painting, dance and theatrical arts, the female messengers have a significant place.

The abstract thinking power of our aestheticians have dimensionalized our art forms and therein lifted the intellectual stagnation occurred inevitably during certain phases in the wide range of time span. The continuity of textual tradition and the tradition of critical theories have undoubtedly made Indian classical arts as the living tradition despite the drastic social changes. One such school of thought is the *Nāṭyaśāstra* and its *prayoga,* the application in both plastic and performing arts of our country. As the Vedic literature is considered as the primordial source for our life studies in general, *Nāṭyaśāstra* has been considered in particular as the fundamental source of reference for any concept to be studied in its propriety concerned with visual or performing arts besides aesthetics.

In the Chapter XXV of *Nāṭyaśāstra,* the verses 9 to 18 discuss the role of female messenger, her qualities and activities. Bharata has identified eleven types of *dutī,* the female messengers as—a neighbour, a friend, a servant, an unmarried girl, a craftswoman, a nurse (a foster mother), a heretic nun and a fortune-teller. He specifically warns about the persons who should not be relied on as *dutī* such as a stupid woman or wealthy or terribly ill.

One has to take care of these conditions while deploying women as a messenger.

It is interesting to note here that Bharata prescribes certain qualities either inherent or to be nurtured in a person who will take up the duty as messenger. A female messenger must be clever in encouraging the beloved, a sweet talker, honest, abiding her time, keeping her own secrets and above all attractive to look at. She should encourage the beloved by giving various reasons, she should report exact words, and be able to describe the emotional condition. She should exaggerate the family status and the riches of the lover. She should be able, by various ruses, to bring about the union of the beloved, who is in love for the first time with her lover. This union should take place during the festivity at night, in a park, in the house of a relative, in the house of a female friend, or in invited parties or under the pretext of seeing a sick person or in an unoccupied vacant house.[1] In any given situation the messenger is expected to behave and act with tact and sincerity of purpose. This would bring the confidence in the heroes and heroines and the very purpose of depending on a messenger for a confidential task is worthwhile.

Kāmasutra of Vatsyayana defines *dutī* as one who entices another man's wife for the hero. Sharadatanaya in his *Bhāvaprakaśana* describes twelve types of *dutīs: Kathinī, linginī, dāsī, kumārī, kāruśilpinī, pāśanḍinī, prativeśyā sakhī, rangopajīvinī, dhātreyi, prekṣaṇikā* and *dutyā*. Damodaragupta in his *Kuṭṭani-mātā* remarks that 'another indispensable aid to a harlot was a sharp, ready-witted and skilled messenger-girl (*dutī*)'. It was through these go-betweens that desired customers were to be approached. The Kuṭṭani by name Vikarāla advises Mālatī to send to her prospective client, Cintāmanī, a clever, bold *dutī* capable of gauging other's feelings and endowed with sarcastic speech (verse - 89). Haralata and Manjari are also said to have sent such messangers to convey their love sicknesses to Sundarasena and Samarabhata respectively (verses 283 and 989). The skill with which they carried out their undertaking is amply illustrated by the speech attributed to them. They first presented flowers and betels to be prospective lovers, gave a graphic account of the physical charms and lovelorn condition of their mistresses, enticed by the words, arousing their passions to a high pitch, and if they found that their speech did not bear the desired fruit, they resorted to sarcasm.[2]

Rudrabhatta in *Ṣṛingāratilaka* depicts eight types more or less similar to that of Bharata's interpretation and adds *kāru,* the labourer to the list. He assigns different duties to the *dutīs* in different situations and they have to handle the situation tactfully. For instance she has to have a great sense of humour to create amusement, sense of beauty. In his opinion she takes important position in the situations of *sanghaṭana* and *viraha nivedana,* and her duties are *manḍana, upalambha, śikshā* and *parihāsa.*

Dhananjaya in *Daśarupaka* identifies the same types but *Svayamdutī* is his own identification where the heroine herself acts a *dutī.*

Bhoja has devoted two independent chapters known as *dutavisesha* and *dutakarmopavarṇa* for the discussion of the eight types of female messengers as listed by his predecessors in his treatise *Ṣṛngāraprakāśa.* Bhanudatta's *Rasamanjari* pictures the messengers as *sakhi, pārśagāmini, sandeśapārāngama, hitakariṇī* and *prasādinī.* Her functions identified by him are similar to that of Rudrabhatta's classification.

Vidyanatha in *Pratāparudrayaśobhuaṇa* refers to nine kinds of female messengers as mentioned by other writers and specifically makes the distinction between *sakhi* as companion and *dutī* as ordinary messenger.

Simhabhupala in *Rasārnavasudhākara* follows the tradition of Bharata in naming the *dutīs* including that of *viprasnika* or *daivagna* signifying the fortune-teller. Visvanatha in his *Sāhityadarpaṇa* recalls the types of *dutīs* as given by Simhabhupala, ten in number. But he brings these characters into three groups, namely *nisrātārtha* - one who speaks, replies, argues with the hero in favour of the heroine, *mitārtha* - one who speak only what is nessessary, *sandesaharaka* - one who just conveys message.

Dutīkarmaprakāśa of Padarika Vitthala is a sole text on the subject and offers interesting aspects of the art of emissary. Pandarika Vitthala belonged to Satanuru, a small village 60 km from Bangalore and his parents and himself were the devotees of Vitthala of Pandarapura, and practised *Bhāgavata Sampradāya.* He composed the text *Dutīkarmaprakāśa* during the period AD 1565-1572. It was written at the specific request of Burhan Khan, who was a young ruler of Ahmadnagar at that time. When Burhan Khan was dethroned he sought refuge under Akbar and Akbar helped him to recover his throne. It gives us a feeling that Pandarika Vitthala left his native place in search of literary patronage and had somehow managed to get closer to Burhan khan who patronized him initially. This helped Pandarika Vitthala to settle himself before entering into Akbar's court and probably the sympathetic patron Burhan Khan must have introduced him to the Emperor. During his Ahmednagar days he composed two texts namely *Dutikarmaprakāśa* and *Sighrabodhini-nāmamālā.* Later his major part of writing covered the dual arts, dance and music from 1572 to 1589 while he was under the patronage of the emperor Akbar. He has authored four texts namely *Sadragacandrodaya, Rasamanjari, Rāgamālā* and *Nartananirṇaya.*

Dutīkarmaprakāśa is preserved in the manuscript form in Bikaner (No. 3801) and in the Nirnaya Sagar Press edition as *Kāvyamālā* no. 13 edited by Sivadatta and Kashinatha Panduranga Parab, published from Bombay in 1903, and later in 1916 Kedarnath Durga Prasad edited it again.

(I acknowledge Dr. Satavadhani Ganesh here for getting me a xerox copy of the text and for his lively discussions on the text)

Pandarika Vitthala talks about twenty-one types of female messengers. The way he gives the examples and the accounts of comparison show his aesthetic temperament. Probably he must have closely watched and observed the significant roles the female messengers played in very critical circumstances besides his own in-depth knowledge the *kāvyas* and the theatrical texts. The characters in the royal household must have motivated him to compose on the subject, which was not treated by early writers on priority and their main concern was the heroine and to heighten her feelings and emotions the female messengers were exploited in a real sense. But Pandarika Vitthala's sympathy towards these go-between characters led him to the composition of *Dutīkarmaprākaśa* through which he carves a niche for the *dutīs* in the hearts of *sahṛdayas.*

Dr. R. Satyanarayana, a renowned musicologist has published recently three volumes on *Nartananirṇaya* of Pandarika Vitthala through IGNCA. In his introductory chapter he has reviewed other works of Pandarika Vitthala. His views are quite significant in knowing the nature of the text *Dutīkarmaprakāśa.* It is a tract on the science (or art) of erotica and deals with, as indicated by the title, functions and duties of the female messenger or go-between *(dutī)* between the separated hero and heroine who are in love with each other. Though not suggested by the title, it also describes the male messenger or confident of the hero, which is added probably as an afterthought or as a separate tact. Pandarika Vitthala states that 'it is impossible for even the creator God Brahmā to know the doings of all types of *dutīs* pertaining to all kinds of heroines; nevertheless, since it affords delight to the excellent aesthetics of the world, I shall describe the functions and duties of the *dutī* as only a fraction of the whole science in both definition and illustration'.

The work commences with brief statement of obeisance, purpose, authorship and title of the treatise. The author then proceeds with a definition of *dutī,* her basic duty, as she has the expertise in conveying messages, communicates to the hero effectively the pangs of separation and brings about their union, etc. Pandarika Vitthala gives an exhaustive list of the types of female messengers. While all the early authors mention some of the common types and the number stops around nine to eleven. But it is really interesting to observe that Pandarika Vitthala comes out with twenty-one types of female messengers. They are:

1. *Sakhi* - a companion
2. *Viprasṇikā* - fortune teller

3. *ceṭī* - maid servant
4. *svayam dutī* - heroine herself functioning as messenger.
5. *śilpinī* - artist or a painter
6. *vicitra vacanā* - expert in persuasive eloquence
7. *gānavati* - songstress
8. *dhātri* - mother, midwife or a female supporter.
9. *kumārikā* - daughter or a girl
10. *prasanginī* - opportunist
11. *mālinī* - garland maker
12. *skhalitā* - strategist
13. *prativeśinī* - neighbour
14. *paracittaviśeśajñā* - expert in the art of reading the minds of others.
15. *cesṭasanketa-kovida* - expert in understanding the body language
16. *rajakī* - washerwoman
17. *saucikī* - the tailor maid
18. *veśadhārinī* - expert in fancy dressing
19. *manihārinī* - seller and maker of beads and bangles.
20. *kathinī* - story teller
21. *nāpikī* - manicurist, hairdresser.

Pandarika Vitthala does not just stop at giving this list but continues to offer his own definitions and illustrations for each of these. The definition includes qualities and functions and duties and is invariably composed in the *anustubh* metre while the illustration contains a situation, circumstances, device or strategy, always composed in the *śārdulavikriḍita* metre.

The way he gives the examples and comparisons show his aesthetic temperament. Being a close associate of the ruler probably he must have closely watched and observed the significant roles the female messengers played in very critical circumstances besides his own in-depth knowledge in the *kāvyas* and the theatrical texts. The characters in the royal household must have motivated him to compose on the subject, which was not treated by early writers on priority and their main concern was the heroine and to heighten the feelings and emotions the female messengers were exploited in a real sense. But Pandarika Vitthala's sympathy towards these go-between characters led him to the composition of *Dutīkarmaprakāśa* through which he carves a niche for the *dutīs* in the hearts of *sahṛdayas.*

He designates them as *narmasacivas.* He snaps with crisp description on each of them; *pītamardha* is a great scholar adept in converting the anger of the heroine into pliable moods, *vita* is a cognoscente in techniques of physical love, *ceta* is skilled in convincing the quarrelsome heroine and *vidusaka* is a jester who dissolves tension, anger, etc. It appears the female messengers have attracted the attention of our author than the male messengers and he has taken great delight in characterising *dutīs* with all his aesthetic pleasure and at times he himself becomes a *rasika*.

The fine arts like dance, music and painting have sensibly characterized the female messengers in the most enchanting way thereby enriched and elaborated the main theme.

Here it is appropriate to observe an important aspect of the whole concept and emergence of the roles played by *dutīs*. Most of the text have used them in the context of romance between a hero and heroine and their services were deployed only with this sense. But when the characters such as of the *sakhī, dāsī, shouchiki* and others were not necessarily seen from this point of view. When taken in the relevance of the *dutīkarma,* their roḷe of going between the characters, the hero and heroine stands as only one aspect of *dutīkarma*. *Doutya* in the sense of emissary has played pivotal roles in many of these and one such example strikes us is Kṛṣṇa playing himself as *duta* of the Pandavas before the Kurukshetra war. Even today the office of embassy is known as *dutavāsa*.

We have grand references of celebrated *dutī* and *sakhis* in our mythology and literature, to name few, in *Abhijñāna Shākuntalam* Kalidasa epitomised the *dutīkarma* in the characters of Priyamvadā and Anásyāyā, they followed the emotions of Shakuntalā as her own shadows. Draupadī's character as Sirendhrī in the royal household of Virāta is an interesting epoch in Virātaparva. In Jayadeva's *Geeta Govinda* the role of *sakhī* stands out by attracting the performers and painters to illustrate her in several ways and we could see in every state of emotions of Rādhā and Kṛṣṇa and their dependence on the *sakhī* as *achārya* leading the *ātmā,* in the form of Radha towards *mukti* by surrendering to *paramātmā* in the form of Kṛṣṇa. The qualities of *sakhī* can be compared to that of Kṛṣṇa's flute, as a constant sharing of his delightful moments and pangs of separation.

Some of the compositions in Indian classical dances commence with the heroine addressing *sakhi.*

Rupagosvāmin is perhaps the last influential authorities in Sanskrit on the subject and considers Kṛṣṇa's flute itself as *dutī*.[3] The sculptures and miniature paintings have immortalized the character of female messengers. The artists have taken delight in portraying them in very interesting ways.

NOTES AND REFERENCES

1. *Nāṭyaśāstra,* translated by Adya Rangacharya, p.137.
2. Ajaya Mitra Shastri, *Kuṭṭni-mātā of Damodara-gupta*, p.122.
3. R. Satyanarayana, *Nartana Nirnaya,* p.37.

22

The Durgā Temple at Aihoḷe and its Sculptures : Style, Context and Appreciation

Shrinivas V. Padigar

It is now nearly a century and a half since the first notice of the Durgā temple at Aihoḷe (pl. 22.1) appeared in print.[1] The temple has been drawing scholar's attention time and now. The research literature on the temple is so copious that recently a work[2] dealing specifically with its historiography has been published. But the interest in the temple has not ceased yet, and rightly so. The purpose of this paper is to view the temple and its major imagery in the perspectives of appreciation, style, possible symbolism and context.

Sculpturally the Durgā temple is the richest at Aihoḷe. None other at that place is blessed with as many sculptures. The themes, forms and styles of the sculptures are also diverse.

There is no image in the temple's *garbhagṛiha* (sanctum) now, but there is conclusive epigraphic and sculptural evidence revealing its dedication to Āditya, the Sun-god.[3] The temple's current name derives from the charming image of goddess Durgā Mahiṣamardinī in one of the *devakoṣṭhas*.[4] It is also known that one Komarasiṅga was its patron.[5]

The temple is curious for its plan (see plan). It comprises of an apsidal *garbhagṛiha* (sanctum) placed within an apsidal *gūḍhamaṇḍapa* (hall). The latter is approached from a *mukhamaṇḍapa* (porch). All these together are accommodated within a cage-like larger structure closely following the contour of the temple so that a verandah (in reality an ambulatory) is formed all around. Hence a set of two *pradakṣiṇāpathas* (ambulatories) has resulted—one around the *garbhagṛiha* proper and the other along the verandah. This is the only known structure with such an elaborate apsidal plan. For an apsidal structure a circular or an apsidal superstructure should be appropriate.

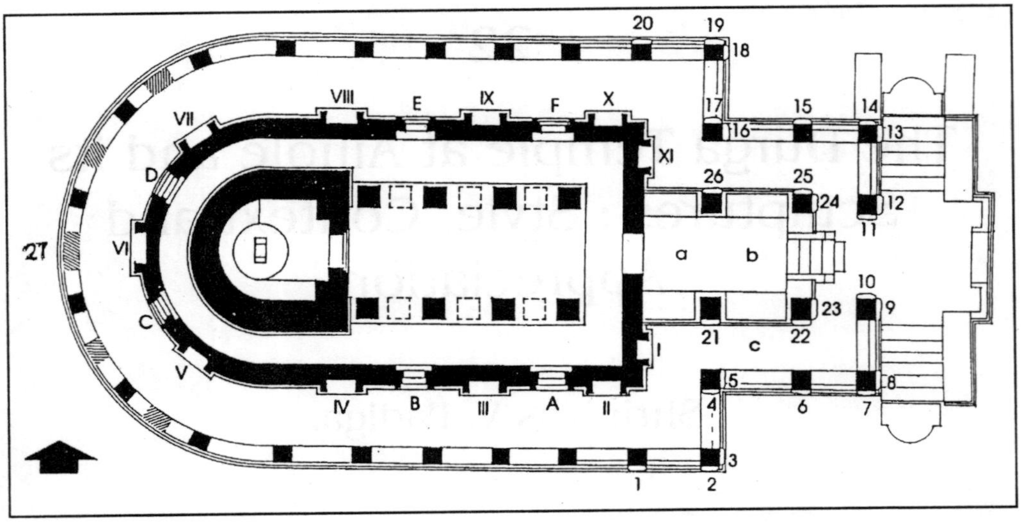

Plan of the Durgā Temple, Aihoḷe, showing the placement of its imagery. (Adapted from G. Michell, *Early Western Chalukya Temples,* London, 1975, Fig. 23)

But this temple supports a *rekhā-śikhara* (curvilinear superstructure of northern order), now only partially preserved. The exterior wall of the *gūḍhamaṇḍapa* is provided with *devakoṣṭhas* (niches for divine images) and ornate *jālavātāyanas* (lattice windows) at well-defined intervals, complete with *udgamas* (pediments) of southern *vimāna (śālākāra* or *kūṭākāra* form) or northern *latā* (formed of *chandraśālā* arches with *āmalasāraka* crowns) superstructure relief models or *makaratoraṇas* as the case may be. The verandah and porch pillars are generally of the southern form while the pilasters of the *devakoṣṭhas,* usually southern in form, follow northern form in certain cases, as, for instance, the one accommodating Śiva-Vṛiṣabhāntikamūrti. Thus there is a conscious blend of northern and southern architectural norms suggesting artist groups of heterogeneous traditions working on the project. This blend, coupled with the sumptuous sculptural decoration, presents the temple in a splendid, gorgeous and arresting form to the viewer as no other temple in Aihoḷe does. The temple appears to have been conceived as god Āditya's chariot, the apsidal form allowing an impression of movement for the temple. This observation also draws support from the fact that the temple staircases are *dviradasopāna* type, so that the votary can enter the temple from north and south as one would climb up a chariot.

The major imagery is found on pillars and in the *devakoṣṭhas.* There are beautiful boldly relieved sculptures (almost approaching round forms in modelling) occupying the *devakoṣṭhas:* Śiva-Vṛiṣabhāṇtikamūrti, Kevala Narasiṁha, Viṣṇu-Garuḍārūḍhamūrti (Karivarada), Bhū-Varāha, Durgā

Mahiṣamardinī and Harihara. The placement of these images seems to follow a conscious logic. To the image of Śiva-Vṛiṣabhāntika corresponds the image of his Śakti (Durgā-Mahiṣamardinī); and to the image of Kevala Narsiṁha corresponds the image of Bhū-Varāha. Extending this logic, one might visualize a syncretic image of Śiva-Ardhanārī in the *devakoṣṭha* (now empty) corresponding to that of Harihara. An image of Śiva-Bhikṣāṭanamūrti, now in the Archaeological Museum, judging from its find-spot, originally adorned one of the *devakoṣṭhas* in the temple. It is possible to speculate further that an image of Āditya occupied the *devakoṣṭha* in the centre of the apse, which should be of cult significance. The *devakoṣṭhas* flanking the *mukhamaṇḍapa* would have held images of *Saura dvārapālas* (Daṇḍa and Piṅgala).

The porch pillars carry images of Narasiṁha and Śiva-Ardhanārī in addition to *mithunas,* usually standing under a tree, on the verandah pillar-faces. The flanking pillars at the entrance into the temple proper carry a *dvārapāla* (south face of the pillar on northern flank) and the "Chastisement of Chhāyā" theme (north face of the pillar on southern flank).[6] A form of Śiva (probably Lakulīśa) is carved on the eastern face of a pillar on the southern side. Similarly there is an unfinished deity occupying the exterior face of the support-slab at the apse end, which is probably an aspect of the Sun god. Like the temple's architecture, its images are also of diverse artistic traditions.

Most sculptures in the *devakoṣṭhas* are superbly finished and are for sure done by master artists. As we move in the temple following the outer ambulatory, i.e., along the verandah, the first image encountered is that of Śiva-Vṛiṣabhāntikamūrti (III) (pl. 22.2).[7] It depicts an eight-armed Śiva leaning on Nandī, his *vāhana.* Standing in balanced and pleasing triple flexion (*tribhaṅga),* Śiva has an elaborately ornate *jaṭāmukuṭa,* complete with crescent moon (*bālendu).* Behind his head is a beautifully finished lotus *śiraśchakra,* against a rather large plain circular *prabhāmaṇḍala* (halo). The lower contour of the *jaṭāmukuṭa* is considerably raised, revealing the broad and prominent forehead showing the third eye. His right ear is adorned with a circular *kuṇḍala* (ear ornament) while the left ear has a *sarpa-kuṇḍala.* He wears a single stringed beaded *hāra* (necklace), a ribbon-like *udarabhandha,* a beaded *yajñopavīta* in *mālākāra* fashion, *nāgabandha*-type armlet, beaded *valayas,* beaded waist-band holding together the *vyāghra-charma* and almost transparent *dhotī,* with no apparent folds whatsoever, closely following the smooth colour of the lower part of the god's person, only its fringe-line being shown in subdued manner. The face is slightly lowered, the raised eyebrows are delicately done, the upper eyelids droop down, the pupils are shown by thin line and look at the viewer, and the lips reveal a gentle sublime smile. The hair-locks fall on shoulders. The overall impression is one of a supremely satisfied sublime divinity looking gracefully at the devotee. The smooth treatment of the flesh adds to the beaming beauty of the god. Śiva's hands, which are spread out in a graceful pattern giving movement, carry an *akṣamālā,* a small *ḍamaru,* a raised cloth *(patākahasta* indicating victory), and *sarpa.* Nandi, against whom the god leans, has a slightly lowered head and his ears and eyes express a disturbed and uneasy mood. A *gaṇa,* true to his naughty temperament, twists Nandi's tail, apparently causing uneasiness and enragement. But Nandi, however, is unable to retort by action, as even a slightest movement on his part would disturb his lord. Thus here is a commendable composition wherein the artist judiciously uses the available space, instills his work of art with a divine, graceful beaming beauty, and introduces a display of the character of a worldly bull in the divine Nandi. The effect is simply enamouring. There is proportion, excellence of composition, imagination, action, grace, sublimity, radiance, revelation, charm, life, all in one. Within him the deity appears to store full energy and release it out simultaneously. This is a creative piece from an anonymous master-artist. Looked at from whatever angle, the image has a superb aesthetic appeal. Only a few sculptures can stand in comparison to it. Though we have described this image as Śiva-Vṛiṣabhāntikamūrti, the piece of fluttering cloth in one of the hands of the deity suggests that the artist presents an aspect of victory and omnipotence of the Almighty, unable we are to understand it though.

The second image (IV) is that of Kevala Narasiṁha (pl. 22.3), carved in pinkish sandstone. The four-armed lion-faced god stands majestically in *dvibhaṅga.* A lotus adorns his head. His manes dangle over his shoulders. A beaded necklace, *nāgabandha*-like armlets, double bead-lined bangles, *yajñopavīta,* and a simple plain ribbon-like waist-band holding the tight *dhotī,* which follows the contour of the lower half of the body, constitute decoration of his person. The lower right hand rests on a *gadā* (now damaged) while the lower left is *kaṭyavalaṁbita.* The upper right and left hands carry *chakra* and *śaṅkha* respectively. The image recalls the Bādāmi Cave III Kevala Narasiṁha which was probably the source of inspiration. But except for the posture, the two images have individualities in presentation of detail. Like its Bādāmi counterpart, this image probably represents Narasiṁha before his combat with demon Hiraṇyakaśipu. The artist has avoided depicting Prahlāda, and perhaps through this technique suggests that the viewer should contemplate himself in place of the great *bhakta* who despite his birth as *asura* overcame ego and ignorance and was graced by the Almighty. The lotus crown, signifying *sahasrāra,* symbolizes the god as *jñānadevatā.*[8]

This is followed by another beautiful composition in the next *devakoṣṭha* (V), that of a four-armed Viṣṇu-Garuḍārūḍhamūrti (pl. 22.4). His damaged upper right and left hands carry a *prayoga-chakra* and a *śaṅkha;* while the lower right is in *varadahasta* and the lower left placed on the thigh. He wears an exquisitely carved *kirīṭamukuṭa* with a pleated fan-type *śiraśchakra* placed against a plain circular *prabhāmaṇḍala.* His ear ornaments differ from each other. A beaded necklace, a beaded *yajñopavīta* in *mālākāra* fashion, *nāgabandha*-like armlets, beaded bangle, a thin ribbon-like *udarabandha,* a beaded waist-band holding the *ardhoruka dhoti,* and another ribbon-like *vastra* passing over the thighs adorn the god's person, but all these are treated with restraint. The smooth modelling of the deity's almost round form is impressive. Viṣṇu's face, slightly lowered, looks down with a subdued smile at the devotee. The eye-brows and eyelid lines are delicately delineated. Viṣṇu is depicted as if he is getting ready to climb on Garuḍa, his *vāhaṇa.* Garuḍa is shown as pot-bellied dwarf of human form with bird's wings and beak. His curled hair is treated with care. A single-string beaded necklace and a ribbon-like *udarabandha* adorn his person. He has lifted his face up and looks at his Lord with a raised right hand as if to enquire where they are to go. Beside, to the right of Viṣṇu, stands *gadā Kaumodakī,* personified as a charming dame in *tribhaṅga.* Her *āmalaka*-like crown reveals her identity. On the whole, this is another sculpture of a master artist who makes judicious use of space for excellent composition, successfully brings out the divine form from its background through a treatment of volume and gives a touch of drama to his creative presentation. There can be least doubt that the image depicts the *Gajendramokṣa* legend, the Elephant-king is not represented though. In that legend, Viṣṇu, as *Karivarada* (One who gave boon of emancipation to the Elephant-king), relieves his devotee Gajendra from the clutches of an alligator (death). By avoiding depiction of Gajendra and the alligator perhaps the artist symbolically suggests that the viewer should imagine himself to be a devotee aspiring release from the cycle of death and rebirth by god's grace. A post-Gupta Mālava art style has been discerned in this sculpture by certain scholars with some justification.[9] In conception and execution the form and style of this sculpture is akin to that of Śiva-Vṛiṣabhāntika image mentioned above, and can be identified as the work of the artist group that worked the latter, though certainly not by the same artist.

After two empty niches, the Bhū-Varāha image (pl. 22.5) figures next (VIII) in the *devakoṣṭha* on the northern side of the temple. The four-armed deity lifts up a personified Bhūdevī on his proper left arm and supports her feet on his left rear hand. His proper right hand rests on hip while the upper right hand carries *chakra.* The *śaṅkha* hangs in background as both his left hands are engaged. The god wears an ornate *kirīṭamukuṭa* without a *śiraśchakra*. There is no *prabhāmaṇḍala*. The ornaments that decorate his person are, as in earlier images, sparse: a beaded necklace, a beaded *yajñopavīta* worn in *mālākāra* fashion, *nāgabandha*-like armlets, a beaded *udarabandha*, a beaded waist-belt that holds the *ardhoruka dhoti*, a ribbon-like band suspended from the waist and falling in a curve between the thighs. His left leg is placed on the body of Nāgarāja (signifying depths of water), who has his hands folded in reverence (*namaskāra-mudrā*). Bhūdevī, who sits on god's left arm somewhat uncomfortably, rests her right hand on his shoulder and places her left hand near her cheek apparently in a mood of astonishment. The smooth modelling almost approaching round form characterizes this image also, but to a lesser extent. The transition from the boar's face to human body is somewhat abrupt and less convincing. However, the ease with which the god lifts the weight of Earth-goddess is convincing. The shape of the stone slab used is also awkward. The floating *śaṅkha* suggests that the artist conforms to a highly localized norm in presenting Varāha image. In all Bhu-Varāha images at Aihoḷe, including the one in the Rāvaḷaphaḍi Śaiva cave, *śaṅkha* is shown hung in background. A lot of surrounding space has been left unutilized and there is imbalance of weight in composition. Thus the composition on the whole is not very impressive. In view of these, the sculpture has to be considered as work of a local apprentice who appears to be under the spell of the artist who made the image of Garuḍārūḍhamūrti of Viṣṇu, but could not rise up to his level. The Bhū-Varāha is a popular theme of the Chalukya artists, for each Chalukya king claimed himself to be *Śrī-Pṛithvī-vallabha* (the lord of goddess of fortune and goddess earth), thus claiming equation with Viṣṇu. Varāha was the royal emblem of the Chalukyas too.

The next *devakoṣṭha* (IX) is again occupied by an excellent piece of composition, depicting Durgā Mahiṣamardinī (pl. 22.6). The eight-armed goddess is in action, slaying the buffalo demon. Her chief hands carry a *triśūla* (trident) and a *ghaṇṭā* (bell) and the remaining hands, some of which are damaged, carry a *khaḍga, vajra, prayoga-chakra, śaṅkha,* etc. while her right leg is firmly placed on ground, she crushes with the left Mahiṣa's back. The dying demon in complete zoomorphic form lifts up his head in pain. Durgā's *vāhana,* lion, which is pushed aside to the right, looks at the shrieking buffalo. The deity wears an ornate *mukuṭa* with pleated fan-shaped *śiraśchakra* held against a large plain *prabhāmaṇḍala,* almost identical to that in Viṣṇu *Garuḍārūḍha* image, apart from two different varieties of *karṇa-kuṇḍalas,* a gemmed necklace, a *chhannavīra,* ornate bangles, *nāgabandha*-like armlets, a beaded *yajñopavīta,* a gemmed waist-belt holding the tight *dhotī,* heavy anklets, and a ribbon-like band that passes over the thighs. Her head is slightly raised and tilted and her face bears a smile of victory. It is a perfectly well-balanced composition, making judicious use of available space. The emphasis of the artist is on the ease with which the inseparable *śakti* of the Almighty overcomes ego and ignorance symbolized by the demon. The fine modelling, perfect proportions, pleasing composition, subdued ornamentation, and above all the style relate it to the Viṣṇu *Garuḍārūḍha* image noted earlier. It is the work of the same artist group if not of the same master-artist that made Viṣṇu *Garuḍārūḍha* image.

The last of the *devakoṣṭha* images (X) is that of an unusual eight-armed Harihara (pl. 22.7) standing in *samapāda* posture. The deity's left hands unfortunately are damaged, while the right hands carry *chakra, śārṅga* bow personified *gadā Kaumodakī,* and *śaṅkha.* There is a vertically stretched oval *prabhāmaṇḍala,* unlike in any other *devakoṣṭha* sculpture. A heavy *mukuṭa* with *jaṭā* and *kirīṭa* parts clearly demarcated, a beaded and gemmed necklace, *nāgabanda*-like armlet somewhat differing from those found on other *devakoṣṭha* deities, a thin beaded *udarabandha,* a long chain-like garland in *yajñopavīta* fashion reaching the ankles, a short and tight *ardhoruka* following body contour, and another ribbon-like cloth reaching the knees in semicircular fashion adorn the god. The *ardhoruka* is covered with closely engraved lines suggesting folds. There is no *śiraśchakra,* but a large plain oval *prabhāmaṇḍala.* The upper corners of the composition are occupied by garland-bearing flying damsels, while the lower corners are filled in by a gaṇa (probably personified *triśula)* and personified *gadā Kaumodakī.* All the three dames are treated alike. *Kaumodakī's* identity is revealed by the *āmalaka* crown hidden from view behind the bow. Her cross-legged posture is noteworthy as it compares well with that of the ladies in the *daṁpati* pairs on verandah pillars. The deity's eyebrows and eyelids are entirely subdued unlike in other images. The height of the face almost equals the torso while the portion from waist below is disproportionately tall. The shoulders are broad. The modelling is smooth and the composition is considerably well conceived, though it lacks proportion. The image is the work of a good artist trained in a distinct school undoubtedly different from that of the remaining *devakoṣṭha* images.

The inner *mukhamaṇḍapa* pillars and correspondingly the outer faces of the pillars of the verandah carry charming sculptural reliefs mostly of *daṁpatis.* There are, however, two sculptures of divinities; one depicting Ugra-Narasiṁha (23) and the other Śiva Ardhanārī (24). Both occupy the east face of the inner *mukhamaṇḍapa* pillars and greet the visitor as he enters into the temple. Ugra-Narasiṁha (pl. 22.8) emerges from the pillar (the *Bhāgavata-purāṇa* depicts Narasiṁha as emerging from a pillar) and tears out the entrails of Hiraṇyakaśipu with chief hands, while the remaining two hands hold *chakra* and *śaṅkha.* Like Kevala-Narasiṁha in the *devakoṣṭha,* he too has a lotus crown. The corresponding pillar on the north side carries almost in round Śiva's charming *Ardhanārī* form (pl. 22.9). These two sculptures appear to have been deliberately positioned in their places greeting the devotee. Ugra-Narasiṁha presents the terrific form of the Almighty and as an omnipresent destroyer of ego and ignorance, while the *Ardhanārī*, whatever its mythological explanation, signifies not only the inseparable union of *puruṣa* and *prakṛiti* (ever united male and female principles of the Universe, *vāg-arthāv-iva saṁpṛiktau...jagataḥ pitarau...Pārvatī-Parameśvarau)* but also the graceful *līlā* of the Almighty. The first represents an aspect of Viṣṇu, while the second that of Śiva, or more appropriately that of Śiva and Śakti. Thus the artists who conceived the plan of placement of images seem to have worked it out beforehand in conformity with the then prevailing concept of various forms of Viṣṇu and Śakti as aspects of the same godhead, who in the present case is Āditya.

The only sculpture depicting a deity on outer face of a verandah pillar is a unique six-armed Śiva, probably conceived as Lakulīśa (3).[10] He carries *varadahasta* (boon-conferring gesture), *paraśu* (battle-axe), *sarpa* (?, snake not clear) and a *kamaṇḍalu* (water jug), while with the remaining two hands he appears to be subduing two demonic forces. The *kirīṭamukuṭa* that crowns the deity, instead of *jaṭāmukuṭa* prescribed for Śiva, makes this image the most unusual. Otherwise he is a *vyāghra-charmāṁbara* and *urdhvaliṅgin* standing in *samapāda* on *apasmāra*. It needs to be seen if aspects of Śiva (attributes, listed above), Āditya (perhaps equated with Viṣṇu; attribute, *kirīṭamukuṭa)* and Brahmā (attribute, *kamaṇḍalu)* are assimilated in this figure to produce a new syncretic deity. In that case the chastised figures could symbolize darkness (ignorance), being dispelled by the advent of the Sun god.

Mithuna or *daṁpati* sculptural reliefs occupy most pillar faces. Those occupying outer faces of verandah pillars along the northern flank of the abutting porch (12-20) contain *daṁpatis* invariably under trees, and may be designated as *Śṛiṅgāra-mithunas.* They contain diverse stylistic presentation. Some (16-20) (pl. 22.10) leave no doubt as to the hand of master craftsmen brought up in situations where *Yoga* based religious systems had strong bases, such as the early Pāśupata caves of Ellorā of the Great Cave at Elephaṇṭā, or even the caves of the Buddhists under the spell of Yogic philosophy as at Aurangabad, all pertaining to *Śramaṇic* tradition; however, chronologically these precede the Durgā temple *daṁpatis.* The voluptuous but introvert dames in some of these *daṁpati* figures stand in a style, posture, gesture and mood that in no way differs from the famous *Vajrasphoṭā* in Cave VII at Aurangabad. The *puruṣa* too stands in the typical triple-flexion posture and introvert mood that have direct parallels in the huge *dvārapālas* and deities of early Ellorā and Elephaṇṭā,[11] noticed also in Cave II *dvārapālas* at Bādāmi. Noteworthy also from this point of view is the typical broad *jaṭāmukuṭa*-like headgear of the *puruṣa*. The most dominating aspect of these figures is that both male and female here are conceived as introvert, in union with Self. The style has to be seen to an extent also in the eight-armed Harihara in the *devakoṣṭha* described above, in particular in the detail of *gadā Kaumodakī* figure. The unidentified and weathered four-armed deity (pl. 22.11) in *tribhaṅga*, accompanied by two maids and hosts of flying Vidyādhara pairs carrying garlands or raising their hands in *vismaya* (gesture of glorification), on the other face of the supporting slab-pillar (27) at the apse end of the varandah also subscribes to this very style, repeated in Kuḍaveli Saṅgameśvara (now in Alampur, Andhra Pradesh).[12]

Other *daṁpati* sculptures on this side (12-15) tend to conform to styles whose genesis may perhaps be seen in the post- AD 650. regionalized local idiom (pl. 22.12). They have eyebrows and eyelid lines clearly demarcated, straight gazing eyes, tapering, cylindrical and dwarfed well decorated *kirīṭamukuṭas* briskly inlaid with gems, three-stringed beaded *yajñopavītas* in *mālākāra* fashion, etc. These features may be detected also in the *dvārapāla* (pl. 22.13) occupying the southern face of the pillar at entrance into the temple (11) as also in the 'Chastisement of Chhāyā', relief (pl. 22.14) facing it on the opposite pillar (10), hands that worked the two sculptures were different though. The sculptures on the other faces of the pillars of the southern flank comprise not only *daṁpatis* (5, 6 and 8) but also include such curious themes as *'Yakṣī* seducing *brahmachārī'* (9) (pl. 22.15) and *'brahmachārī* haunted by nude *Aśvamukhī Yakṣī'* (7) (pl. 22.16). The female form in these cases is fleshy, bounteous, voluptuous and dominant, dwarfing the disinterested *brahmachārī*. There is also a beautiful presentation of a *daṁpati* pair of whom the female has a child on her (4). The plump fleshed lady with child on her stands cross-legged, wearing an *ardhoruka* and a hairdo in the manner of a tribal, and looks up at her spouse who holds her left arm (pl. 22.17). All these charming pairs betray masterly calibre, imagination and creative genius on the part of the artists.

The boldly relieved sculptures of *daṁpati* pairs on the faces of pillars of the *mukhamaṇḍapa* inside (21, 22, 25 and 26) differ from those on the verandah pillars. They represent the *āsakta-mithuna* class (pls. 22.18, 22.19) in contrast to the *śṛiṅgāra-mithunas*. Most of these are damaged but lively and charming. In style they conform to a regionalized idiom.

Two short label inscriptions on the temple deserve attention here. One of these found on the *kapota* moulding of the *adhiṣṭhāna* south side, is in Kannaḍa language and Kannaḍa script of 8th century and reads *Śrī-Jinālayan*, the proper name of a craftsman named Jinālaya. His name recurs on a contemporary temple, called Pārvatī temple, at Saṇḍur in Bellary district. It is of twofold importance. First, since it is in Kannaḍa, it suggests an artist of the Kannaḍa region. Secondly, its recurrence at another place suggests movement of artists. Noteworthy is also the fact that the style of the pillar sculptures found on southern side of the temple verandah conforms essentially to a regionalized idiom. The second inscription is in *Siddhamātṛikā* characters (which later on gave rise to the *Nāgarī* script) of 8th century and Sanskrit language and it is found on the east face of a verandah pillar on the north flank of the porch. It reads *Śrī-Surendrapādaḥ,* the proper name of a craftsman named Surendrapāda. Like the above inscription it is of twofold importance. Firstly, since it is in Sanskrit language and *Siddhamātṛikā* script, it suggests that the artist came from a region outside the Kannaḍa-speaking area, apparently northern Deccan, for the Chalukyas preferred Kannaḍa script for even Sanskrit inscriptions, including copperplate records. Secondly, it suggests the movement of artists from elsewhere to participate in the ambitious project of building, the Durgā temple. It may not be without significance that most pillar sculptures in northern Deccan style, including the Harihara referred to above, are found on this flank of the temple. Like the temple and its sculptures, these inscriptions suggest heterogeneous artist groups cooperating consciously on the project.

The above review should make it clear that the Durgā temple though dedicated to god Āditya contains less of *Saura* imagery and presents more of an imagery comprising forms of Śiva, Viṣṇu and Śakti and syncretic forms like Harihara and Ardhanārī. The reason for want of *Saura* imagery is understandable: there are only few popular myths and iconographic forms of this deity. These have found placement in appropriate and significant situations on the temple: a standing two-armed Āditya with lotuses in hands in the miniature shrine arch *(chandaraśālā* motif) in the architrave over doorframe of the *gūḍhamaṇḍapa;* a similar miniature form (facing west) with *Saura-dvārapālas* on the inner face of the architrave of the *mukhamaṇḍapa* entrance; 'Sūrya chastising Chhāyā theme' on the north face of the pillar at the entrance into the temple and facing the *gadā*-bearing *dvārapāla* on the opposite pillar; a possible standing Sūrya image in the empty central *devakoṣṭha* of the aspe part; an unfinished seated two-armed Sūrya once adorning the *śukanśa* of the temple; and a seated two-armed Sūrya in the trefoil arch over the *pratolī* (gate-house) on the south side of the temple.[13] There seems to be an equation of Āditya and Brahmā in the placement of a three-faced standing Brahmā figure within the miniature shrine motif and an Āditya figure in the *chandraśālā* arch motif (acting like a dummy *śukanāśa)* on the same shrine motif in the architrave over the doorway of the *gūḍhamaṇḍapa*. The equation is well founded as Brahmā is *Hiraṇyagarbha* (golden egg). The inclusion of a good number of forms of the other major deities, viz., Śiva and Viṣṇu implies a conscious attempt to identify them with god Āditya. This probably hints at the context of the Durgā temple. The temple was conceived at a time when a new wave of Pāśupata Śaivism was rampant in the core areas of the Chalukya territory in Andhra-Karnataka. Its force and manifestation are discerned in the numerous temples that cropped up in centres like Ālaṁpur, Mahākūṭa and Paṭṭadakal and no less in Aihoḷe itself. It appears to be a development from the middle of the 7th century. In AD 659 Vikramāditya I, as recorded in his Āmūḍalapāḍu plates[14] and apparently unable to ignore the force of this Pāśupata Śaiva wave, became a Pāśupata Śaiva votary ritually by taking *Śivamaṇḍala-dīkshā.* Judging from the nature of the Śaiva monuments particularly at Ālaṁpur and Paṭṭadakal, this sect though it accorded Śiva the central place allowed liberally for presenting Vaiṣṇava imagery that would otherwise stand testimony to greatness of Viṣṇu. The ceilings of most temples depicted prominently images of Brahmā, Śiva and Viṣṇu with Śiva always at the centre. In the Virūpākaṣa temple (AD 733-744) at Paṭṭadakal the chief (east) *mukhamaṇḍapa* ceiling carries a gorgeously treated image of Āditya on chariot and a corresponding inscription prefers to describe the *mukhamaṇḍapa* as *Ādityagṛiha* (house, i.e. shrine, of Āditya) instead of *mukhamaṇḍapa.* Thus there is a forceful suggestion in these Śaiva monuments that the sect treated the Trinity (which can be Brahmā, Śiva and Viṣṇu, or Surya, Śiva and Viṣṇu) on par or accepted them as aspects of Śiva performing the three-fold deeds of creation, sustenance and destruction. Later on, at least from the 10th century to the 14th, the Pāśupata Śaiva *āchāryas,* who expressly claimed *Lākula āgamas* as their religious manuals, virtually flooded northern part of Karnataka with temples of *Trimūrtis,* called *Traipuruṣas* in epigraphs. The *Traipuruṣa* temples, which were usually *trikūṭa* (triple-shrine) temples, enshrined images of Brahmā, Viṣṇu and Śiva or Āditya, Viṣṇu and Śiva, the latter combination being preferred in most cases. An early Chalukya precedent for this may be seen in the triple-shrine temple of Brahmā, Viṣṇu and Maheśvara erected in AD 699 at the request of Vinayavatī by emperor Vijayāditya at Bādāmi, the capital. I should suggest also in this context that the appearance in plenty of the temples of northern *Latina* form in Karnataka during this period has a nexus with this new Pāśupata wave. It is in this context that the Durgā temple, its form, its imagery, the style of its imagery and the like should to be seen. Though it cannot be branded as a Pāśupata work, it reflects that the *Saura* votaries shared with contemporary Pāśupatas the ideology of equality and inevitability of the Trinity.

NOTES AND REFERENCES

1. The temple was first noticed as the 'Śaivite' temple of 'lwullee' in a collection of photographs by Colonel Briggs sometime in mid 19th century. These were included in the work entitled *Architecture in Dharwad and Mysore* published in 1866 from London by Meadows Taylor and James Fergusson.
2. Gary Michael Tartakov, *The Durgā Temple at Aihole : A Historiographical Study*, Delhi, 1997.
3. Shrinivas Padigar, "The Durgā Temple at Aihole: An Āditya Temple", *Archaeological Studies*, Vol. II, Mysore, 1977, pp.59-64.
4. Scholars have floated the view that because the temple is within the fort and in the proximity of the fort wall, the temple has acquired its name 'Durga temple', meaning 'Fort temple'. But the facts that to obtain that meaning in the vernacular the form of the world has to be *'Durgada-guḍi'* and that the term *"Durga"* in the sense of a fort is scarcely in use in the northern part of Karnataka where its vernacular equivalent *'koṭe'* (colloquially *kvāṭi*, in which case the word form would be *kvāṭi-guḍi* for 'fort temple') is widely current has been grossly overlooked by them. When I launched my study of this temple during the latter half of 1970s the villagers still preferred to call it *'Durgī-guḍi'*, or *'Durgā-guḍi'*, meaning 'temple of goddess Durgā'. The only deity in the temple with which the villagers were well acquainted and which they could easily identify was the one of Durgā Mahiṣamardinī in the *devakoṣṭha*, the 'living' goddess 'Durgā', colloquially 'Durgi'. For that goddess is a popular deity in countryside even today.
5. Shrinivas Padigar, *op.cit.*
6. For details, Shrinivas Padigar, "Some Sculptures of Malegittiśivālaya and their identification", *Journal of Karnatak University, Social Sciences*, Vol. XIII (1977), pp.62-64; also G.M. Tartakov, *op.cit.*, p.85.
7. The numbers in brackets (Roman or Arabic) indicate the position of the respective image on the temple shown on the plan.
8. A curious feature observed in images of certain deities is the lotus crown. Gaṇeśa and Narasiṁha in early iconography invariably have this feature. Interestingly both have human body and animal head and in later understanding at least both have acceptance as *jñā-devatās.* The presence of lotus on head therefore appears to signify the *sahasradala-padma* (symbolizing *sahasrāra-chakra)*, located in a crucial position in head, which in *tāntric* perceptions is believed to bloom out in a *jñāni.*
9. J.C. Harle, "Some Remarks on Early Western Chālukyan Sculpture", in P. Pal (ed.), *Aspects of Indian Art*, Leiden, 1972, pp.65-69.
10. For illustration see G.M. Tartakov, *op.cit.*, pl. 51. Susan Buchanan identifies this as *Śiva Bhikṣāṭana* attacked by *Ṛishis* in pine forest; cited by G.M. Tartakov, *op.cit.*, p.84.
11. For illustrations of Elephaṇṭā see George Michell, O'Flaherty and C. Berkson, *Elephanta: The cave of Śiva*, Delhi, 1983.

12. Carol R. Bolon, "The Durgā Temple, Aihoḷe, and the Saṅgameśvara temple, Kuḍaveli: A Sculptural Review", in *Arts Orientalis*, Vol. XV (1985), pp.47-64.
13. The reader is referred to G.M. Tartakov, *op[. cit.*, for illustrations of these subjects. The ceiling in the *mukhamaṇḍapa* carries sculptured reliefs of Nāgarāja (whose sculptural style has been equated with that of Subrahmaṇya on peacock in the *mukhamaṇḍapa* of Huchchimalliguḍi at Aihoḷe by C.R. Bolon, *op.cit.)* (position 'a' on plan) and *matsya-chakra* solar symbol (position 'b' on plan). There were also fine flying *Vidyādhara mithunas* of which one is preserved (position 'c' on plan).
14. *Epigraphia Indica,* Vol. XXXII, pp.98-102.

Late Prof. K.D. Bajpai Memorial Lecture

Indian Art : Some Issues

Kapila Vatsyayan

President of the Indian Art History Congress, Dr. M.L. Nigam, distinguished Vice-Presidents and the Secretary-General of the Indian Art History Congress Dr. R.D. Choudhury, eminent scholars and young art historians present here.

Allow me to thank you for the singular honour you have bestowed upon me by inviting me to deliver the K.D. Bajpai Memorial Lecture. Prof. K.D. Bajpai's contributions to the field of Indian studies generally and archaeology is of great importance. He discovered many new sites, provided the basis of understanding many aspects of regional architecture and sculpture. All these studies were of great value because Prof. K.D. Bajpai combined in himself the knowledge of Indian texts, the exacting techniques of archaeology and a perceptive insight into artistic traditions. I pay my respectful tribute to him. Like many others of his generation, he was a polymath combining many disciplines. Over these years while there has been greater specialization, sometimes this has been at the cost of not having a full peripheral vision of the material studied.

When Dr. R.D. Choudhury requested me to deliver the lecture, I asked him if he had any particular subject or field in mind. Graciously he responded that he would leave this to me. I suggested a few titles, e.g. Whither Indian Art History? Indian Art History Beyond Chronology, and perhaps one or two others. I could have taken the comparatively easier path to speak about either the inter-relationship of the Indian Arts or the Gita Govinda, the two themes I have perused with some tenacity over these decades. However, I did not suggest either of these because whatever little I have done in these areas is perhaps known to some if not all of you. There are many areas yet to be explored in regard to both these themes. I am aware of the vast expanse which has opened up. I chose to speak about the state of scholarship in the discipline of Art History today because perhaps it is time to overview the several concurrent and often contradictiory positions which have taken place in respect of both the discipline of Art History as also the methodologies which have been employed in a critical appraisal and interpretation of the 'materials', be in architectural edifices, sculptural remains, paintings or other objects. Also, I thought it may be pertinent to pursue the very important issues which were raised by Prof. M.A. Dhaky in his most perceptive address at the Hyderabad conference.

First and foremost, the question of 'Art History' as an autonomous discipline continues to be a subject of debate. Undoubtedly, there are half a dozen departments of the History of Art and a few institutions in India. There is a lurking scepticism by the archaeologist, anthropologist, historian, sociologist, literature scholar, even aesthetician, whether there is any indisputable necessity for such a discipline. The archaeologist, anthropologist, the historian and sociologist and literary savant, have all dealt with, or deal with, a body of expression of the human mind individually or collectively called 'art', therefore it is argued that since cultural or artistic expression penetrates all dimensions and many disciplines, 'art-history' is redundant or at best a misnomer. This has been a central argument in not according priority to the discipline of 'art-history' within the Indian University system. There has been a marked resistence from the departments of archaeology, history, anthropology, sociology and even philosophy alike. This I know from my personal involvement in the debates at the policy level over decades. Be that as it may, it is today accepted as a separate and distinctive discipline to be pursued with rigour and precision. So, then, what is Art History, specially in the Indian context, as distinct from the disciplines mentioned above, not to mention 'religion' and 'theology'? A concentrated attention to the question will make it clear that although individuals and societies are situated in linear time and are subject to the inner dynamics of reflection, they express themselves in diverse ways, forms and styles. The social structure, the patronage or the lack of it, undoubtedly condition or affect the nature of the 'experience', but the expression, the art piece, be in monument, sculpture, painting or for that matter music or dance, its ultimate efficacy lies in its power to encapsulate all dimensions of life in a 'single-whole'. It is the art piece or art expression which has the in-built capacity of polyvalent multilayered meaning and significance. The artistic expression thus, although situated in time and in specific time and place, is the symbiosis of the historical, social, ideational, symbolic into a single meaningful whole, which transcends all these dimensions beyond time and place.

A comprehension of the processes by which the 'experience' takes form or significant form has to take into account many dimensions and not any single dimension. Art History thus in its very nature has to be multidimensional and multilayered. It has to address itself to all that is not only embedded in the particular manifestation, but also much that is around it, behind it, all that was before it. While the artistic expression is the work of an individual or a group of individuals, it is affected by the socio-cultural context, the patron or the occasion, and is part and parcel either in agreement or in opposition to the contemporary discourse. The artist or creator imbibes both consciously and unconsciously the 'ideas' inherited and makes an attempt to give shape and form and voice in a style and mode which evokes 'response', positive or negative, both in time and place and beyond it. The ultimate value of artistic creation is its potentiality to communicate beyond the specificity of time-place context. In turn, the artistic creation affects life at many dimensions, and Art History has thus to be that enterprise which can carefully sift these many dimensions and levels of the artistic work and yet focus attention to the power of the artistic creation to communicate at many levels both of meaning and form. No single discipline, be it of archaeology or history, anthropology, sociology, linguistics or prosody, philosophy or metaphysics or cosmology can be used as a 'tool' for comprehending the apparently simple and spontaneous act of art creation. Indeed it is the unmanifested complexity which accounts for the apparent simplicity and beauty of the manifested art creation. While it may not be particularly fruitful to provide a new definition to Art History, it would be relevant to state that artistic creation and its history or dynamics, cannot be considered an appendage or sub-division of any of the disciplines mentioned above.

In the Indian context underlining this inherent multidimensionality and polyvalence is particularly important, because the critical discourse on art and its history has had a legacy of being inextricably linked with archaeology or political history or being comprehended only against a never-changing perennial tradition of seminal principles and metaphysical preoccupations.

This fact is more than evident if we pause for a minute to overview the nature of discourse in Indian art since the nineteenth century or early twentieth century. From a perusal of the literature it becomes clear that while on the one hand the concern of the art historian could hardly be distinguished from the archaeologist in respect of identification of dates, provenance and establishment of linear chronologies, on the other there was the assertion of some perennial metaphysical ideas which sought to be identified in all forms of art in the Indian tradition. This history is well known to the historiographers of Indian Art History and has been outlined by Pramod Chandra on the studies in Indian Art, 1983, and by Bhuvanendran in his book *Interpretations of Indian Art*, Delhi, 1995 and by Gary Michael Tartakov

(1994). From another point of view Partha Mitter has brilliantly traced the history of European response to Indian Art in his popular and much quoted book *Much Maligned Monsters: A History of European Reactions to Indian Art* as far back as 1977. I do not therefore have to recount the history of either the contributions of Fergusson, Cunningham or Burgess or Cousens, for that matter the continuation of the tradition in Indian archaeologists, ranging from Dayaram Sahani, Hirananda Shastri to Banerjee, C., N.R. and P. or A. Ghosh, or Vasudev Saran Agrawala and C. Sivaramamurti to an extent. All these persons were primarily archaeologists or epigraphists, but what distinguished the Europeans from the Indians of this century was the latter's command over one or more Indian languages. So while one group of scholars attempted to reconstruct the past through material remains, the other added to this both inscriptional evidence and other literary evidence. The focus of both groups with varying degrees of emphasis was on the identification of dates and the establishment of chronologies. Vasudeva Saran Agrawala and Sivaramamurti were different in many ways but that we will come to later. Dating and establishment of chronologies and identification of provenance became a central concern by and large not only of the archaeologist but also of the art historian. Often, though not always, the art historian considered or still considers his task accomplished once he/she has been able to place the art creation in a chronological sequence, ascribe particular dates and locate provenance of the objects not *in situ*. I do not have to give specific examples of this approach, which continues to dominate the field to this day. While archaeological evidence supported by literary evidence is an essential pre-requisite, it cannot be the final aim of the art historian. M.A. Dhaky most effectively drew attention to this when he remarked in his presidential address at the Hyderabad conference.

But an exclusively archaeological approach is not intrinsic to, nor is it a prime objective of the discipline of history of art. As a result, the classificatory, nomenclatural, and metrographical aspects of buildings, and iconographical/icononomical, even iconological considerations for sculptures or for that matter the pigments, the techniques, the typology of attires of human figures and accoutrements of animal figures and related matters in paintings, lose centrality and become somewhat secondary in importance even when they can never be neglected since they provide firm fixtures for the art historical constructs. They are auxiliary agents but not the ultimate determinants in the domain of history of art.

It is of course known that, against the political, socio-religious and ethnological background, the generative factors and processes which led in the past to the manifestations of regional and period styles of art and architecture, the style's origins, evolution, culmination, degeneration and decay (or in some instances abrupt termination) usually are the basic concerns for an art historian. Next in order are their special visual features, qualitative/expressive aspects, and of course their interrelationships, interactions and cross-currents which lead to the sharing of elements or to the influx or radiation of influences, be they superficial or deeper; these are some of the major aspects involved which today engage the minds of most historians of art. This is particularly so for those who are schooled in the 'classical' Western academic methodology of investigation. As art history uses archaeology, art interpretation—or for that matter art criticism—often uses art history, even if at times minimally, as its basal structure. And next, depending on the one hand on author's perceptions, predilections or proclivities, and on the other hand on the qualitative aspects of the object discussed, the approach leans either toward aesthetics, or to core-concepts, in some cases also searches the metaphysical meanings inherently present or reflected, be it incidentally or accidentally, in the formulations and visual manifestations of art and architecture. In some cases, there can be textual authority to back it. In some art historical writings, history of art and art interpretation are interlaced and rolled into a single undifferentiated whole, a happening which often consequences in highly readable, enjoyable as well as memorable, instructive and enduring pieces of writing. (In a few cases, the newer approaches to art-understanding lead to the fresh vistas of looking at art, the very thinking in the history of art somewhat changes and consequently new concepts have emerged).

In contradistinction has been the view point of another group who has focussed attention on the metaphysical and even philosophic ideas which are relevant for understanding the value of the art piece. This approach also has a long and complex history. Today the evaluation of the work of E.B. Havell, A.K. Coomaraswamy, Mercia Ghade and Sri Aurobindo and the later writing of Vasudev Saran Agrawala has to be viewed against the background of the history of the European reaction and response not only to Indian art, but more—Indian Civilization, culture and philosophy. The critical evalution of these scholars, none of whom can be termed as professorial art historians because they were more, has to take into account the then prevailing debates on Indian civilization and its values and its world view. If at times their stance was assertive in affirming the perennial and the metaphysical, it has to be appreciated that they too were responding in one manner or another to the scathing attacks on the nature of Indian art by Europeans. I do not have to recount the history of the exchanges between Sri Aurobindo, Birdwood, Cole, Smith and others. The next generation of scholars or slightly younger scholars, then specially Stella Kramrisch and later Alice Boner, despite their careful and insightful analysis of 'form', have been grouped along with the 'essentialists' and 'symbolists', while this is far from the whole truth in respect of either Stella Kramrisch or Alice Boner, their names need to be mentioned only to clarify the differences in the two approaches. We must remember that the approaches often interpenetrate and are not insular categories.

The point that I am trying to make is that Indian Art History and its discourse has been entangled with the history of establishing a chronology of history of India and of articulating an Indian 'metaphysics' and world view, both linked with the scholarship of the European/or West on India. This is a historical baggage we still carry in respect of both chronology as also assessments on what may be terned as an Indic world view. Naturally, in evaluation thus we have the polarities of a Fergusson and A.K. Coomaraswamy both in terms of chronology as also critical appraisal. One group tried to evaluate all Indian Art with the yardstick and the subscription to a linear progressive path with a clear cut movement of evolution, development and degeneration, and the other sought to identify the special nature of this art from the point of view of world view, metaphysics and 'symbolism'. Implicit in the first was comparison with Europe, explicit in the second was distinctiveness.

While the differences in these two viewpoints have been the subject of dissension and there is a recent critique of the second viewpoint by some younger scholars as amounting to the reconstruction of a nationalist agenda (see Partha Mitter's text Tapati section, and Gulia Thukarta's work on the Bengal school). Perhaps there has not been an equal sensitivity to identifying the basic categories of 'thought' and perception in different cultures. If the first group tried to evaluate Indian art though the application of Greco-Roman parameters and later of medieval European Art, the second group including Havell and Coomaraswamy to an extent also tried to evalute Indian art through a comparison with other traditions. The journey of A.K. Coomaraswamy from his early writing to the last essays was a complex one. This is not the occasion to traverse that ground. I have tried to do this in my essays on A.K. Coomaraswamy in the Lalit Kala Akademi publication, as also my forewords in the reprint series of the IGNCA publications. Pramod Chandra has also traced his trajectory in a convincing manner. Even for his vehement critics his contribution to the field of Indian Art History is a milestone of the greatest importance. It would be incorrect to confine evaluation of his work as only the metaphysical and symbolic or, as an eminent scholar recently points out, his Christian bias, overlooking his contribution to the understanding Indian architecture, sculpture and painting. It was he who first drew attention to the humble beginnings of early Indian architecture and to the evidence of architectural edifices in the Bharhut reliefs. *The History of Indian and Indonesian Art* laid the foundations of a chronology based not only on archaeology but also artistic principles and it was he who spearheaded the debate on the Indian origins of the Buddha image. He was the first to distinguish Mughal painting from Rājput, even if we have learnt much about Pahāri paintings as a separate genre with sub-schools. These were not merely metaphysical speculations and application of abstract principles to concrete form. They were grounded in acute observation and analysis of the artistic form in a historical perspective. One would respectfully have to differ from Partha Mitter's evaluation in his otherwise brilliantly argued analysis of the history of the discourse on Indian Art History. I mention this because I find that a school of younger scholars has been trained to overlook some of these contributions as pointed out by M.A. Dhaky. To my mind some younger scholars have essentialized the contribution of A.K. Coomaraswamy and even Stella Kramrisch in their enthusiasm for an unidimensional socio-political understanding of the monument, the sculptural piece or painting schools.

It was important to take this brief look back before focussing attention again on the interdisciplinary and multidisciplinary nature of Indian Art History as a discipline.

In any case nearly five decades or more have passed since the writing of *History of Indian and Indonesian Art* (1927) and the *Hindu Temple* (1946) and there has been considerable expansion of the fields and sub-fields. Both Indian and a significant number of foreign scholars have explored both new areas as also new approaches, beyond the discourse of 'Orientalism', foreign-Indian, Aryan Dravidian and neat categorization of periods into Ancient, Medieval and Modern, etc.

Art as I said is not unilinear one-dimensional. Any attempt to draw up purely linear graphs in the basis of neat catagories set up by historians is not likely to be an entirely successful excercise in evaluating artistic excellence or for that matter identifying development. This is evident in some recent writing on tracing the historiography of the assessment of the Durgā temple in Aihole and in respect of Ajanta and Ellora. Pertinently the scholars have pointed out the aspects of overlap of historical periods. Also, as we know the periodisation of Indian history has undergone many changes both on account of the discovery of new evidence, as also radical differences of perception and opinion, now even in ideology. The question before the art historian is whether he or she will accept one or the other school of historians for evaluating the art creation, or will use his discretion and distinct tools of analysis and interpretation of another order. While it is time that the art historian builds on the archaeologist and the historians' primary data, the art work can often transcend the confines of archaeological or historical importance. Also, it is only in the realm of art one can discern the possibility of a creative dialogue between and amongst dogma or prescriptive rules. The dynastic categories of Indian Art and pure watertight compartmentalization of historical periodisation have proved inadequate.

For the art historian they are the springboards of enquiry but not the enquiry itself of the artistic creation, singly or in a collectivity in a site.

The purely historical approach and confining discussions and critical discourse within the confines of dynasty and period is as delimiting as the approach to analyse all art creation on the basis of the patrons' taste and predilections. Often the art historian has forgotten that in the last analysis it was the artist and the craftsman who was the creator even if he was comissioned, governed by the dictates of the patron. Several recent studies have focused attention only on the patron to the exclusion of artists' prediliection. This is then not the history of art, it is the history of the religio-political-social history of the patrons. This is one dimension to be taken into account but not the only one.

The historical dynamic framework has also given rise to a greater consideration within the domain of art-history to socio-political movements, sometimes called mass movements or dynamics of social change and issues of power, enforcement and oppression, and now gender issues. This is indeed a welcome development. Many recent studies on regional schools styles have been correlated to socio-political movements as also voices of revolt, reform and dissent. While artistic creation and the artist is certainly a participator in the dynamics of social change, it remains to be proved that all artists in all eras and cases reflext this. The purely sociological approach begins with a hypothesis outside the piece of art and then endeavours to assess the artistic creation to social movements. While this may be applicable to some aspects of modern Indian art, it may not enable the art historian to comprehend the totality of miniature painting, sculpture of architecture of all periods. To cite only one outstanding example of the difference of perception and analysis in the recent past in respect of power, is the on-going debate between Dr. Champakalakshmi and Dr. Nagaswamy on the appearance of the Tripurāṅtaka figure in the Brahadesvara temple, as also the repeated reference to Dakṣinamurty. While one scholar interprets it at the level of Indian myth and Śaivite ritual, the other sees it as an expression of the assertion of power. A more comprehensive view of the art historian would be to see the scheme of visual imagery of the Brahadesvara temple at all levels of the conceptual, metaphysical, religious as also political and social. The temple no doubt is situated in time, i.e. Raja Raja Chola, and is an intrinsic part of the rise of the Chola kingdom. It is an important socio-political statement in respect of the alignment of the temple complex and the city plan. Nevertheless, the temple has an undeniable presence, as a replication of the cosmos on earth. It is indeed the replication of the concept of Mahā Meru, and brick, stone by stone, image by image the temple stands as a 'whole', embodying multiple levels of thought and perception. It is the artistic skill of design, layout, geometry, mass and volume which makes this possible. If Ganapati Sthapati understands the temple as representing the three *gunas,* from a traditional point of view, and equates the elevation to the three *gunas,* he is neither incorrect nor biased. Ganapati Sthapati's analysis of the Brahadesvara temple comes from a long tradition of sthapatis' comprehension of the temple at the level of ultimate value, symbolism, the several types of coordinates, which are built into the structure. All this is most valuable both from the point of view of the material that he presents as also the attitude of the conceivers of these monuments even if they were dealing with concrete material.This interpretation cannot be discounted. Dr. Nagaswamy speaks of the temple in terms of the concepts of *ākāsa, bhutākāsa* and traces the elevation plan from the level of *bhutākāsa* to *paramākāsa.* Dr. Champakalakshmi on the other hand adopts the methodology of socio-political interpretation and understands the temple as a statement of political power. Now, the question is whether these are contradictory positions or these are multiple levels of understanding a great artistic piece. The answer quite clearly is that the total structure and presence of the temple has to be seen as conceived to communicate different levels simultaneously. This is what gives it a perennial significance. The language of Indian art is in its very structure polyvalent and multidimensional. The challenge before the artist, the conceiver, as also the builder, is how to encapsulate different dimensions from the cosmic, astrological, metaphysical to the social and political. The astronomical significance of the temple has been studied very carefully through modern instrumentation. Thus, the temple can neither be purely metaphysics nor politics.

And finally the structure is enlivened and govern life and breath through a well-structured ritual. Here all the arts have a definite and precise role to play. Any unidimensional understanding of this great piece of art which is neither archaeology nor history would be a partial understanding of the significance of the monument at the level of meaning and form. It was therefore with a purposeful design that as former Academic Director of IGNCA, I conceived of a multidisciplinary integrated project on the Brahadesvara temple, so that all dimensions, material, geometrical, historical, conceptual and ritual should be studied with a view to uncode the grand schema. Some modules were complete, others continue to linger. It was my hope that the function of this project would lay the foundations of a new holistic methodology of Indian Art History. Alas it is incomplete. The multidisciplinary project on Vijayanagar and Hampi and the University of Cambridge and London are other such attempts in this direction.

From history and socio-political movements, let me now turn to interface of art history and anthropology. Just as art history was intrinsically linked to archaeology, it has also been and is related to anthropology. If the archaeologist excavates "sites" and opens the different strata in a given "field", the anthropologist goes into the field to collect data on the human species and does field work. Both are exploring a field, one of the past and the other of the present. And both deal with Art. However, we must remember here that both 'archaeology' and 'anthropology' as disciplines arose in the era of enlightenment and with the growth of colonial power. If archaeology sought to know the past of the ancient world so as to illumine the past of the new world (i.e. Europe then), anthropology was the domain of studying the culture of the 'other', those others, sometimes called primitives world. In short the focus was on the study of the life and customs of those others—the Asian, African and Mesoamerican people. The complex discourse on definitions of civilization itself became relevant. There would not be time dwell upon this. However, in this case also Indian anthropology carries the baggage to a large extent. Indian Art History also adapted a similar if not identical view. The art historian seems to have been conditioned by the history of the establishment of the Archaeological Survey of India and the Anthropological Survey as institutions in India. Thus the two disciplines thus hardly ever met. While archaeologists looked at archaeological remains and reconstructed the past, the anthropologist looked at 'tribes' (those others) in the mistaken belief that their past was not of any great consequence or related to archaeological monuments. Also, except for the very recent past, anthropology continued itself to study of those others, the tribes, and communities normally considered outside the normative structure of Indian society classified either as 'castes' or on the basis of denominational classification of Hindus, Muslims, Parsis, Christians, etc. The 'Orientalism' view was evident. The results of these classificatory system were far-reaching when extended to the domain of artistic creation. On the one hand it led to categorizing classical and folk on the basis of either 'time' bracket or category of artist, and on the other it viewed the art of so-called tribal India, later extended to rural India as insulated and separate from the classical high tradition. Now it is well known that Sanchi reliefs were the work of ivory carvers, and that the terracottas of Kosambi or, for that matter, Śuṅga art can be made in perfection by the modern craftmen. Stella Kramrisch pertinently gave the appellation 'dateless art' and 'dated art'. It was the anthropologist and the social scientist who propounded the theory of the great and little traditions, and many Indian art historians with notable exceptions accepted the classificatory system. The Museums continued to follow the divisions of archaeology and history and reluctantly included anthropological galleries in museums of art, when some continued to believe that they should continue in the museums of natural history and ethnology.

Here, too, the acceptance of interpretative categories of European discourse on Indian society was evident and continues to be unquestioned by and large.

Thus it will be conceded it was restrictive if not inimical when extended to the field of art history as it was disrespectful in a manner of speaking to groups of people called 'tribes'. They were not and are not those 'others' reserves of mono cultures, they were and are those who have provided an unparalleled continuity and vitality to artistic creation in India. Indeed they and their art are givers of an Indian identity which we acknowledge indirectly by appropriating the exquisite creativity as 'craft' for decorating ourselves and our homes. The anthropological categorization of material culture, value-culture, the division into tribes and sub-tribes, left little room for a further comprehension of a unique, pervasive and vital stream of the Indian artistic tradition. A large body of this art in all its variety, diversity and yet Indian identity was for the most part excluded from the discourse on Indian Art or Art History per se. At best the art historian spoke of 'folkish or tribal elements'. This is still evident in many critical studies. No, or little, attempt is made to explore the connection between the artistic expressions of what is concerned high art and folk and tribal art. There is indeed a connection, an area which demands further exploration. Prioritization has only been given when individual creativity is recognized as in the case of paintings of Gangadevi from Madhubani and others from Manipur. In a recent presentation by Jyotindra Jain, some years ago, this was clear evidence why it became necessary to use the term, 'the other traditions. Impressive and deeply moving as the show was, the emphasis was on proving individual creativity in, what has so far been termed largely as the anonymous tradition. Convincing and commendable no doubt, but equally important continues to be the necessity to link the so-called anthropological art (the dateless) with what is concerned the mainstream classical art, or high art. The interpretation between and amongst these is of great significance in a country with long continuities of cultural patterns and an active dialogue between different strata of society. There were many different currents of such dialogue which manifested themselves in the artistic creations both of what are called classical arts, those others called folk and tribal. Elsewhere, in the context of the performing arts, I have interrogated the classification and resultant insularity in critical discourse. Also, the oral tradition and contemporary practice may well illumine the historical.

A very important case in point is the tradition of *dhulicitra*. In the field of textual studies we are aware of the mention of the tradition of *dhulicitra* both in the north as also south. While there are earlier references specially in Someshwara's work of the *abhilāsitārthacintāmanī* (Manasollasa) of

Someshwara, there is a detailed description in the Kerala text of Sri Kumar, viz., *Śilparatna*. It is also mentioned in *Narad Shilpa*. However, we know the study of *dhulicitra* has been restricted to the field of crafts and what are called folk and tribal arts. In Kerala there is a very distinct and a highly developed tradition of what is called by the generic name ' *Kolam*'. This is quite distinct from the other traditions such as *Alpanā* in Bengal and *Sanghi* in North India particularly Vrindavan. Now, as we know, the *Kolams* are made by a class of people who are generally at a lower level of social hierarchy. This is not a complete statement because many people are required, ranging from the Namboodiri to the Kurups to others. The entire ritual is a complex artistic whole. Our understanding of the tradition of Ayyappan and Bhagawati Kolams, their making as also the ultimate dissolution of the artistic work has been studied in the field of anthropology and social studies. It has not been considered, naturally, as an aspect requiring the traditional art historian's concern. However, if we pause to study this contemporary ritual carefully, we will be immediately struck by the fact that what has been executed by the artists of folk, or tribal artists we call them, is in fact a continuation of the traditions of Kerala mural paintings of Vadakkanathan, Wadakkancheri, Padmanabhapuram and others. The question at the critical level to be asked is whether we will classify the murals within the precincts of the temple as folk or tribal or call the contemporary practice of making of the *Kolam*, its consecration ritual and performance as classical. Any in-depth understanding of both the murals and the contemporary practice will show dynamics of interaction and the non-insularity of the social context. There is room here for major modifications both in approaches as also methodologies of the study of some aspects of Indian art. Some years ago, Clifford James had drawn attention and in a recent volume Balan Nambiar, a modern artist, has drawn attention to the contemporary practice and its relevance to modern art. In my own little way I have written fairly extensively on the forms of Mudiuyettu both in relation to the nature of the performing art as also the nature of what can be called visual culture of a highly-stratified Kerala society.

In another context, Joanna Williams was drawn to the study of the contemporary practice both as attitudes as also technniques of the *pat* painting of Orissa. She has made some very interesting observations on contemporary practice which illumines our understanding of Orissan miniature paintings. There are other areas also.

At another level an extreme and brilliantly successful case is of a very distinguished American scholar Dr. lrene Winter who observed the rituals at Vrindavan temple and used the documentation of her fieldwork to reconstruct the ritual context of the archaeological remains of Ur. These are positive areas of further work both within a cultural area or for cross-cultural studies. Of late there has been a welcome attempt to employ one discipline to illumine the other. Art historians are often encouraged to look at their material often decontextualized and not encouraged to observe contemporary life function and art practices of communities, perhaps an exposure with methodology would help.

Having spoken about the interdisciplinary nature of art history, let me now turn my attention not to the archaeology, history, social structure, the social status of the artist, but to the work of 'art', the object, the final expressions, to move from the outside and around the artistic creation to the inside, be it architecture, sculpture or painting, or for that matter all that we term as decorative, again following the classification.

Since I have taken the example of Brahadesvara temple to illustrate one issue, let me draw attention to the phenomenon of sculptural reliefs or a piece of sculpture, stone or bronze to identify the many levels and dimensions of a single sculptural figure. First and foremost, the art historian asks the question of meaning or the theme in short context. Now this context except in the case of 'portraiture' in Indian painting is mostly a-historical. It is either myth or 'narrative' or a literary text which provides the clue to meaning and identification of content. Buddhist Jātakas, Jain texts, Purāṇas, Kāvyas and *nātak* or lyrical poetry or historical texts—*Baburnāmā, Akbarnāmā.* The history of identification of meaning and content has been understandably a major preoccupation of the art historian. All scholars from the most erudite to the novice have been compelled to go beyond titling, to identification of the literary source for a fuller comprehension of the visual 'text' as constructed by the artist in two dimensional or three dimensional form, line, colour, mass volume proposition. Often, not always, just as dating and establishing of chronology becames a final goal, so also identification of 'theme' and possible literary source becomes a final goal of the art historians' critical appraisal. This in itself is not an easy excercise, as is evident from the recent article of Dr. N.P. Joshi in *Kalā* entitled 'Purāṇas as Interpreters of Icons'. Scholars of the eminence of Dr. Vasudev Saran Agrawala, Dr. Motichandra, Dr. C. Sivaramamurti were deeply steeped in literary texts in Sanskrit, Pali, Prakrit, and could with felicity make the one to one co-relation. Even with them there was room for difference of opinion, as I know as a student of Vasudev Saran Agrawala. I have been a silent listener to the many stimulating discourses between Vasudev Saranjee, C. Sivaramamurti and Motichandra. What I learnt, and which continues to be valid for the art-historian of today, is that there has to be cultivation of unceasing curiosity in not only keenly observing the visual image, but an equal perseverance and ability in pursuing the trajectory of the variations in the development of a particular narrative, myth or even theme. There are more than one version, and in course of time many accretions and interpretations. To co-relate the version, identification of the text with the particular piece of sculptural relief or a stone or bronze image precisely is a difficult and certainly a task of perseverance. With notable exceptions (e.g. P.K. Agrawala) the younger generation, perhaps for lack of time or training in access to language, literature or scripts, appear to be somewhat handicapped. I hope I am wrong. Anyway this exercise of identification of text, version over, the art historian's next task is to analyze the relief or the sculptural image. In the case of reliefs ranging from Bharhut to Amravati and some of the Chalukya temples, commendable work has been done on how time and space move within the visual text. Two excerpts amongst others may be cited, i.e. Vidya Dehejia's and Rattan Parimoo's. Adopting very different approaches and methodological tools, the scholars have succeeded in identifying the processes at work within the art piece of dealing with time-space place. A.K. Coomaraswamy and Stella Kramrisch in their different ways had drawn attention to the Indian artists' techniques of dealing with multiplicity of human forms, relative importance rather than perceptive. The scholars of this generation have gone further in tracing the different methods of dealing with time and movement within a specified sculptural field. Both these and some others have gone beyond identification of text and linear time to point multiple orders of time-space within the same frame. Dr. Parimoo has extended his interest to Indian painting specially Sahibudin's *Rāmāyana*, judging from his highly insightful article in *Kalā*.

From identification of theme, literary source and also juxtaposing rough dates of text and image, the art historians' concern has been with style and school, region and sub-regions, and finally to the question of the sculptor or painter. Now, Indian Art History has been concerned for decades on identification of school and style, both to argue specificity and distinctiveness as also intra-regional influences or dialogue. Indeed, 'style' has been considered a very important criterion for 'dating' and chronology, both in respect of sculpture as also architecture. As in the case of text and version, the question of style is not a simple one. It is a fairly vexed one. While a distinctive character is in evidence, in particular monuments and reliefs, and a regional style is in evidence, at no point it appears insular or the changes dramatic.

In recent scholarship there has been a marked enthusiasm for dividing regional characteristics into smaller and smaller geographical or time units. While these microstudies are welcome, sometimes on the basis of isolated pieces of sculpture or single or a few folios of paintings, deduction on the basis of stylistic identification or cultural traits is fraught with some dangers.

Let me however move on to the sculptural image, specially the complex images with seeming simplicity based on or evoked by Indian or more specifically Hindu mythology. The case of the analysis and identification of the most popular and well-known image of the *Naṭarāja* is a case in point. Each *Naṭarāja* image (i.e. the generic term used for Śiva in a movement of the dance) is a visual counterpart of a specific myth which locates the dance in context, i.e. the occasion purpose mode. The art historians again from the days of Coomaraswamy to C. Sivaramamurti to Nagaswamy to others have tried to identify the 'context' of the dance by relating the image to the particular text, the specific Purāna or Tamil source or literary piece, both the questions of where the dance took place and who else was present and what happended during the dance are addressed. Further, the mode of the dance is identified. However, when we look at the image closely, we realize that the artist does not only embody the myth in its generally or specificity but further collapses several myths into the body of a single image. The particular *prabhāmaṇḍale,* the open *jatās* and the *Gaṅgā* poised in the *jatās* are a familiar example, taken altogether too much for granted. No well-known text that most scholars have alluded to speak of Gaṅgā being hidden or sitting demurely in the *jatās* at the time of the dance. Our familiarity with the myth of the descent of the *Gaṅgā* so powerfully articulated in many reliefs including the controversial Bhagirath or Arjuna's penance and with Śiva images as *Gaṅgādhara* is possibly responsible for our overlooking the fact this is the very special ability and dexterity of the artist to collapse one or more myths into a composite whole. Indeed, each part, limb, attribute of the *Naṭarāja* is a window opening to another myth of another aeon or place. Despite the most outstanding and deeply moving and evocative descriptions and analyses of this and other images has not been given sufficient analytical attention on the power of the artist to collapse and encapsulate several texts into a single visual text.

However, let us move further, because the dance is in 'time' and 'space', but also in no time and space. Under the surface propotions and the adherence or departures from the *sastric* prescriptions is a deeper sacred geometry which provides the basis of the powerful impact of the sculptural form. It is at this level of sacred geometry that the work of A.K. Coomaraswamy in some measure and of Alice Boner in a much greater measure becomes important. The unraveling of sacred geometry (overlaid on the fundamental skeleton structure of the *manas, sutra-s* and *bhengas)* has validity and significance. Mercia Ohade had attempted it in respect of Buddhist sculpture, but Alice Boner first in her work 'Principles of Composition' and later supported through the *Vastirepanisad* continues to be of significance. Thomas Maxwell's analysis of the Sarnath Buddha and now his continuing work on the *Visvarupa* is an extension of the approaches intiated by Stella Kramrisch and Alice Boner. With hesitation I may also refer to my own work in the 'Square and the Circle of the Indian Arts'. The identification of the implict geometry and the relationship of the point, line, shapes – circle, square, triangle – has been undoubtedly considered in the context of what is termed as Tantra Art, and Yantras, but what attention is being drawn to it is pervasive employment of a geometric grid full of meaning and significance at both the narrative and structural levels. Few young scholars appear to have ventured on this path of discerning the essential geometry within the work of art, which has the power of both containing meaning and evoking emotion. The grammar of the *Sutra-s, mana-s* and *bhenga-s* is a tool kit, but it is the individual artist who elaborates or departs from it or superimposes upon it to create a new whole, never of course violating the principle of the *bindu* and the *brahmasutra.*

If at the level of meaning it is myth and at the level of form it is sacred geometry, then the two together provide the basis for the evocation and containment of the metaphysical in symbolic form. The Natarāja image like the Brahadesvara temple is also the *gunas* and the *paneakratyas* and the manifestation of *Śṛisti, Sthiti* and *Sanghāra.*

So then what is the *Naṭarāja's* archaeology, history, myth, geometry, metaphysics or symbol? It is each of these, not to mention technology of metals and casing and more. In turn it evokes responses when in context of rituals, is the subject of liturgy, of music and dance. Tagore and Rodin respond unlike academic art historians with equal conviction and force. It is the art historian's responsibility and task to bring his/her analytical skills to a fruition in a manner that the whole, the multilayered and the polyvalent can be reinvoked. The art historian's final vocation is akin to the artist to evoke the *rasa,* the sap imaginable as experience, with all the concrete tools of scholarship. I have not with purpose brought into this presentation the role of theory and particularly the many dimensions of *rasa* as a theory. This would be another lecture.

The multilayering of the analysis of the Natarāja figure is equally applicable to the study of most Indian structures, specially temples. The work of scholars such as Michael W. Meister in the analysis of temple plans, such as Mundeswari, and others clearly shows that while there were some standard grids, the conceiver or the visualizer played with the basic form of the *Vastu Puruṣamandal* in a variety of ways. This gave rise to a very complex geometry, where circles were superimposed on squares and many other configurations were developed. What the Indian musician then does at the level of structure is parallel to what the Indian musician does with a given set of notes in a given *rāga*. Just as the Indian musician can improvise within a given structure of the *rāga* and the *tāla*, so also the Indian *stapathis* improvise on the basic types of geometrical grids given to him whether in the field of architecture or sculpture. This is the fascination. There is no time to now interrogate the problem area of what is called the *Śāstra* and the *Prayoga*.

Perhaps I should stop although I could go on. However, before concluding, there are one or two issues of the contemporary discourse which must be mentioned if not elucidated upon.

Among these is the issue of religions, secular, ascetic, erotic, sacred and profane. We have gone a long way from absolute dichotomies, but the issue is of continued importance notwithstanding the important contribution of Devananga Desai in respect of religious imagery and eroticism. She idealizes *Sandhyashesa* as an important factor. Much earlier Hazari Prasad Dwivedi had drawn attention to this. In a recent publication edited by Professor B.N. Goswami under the project of the History of Science, Civilization, there is a record of an animated discussion on the subject amongst Dr. Desai, Gulam Sheikh and Professor B.N.Goswami. This is relevant and illuminating. This dicourse again has to be situated not only within the discourse of the Indian tradition but also the discourse by western scholars ranging from Dr. Wendy O'Flaghtey to the writer of *Eye of Look* and the active debate in religious and ritual studies specially in USA. Alas there is no time to elucidate on it, except to say that the sacred-profane are not binary opposites in this tradition or for that matter many other mystical traditions. Indian Art reflects that as much the difference between attitudes to the body. How the art historian will distinguish between eroticism in Indian Art and the outrageous profanity of contemporary advertisements is not a matter totally out of place for modern urban sensibilities.

The other issue of great importance is that of anonymity vs. individuality. Dr. Salter's work and specially Prof. B.N. Goswami's work and of others in the context of Indian painting, Mughal, Rājasthāni and Pahāri, has indeed proved the presence of the stamp of excellence of the individual artist. This is as evident in the sculptures of Khajuraho as in paintings. When Coomaraswamy spoke of the tradition of anonymity, he was referring to another level. It was the attitude of the artist towards the artistic creation. Also, just as meditative techniques *Yoga* cannot be applied to the whole field of Indian art, that was the idea, so also while genealogies and individual creativity is important in any living tradition, *gharanas* and *sampradayas* of music, dance, painting, the art historian may and should recognize individual creativity and excellence and power of improvisation, new configuration and most of all establishment of new *sampradāya* or school as Nain Sukh or Sen, this is perhaps not identical with notions of individuality in confrontation with society or assertion of individuality as a modern art. This is another important area for further investigation.

Finally there is the question of inter-relationship of the arts and the parallel visual or aural image the artist makes from simile, metaphor. In Indian art, specially miniature painting, this identification is of essence as the work on the analysis of Nala Dayamanti or the several sets of Gita Govinda have convinced, particularly the Marwari *Gita Govinda.* But that will take us back to re-examine classificatory categories and the important question of the autonomy or interpenetration and interdependence of the arts. I promised not to speak about it.

I hope I have been able to touch upon some issues which preoccupy the young art historians' mind. There are no absolute answers, as there are no absolute categories in the Indian tradition. Flexibility Flax, continuity and change in concurrency is of essence. Art History is an exacting, engaging journey of a life time or more. No wonder the *Viṣṇudharmottara* story of the conversation between Vajra and Markandeya continues to be of relevance in the pedagogy of art criticism.

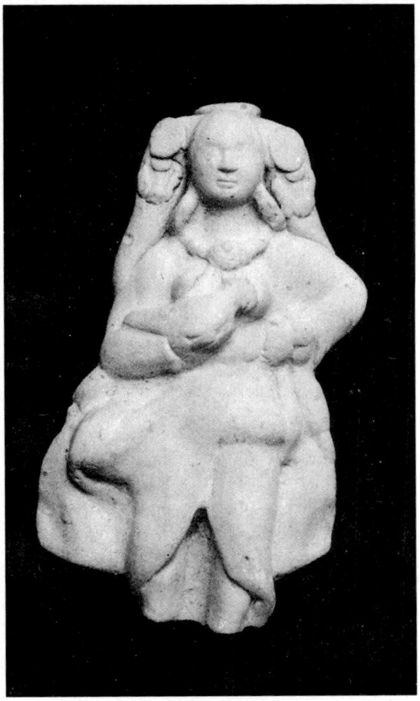

Pl. 1.1 Mauryan figurine, Chandraketugarh.

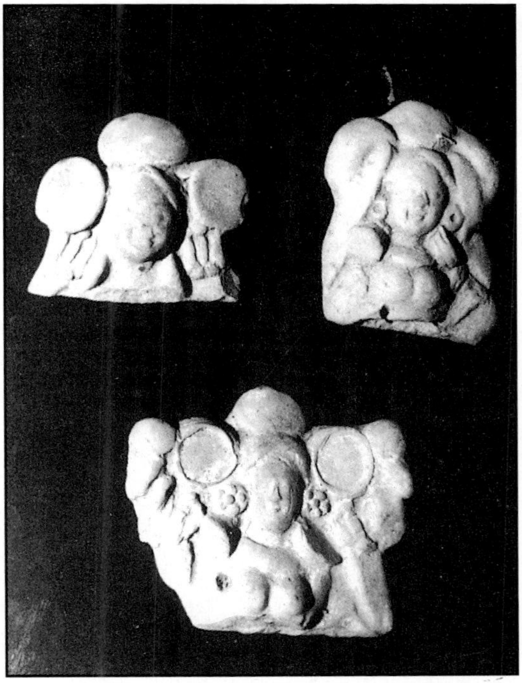

Pl. 1.2 Female heads, Chandraketugarh.

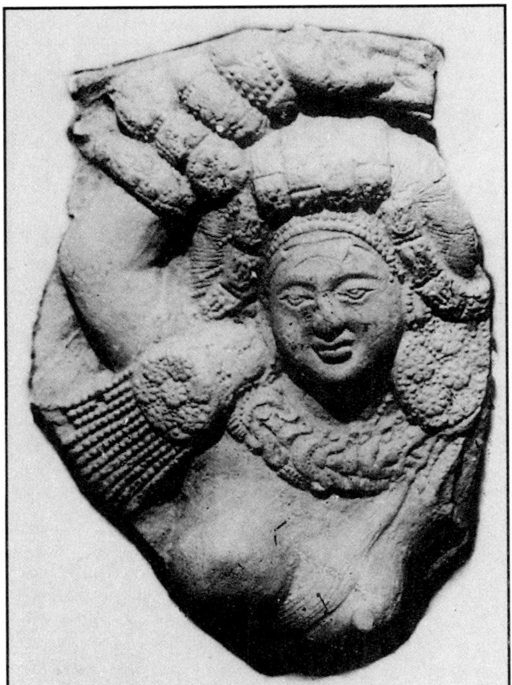

Pl. 1.3 Dancer, Chandraketugarh.

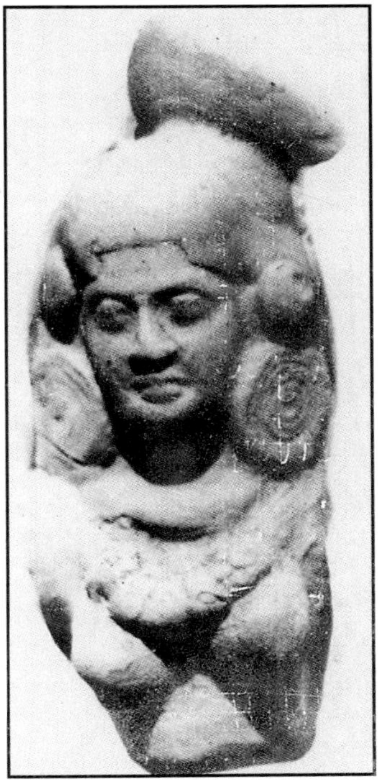

Pl. 1.4 Young damsel, Chandraketugarh.

Pl. 1.6 Male figure with bird, Chandraketugarh.

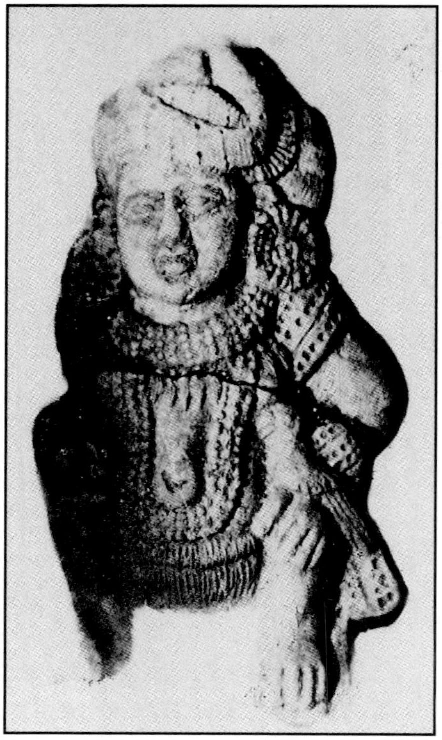

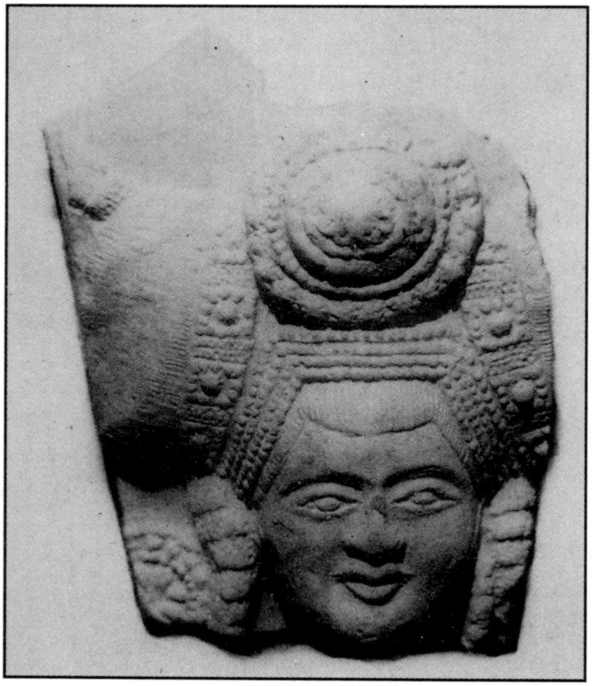

Pl. 1.5 Female head, Chandraketugarh.

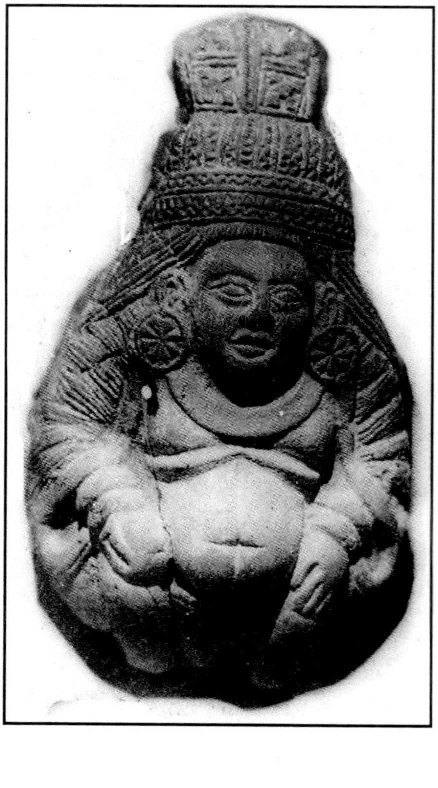

Pl. 1.7 Kuvera, Chandraketugarh.

Pl. 4.2 Rāvaṇānugraha, Kailāśa Temple (Cave 16), Ellora.

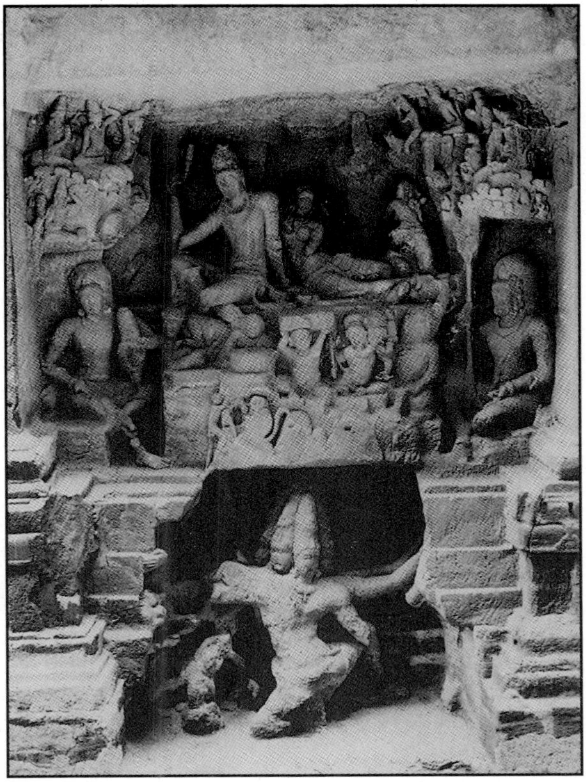

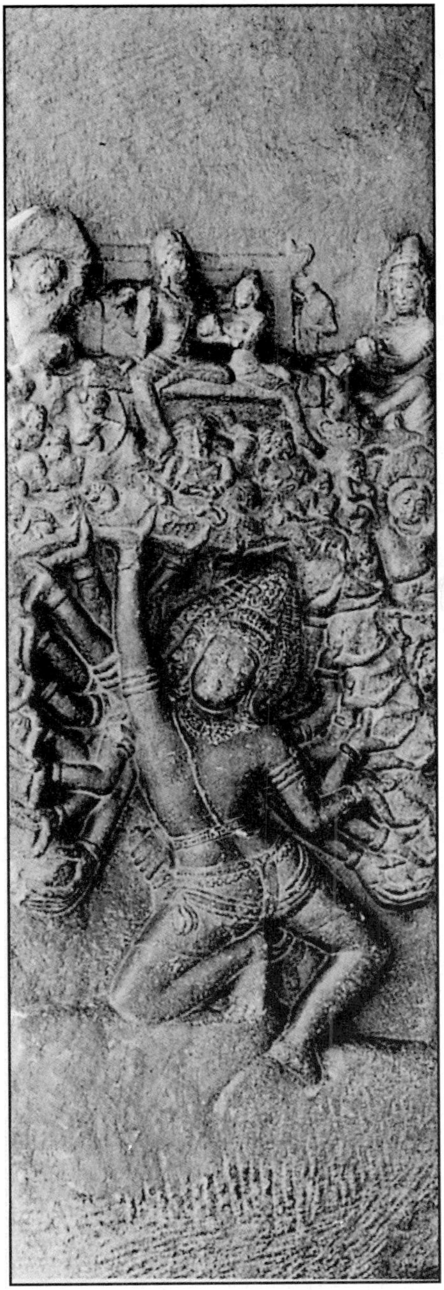

Pl. 4.1 Rāvaṇānugraha, Virupākśā Temple, Paṭṭaḍakal.

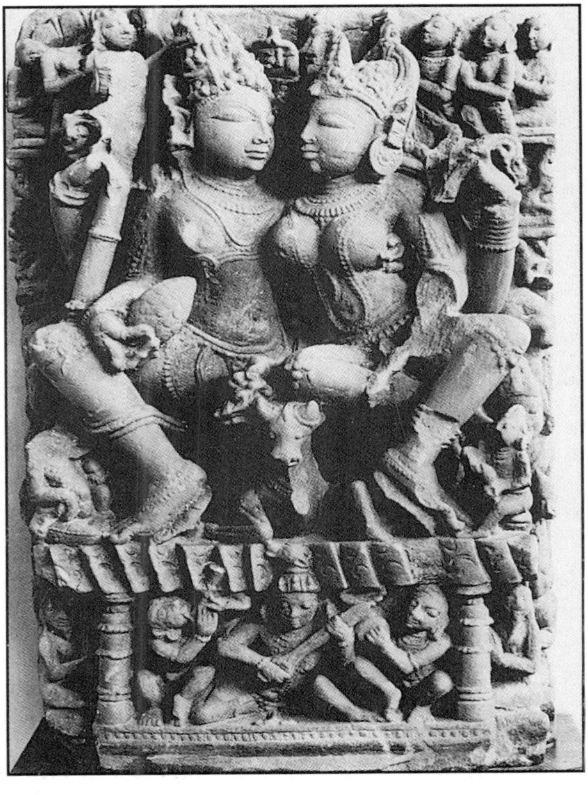

Pl. 4.3 Rāvaṇānugraha, Tevar (M.P.).

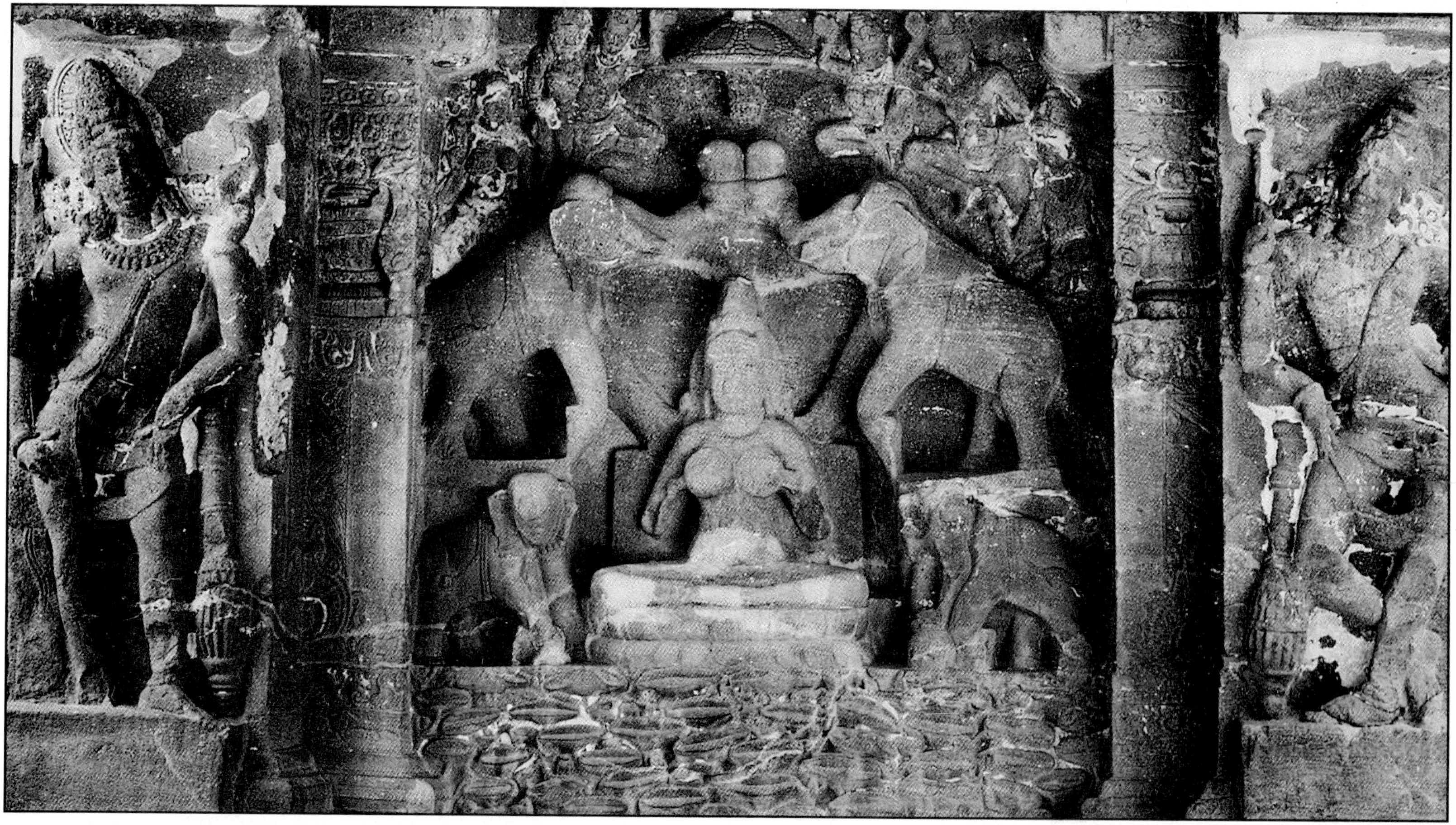

Pl. 5.1 Four elephants flanking Lakṣmī (KailāśaTemple).

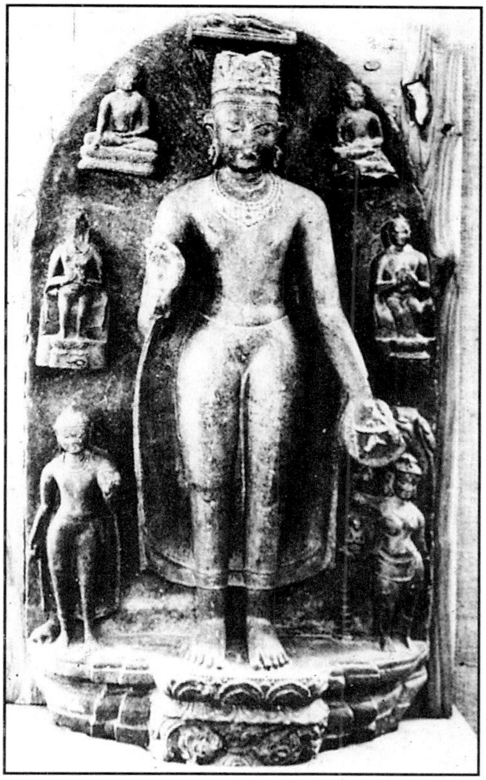

Pl. 8.1 Buddha with *mukuṭa* and ornaments, Bihar.

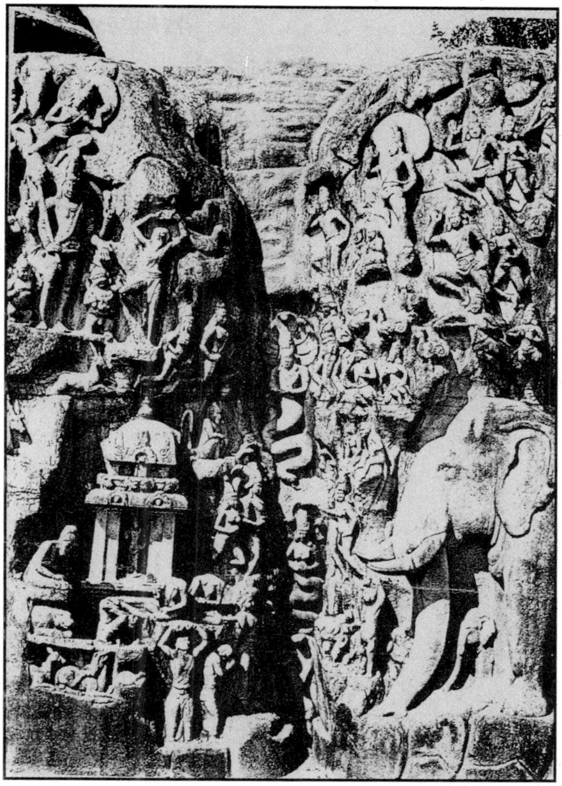

Pl. 8.3 Gaṅgāvataran panel, Mahabalipuram.

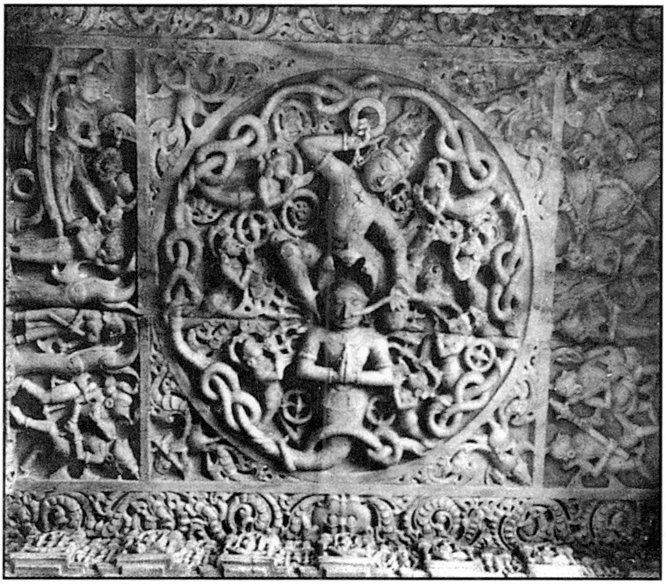

Pl. 8.2 Kaliyamardana scene, Vimala Vasahi, Delwara, Mt. Abu.

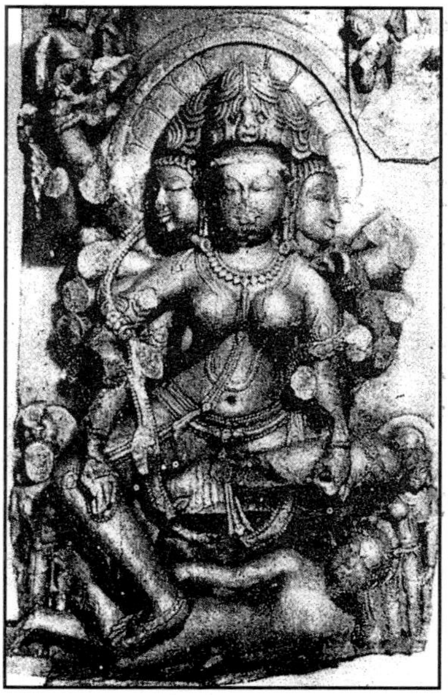

Pl. 10.1 Māheśvarī Trimurti, Hingalājagarh.

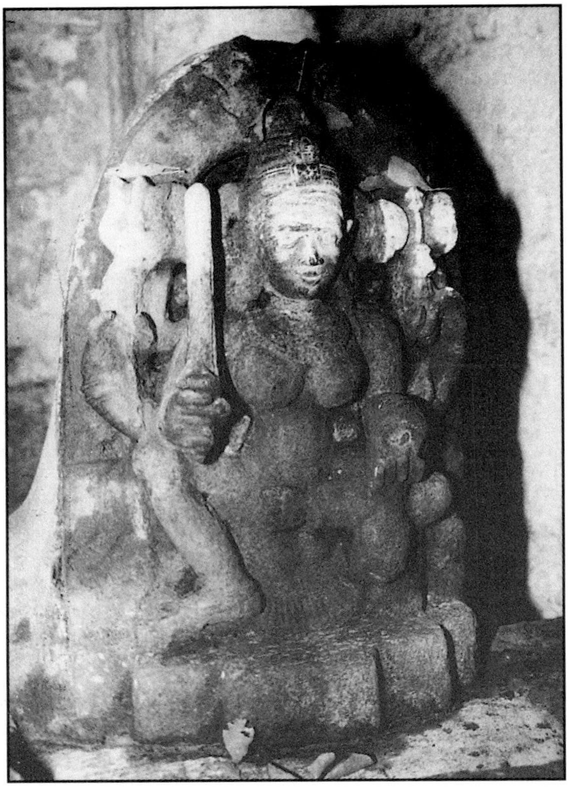

Pl. 11.1 Bhadrakālī, Vīrabhadra Temple.

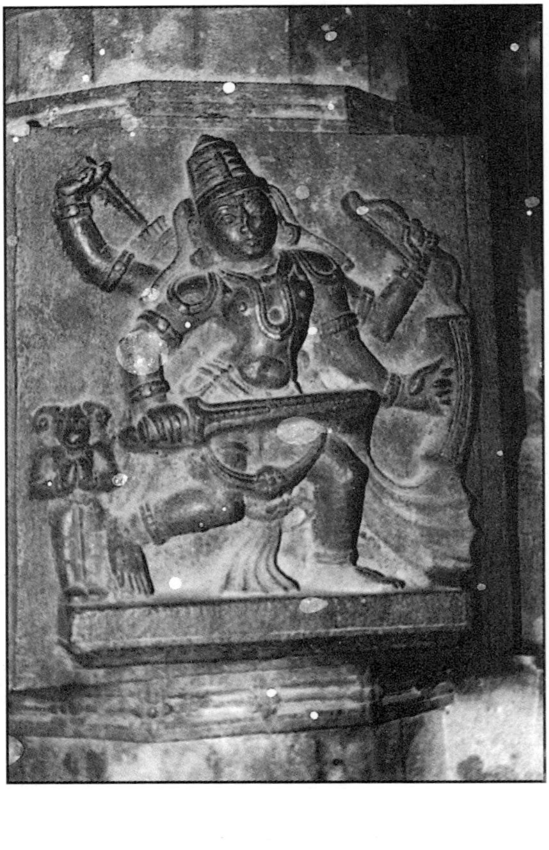

Pl. 11.2 Vīrabhadra.

Pl. 11.4 Markaṇḍeśvara Temple.

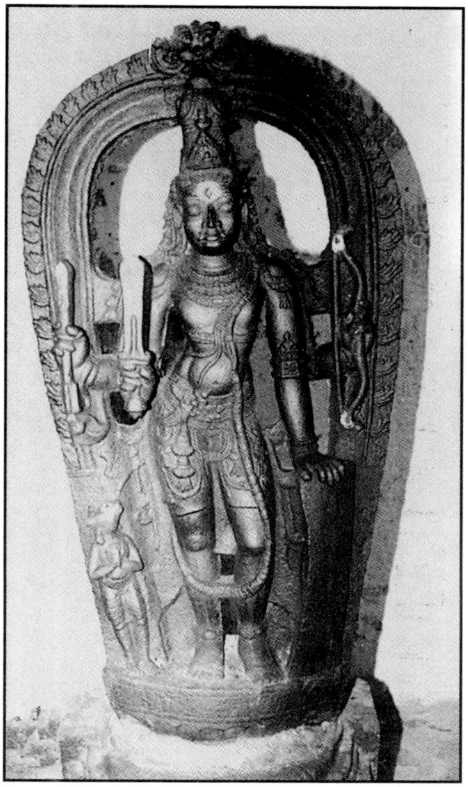

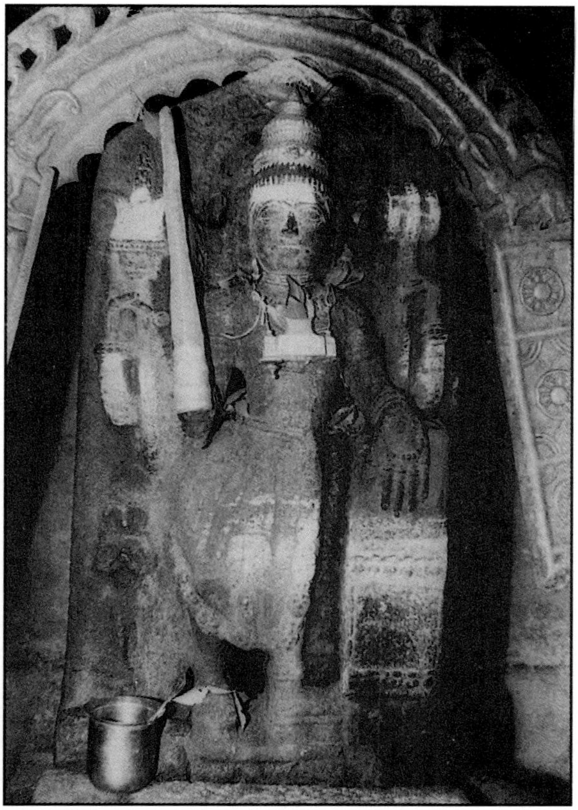

Pl. 11.3 Vīrabhadra.

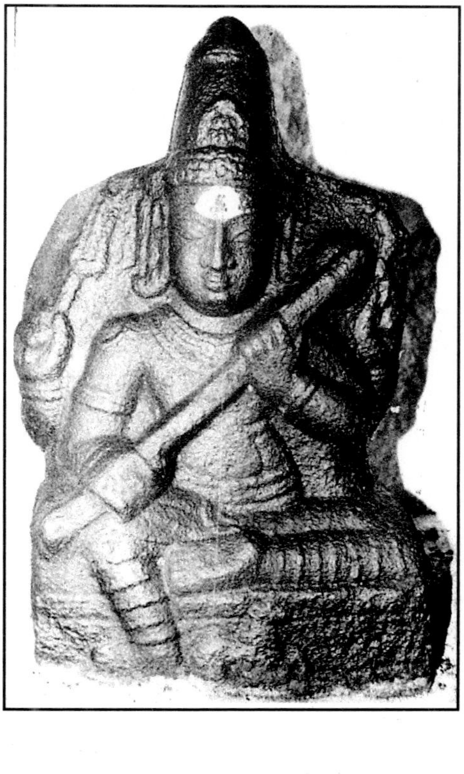

Pl. 11.5 Vīnādhara.

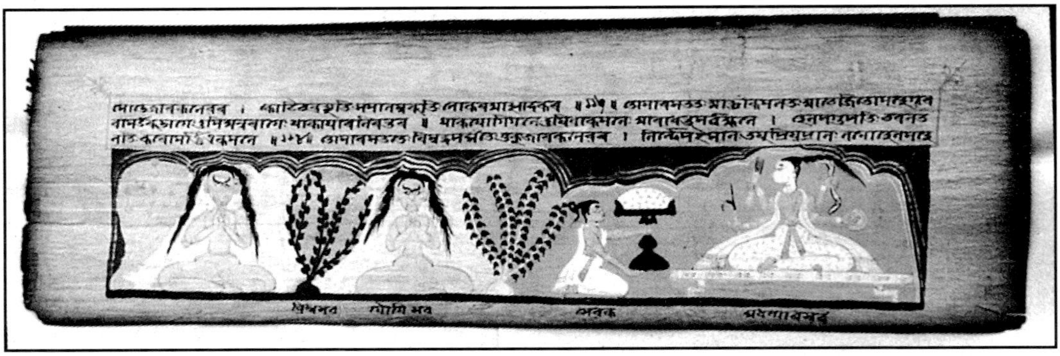

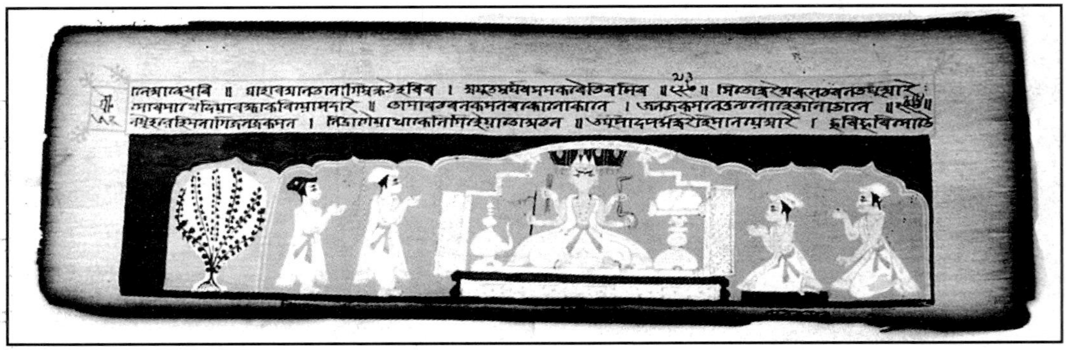

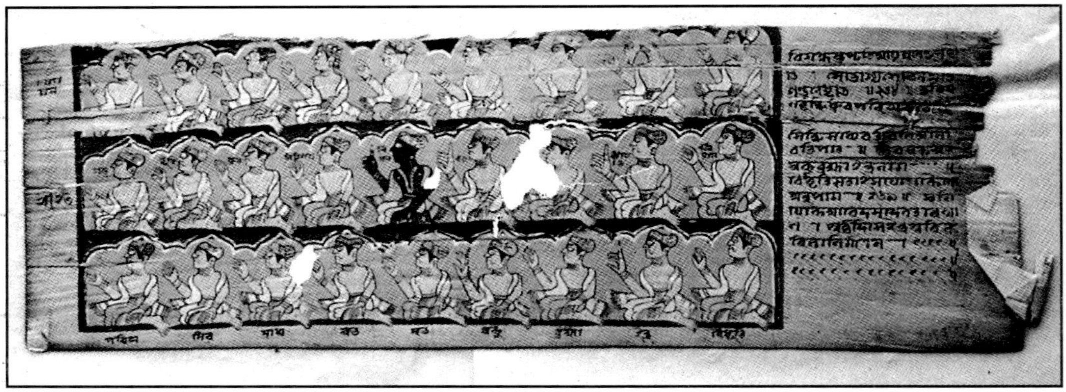

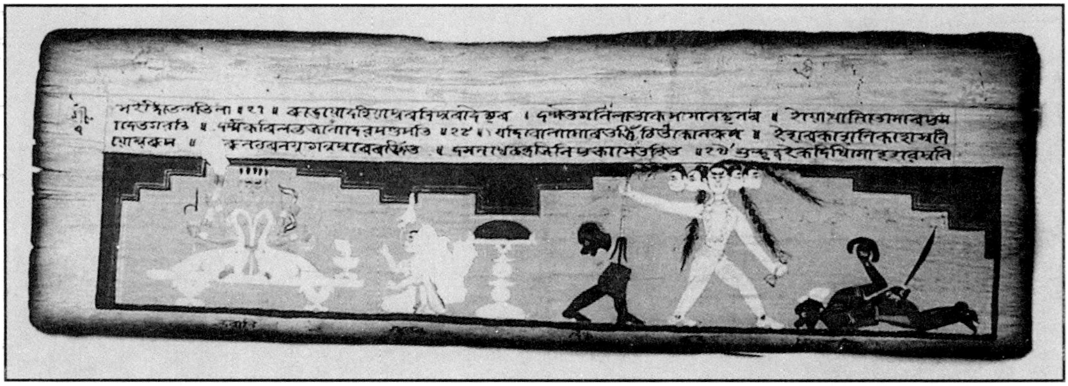

Pls. 15.1 – 15.4 Miniature paintings.

Pl. 17.2 Bust of human head.

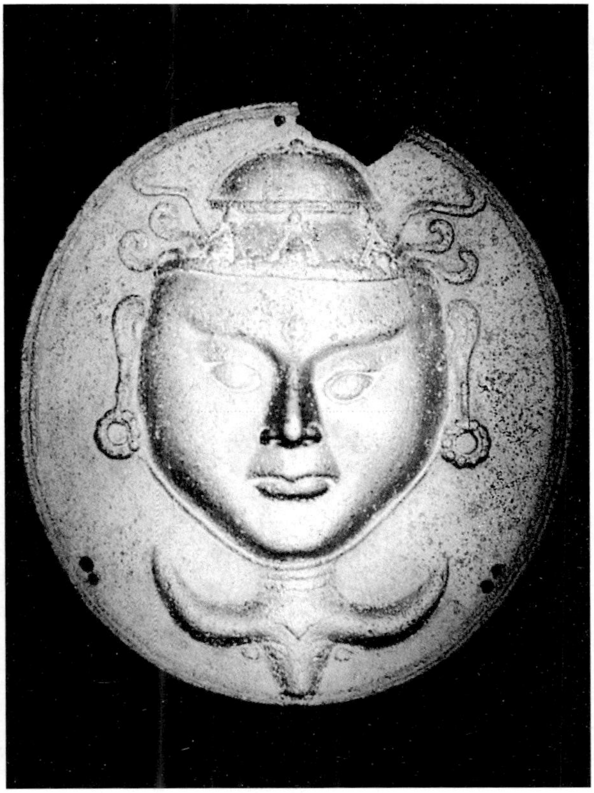

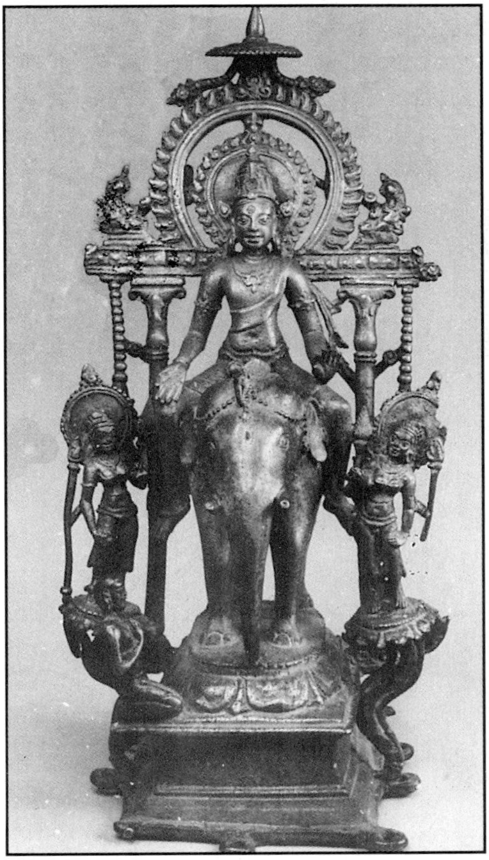

Pl. 17.1 Indra.

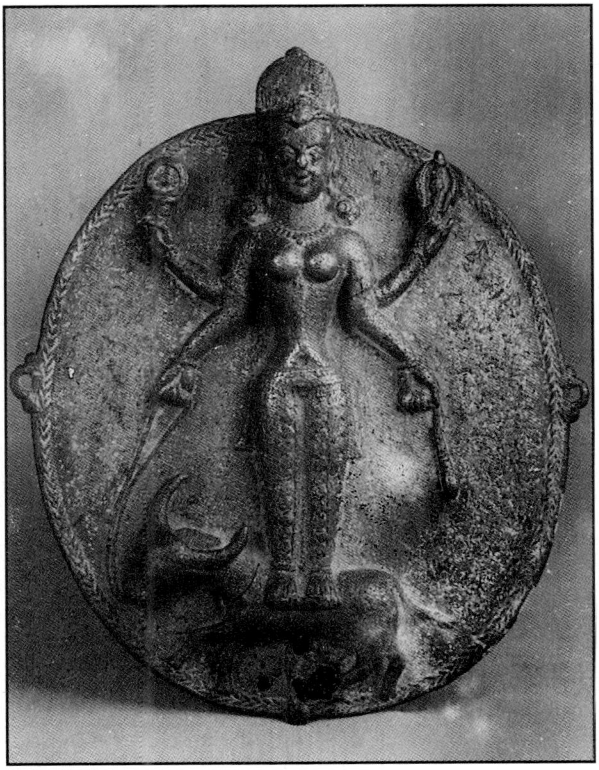

Pl. 17.3 Female deity.

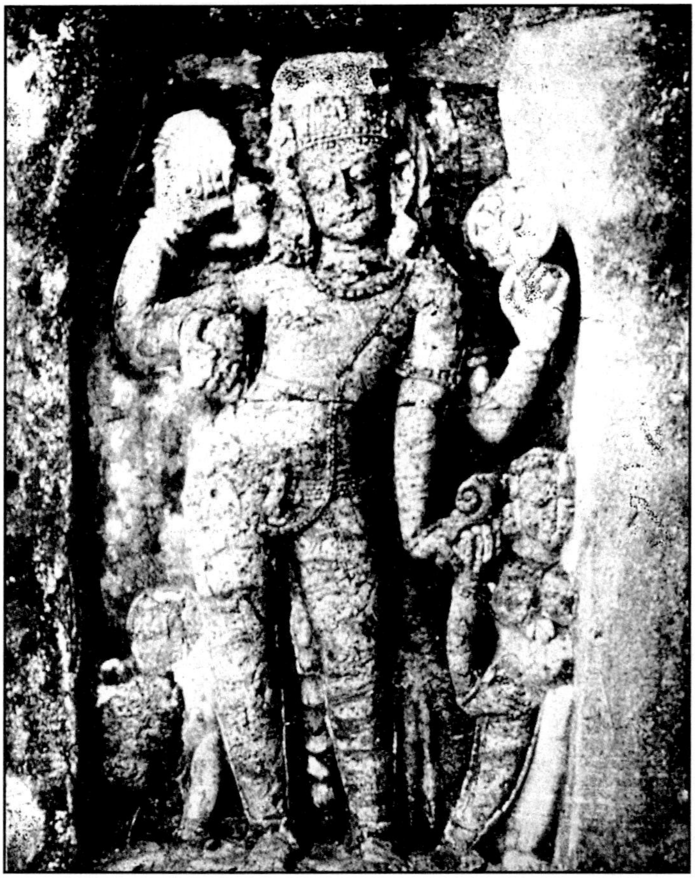

Pl. 19.1 Harihara, Madhukesvar Temple, Mukhalingam.

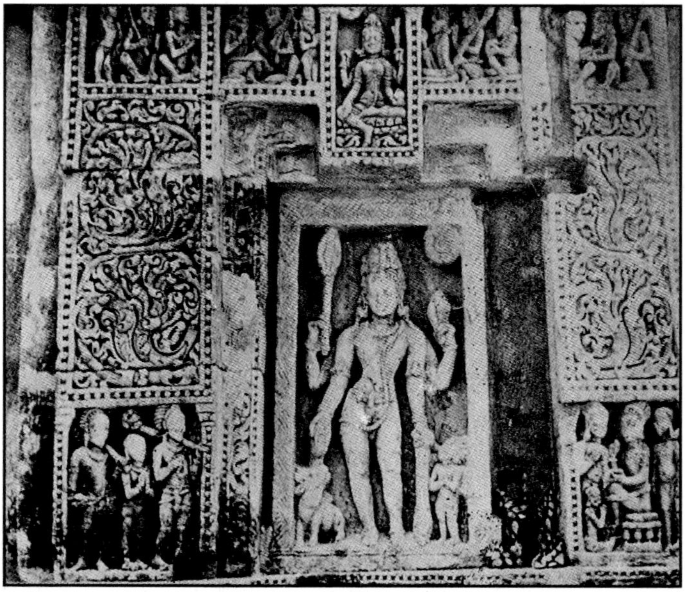

Pl. 19.2 Harihara, Somesvara Temple, Mukhalingam.

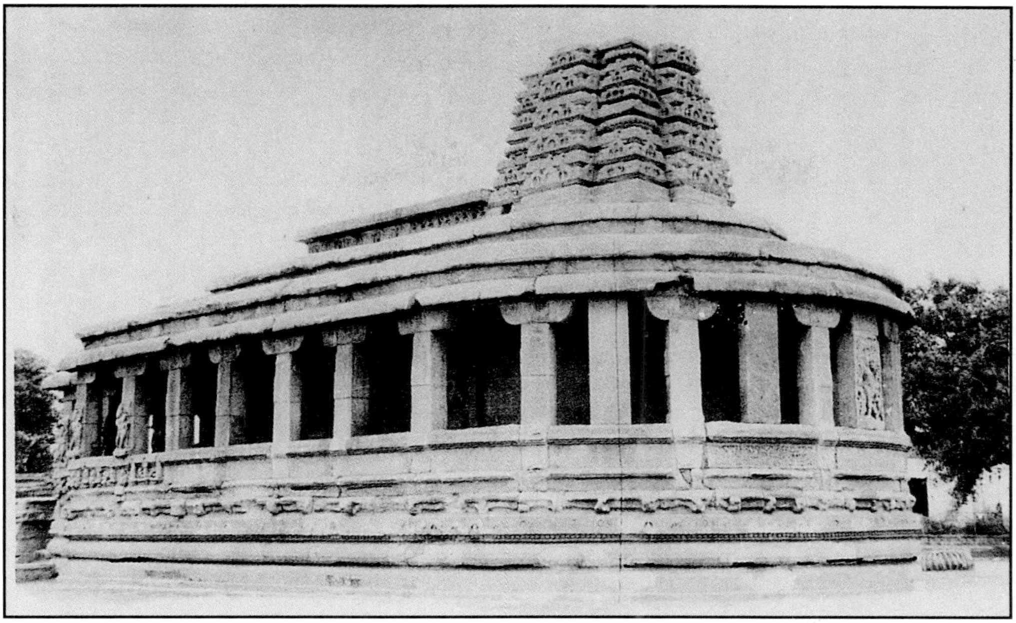

Pl. 22.1 Durgā Temple, Aihoḷe: General View.

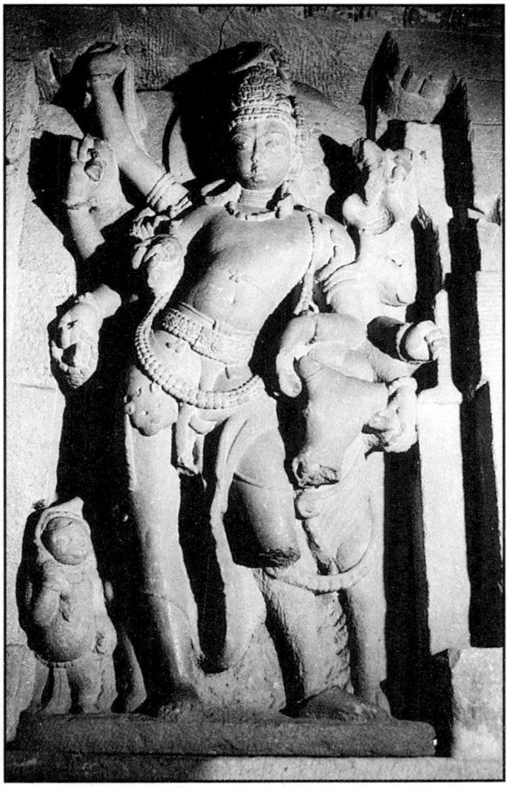

Pl. 22.2 Durgā Temple, Aihoḷe: Śiva-Vṛishabhāntikamūrti.

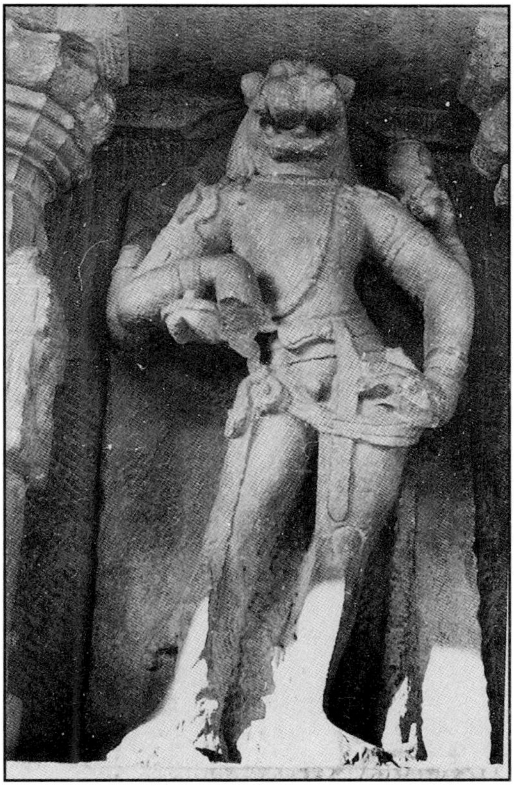

Pl. 22.3 Durgā Temple, Aihoḷe: Kevala Narasiṁha.

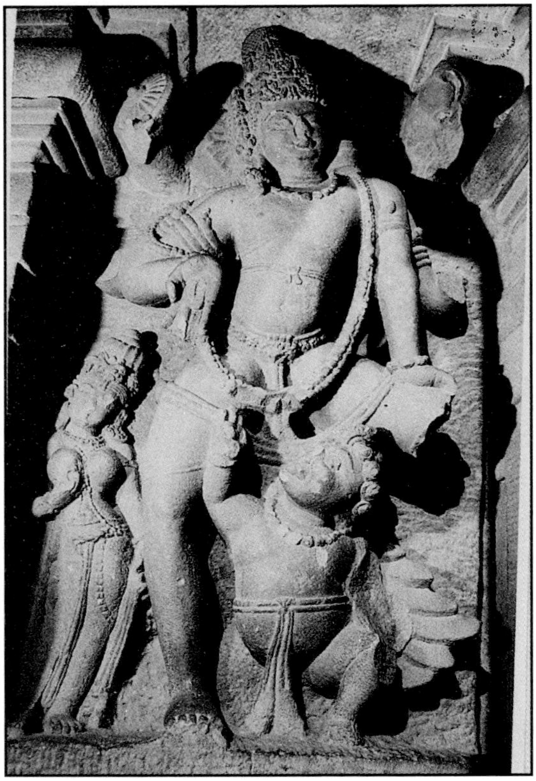

Pl. 22.4 Durgā Temple, Aihoḷe: Viṣṇu-Garuḍārūḍha.

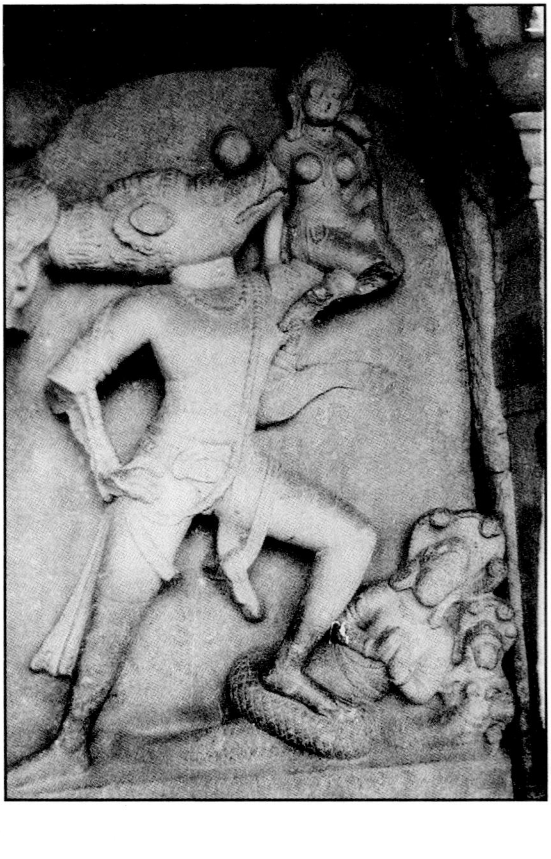

Pl. 22.5 Durgā Temple, Aihoḷe: Bhū-Varāha.

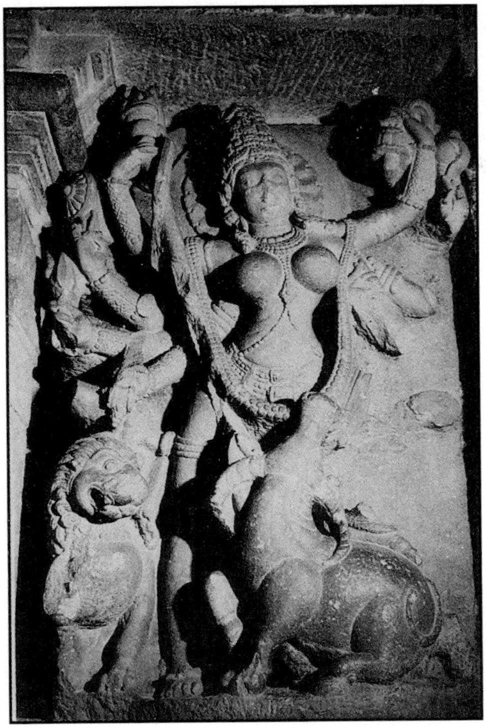

Pl. 22.6 Durgā Temple, Aihoḷe: Durgā Mahiśamardinī.

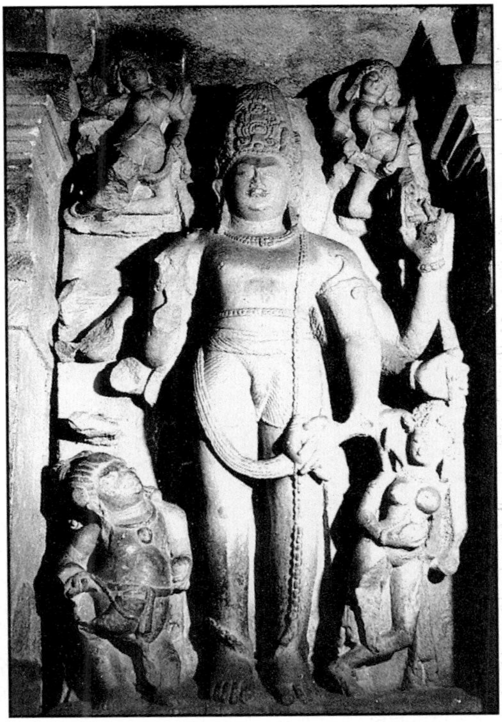

Pl. 22.7 Durgā Temple, Aihoḷe: Harihara.

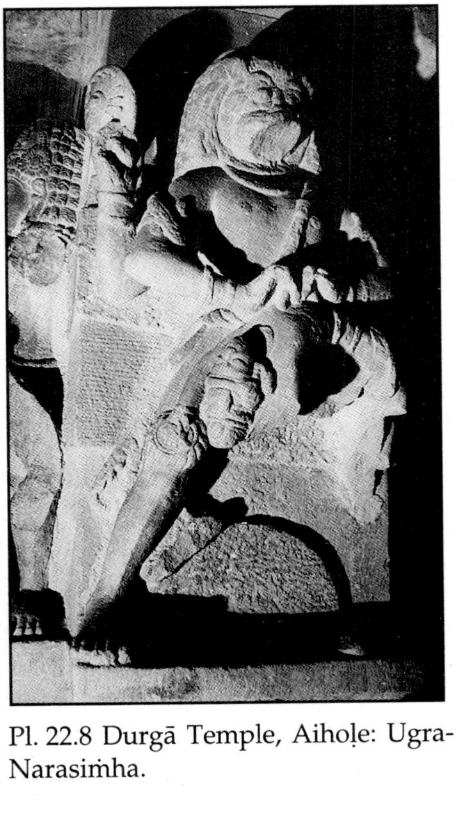

Pl. 22.8 Durgā Temple, Aihoḷe: Ugra-Narasiṁha.

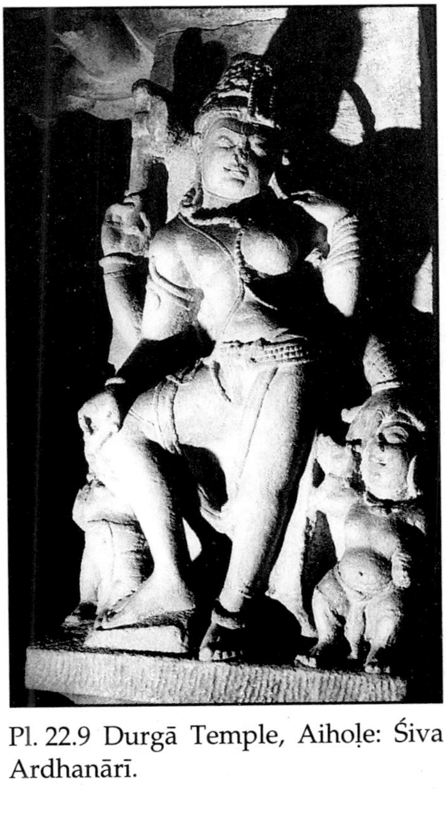

Pl. 22.9 Durgā Temple, Aihoḷe: Śiva Ardhanārī.

Pl. 22.11 Durgā Temple, Aihoḷe: Unidentified deity at position 27 on plan.

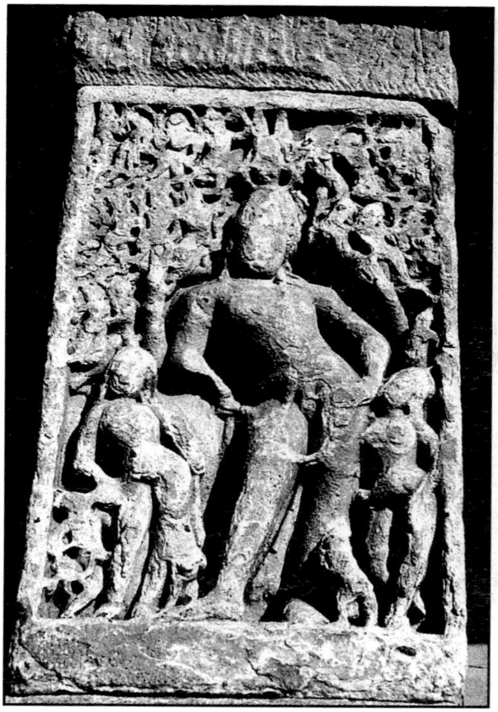

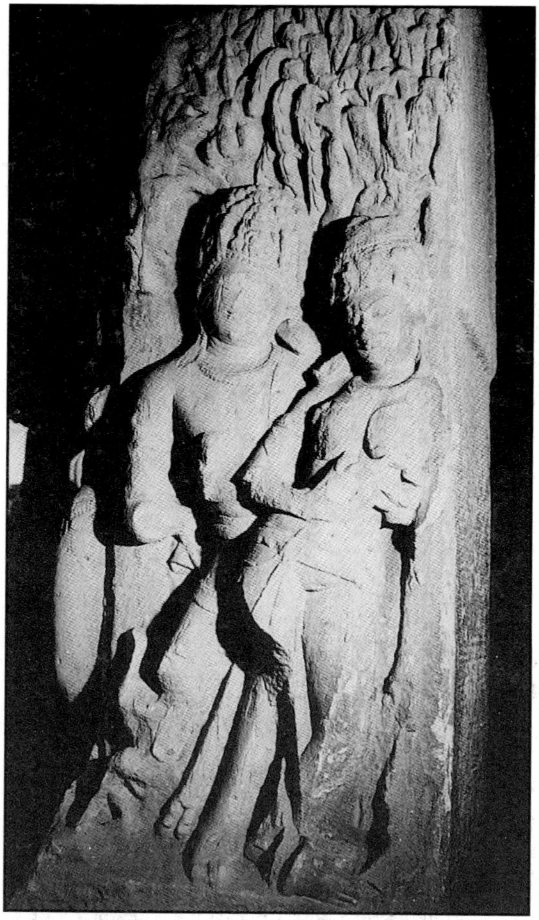

Pl. 22.10 Durgā Temple, Aihoḷe: *Daṁpatis* as *śṛingāra-mithuna* at position 17 on plan.

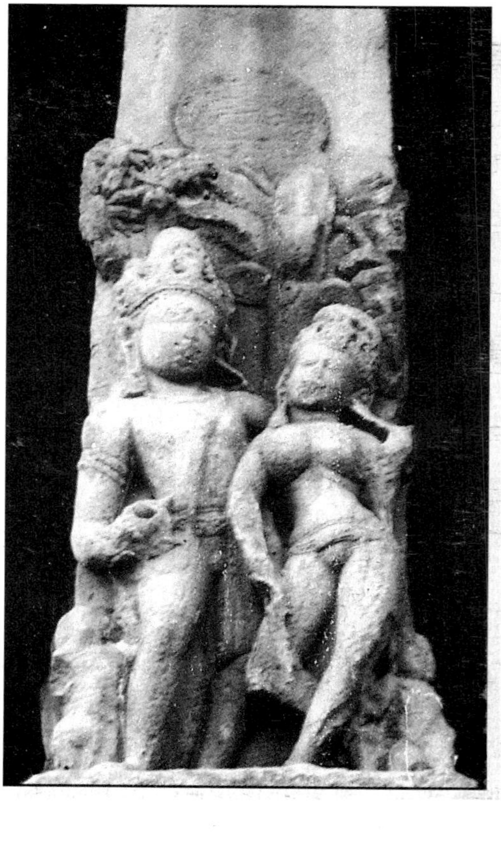

Pl. 22.12 Durgā Temple, Aihoḷe: *Daṁpatis* as *śṛingāra-mithuna* at position 15 on plan.

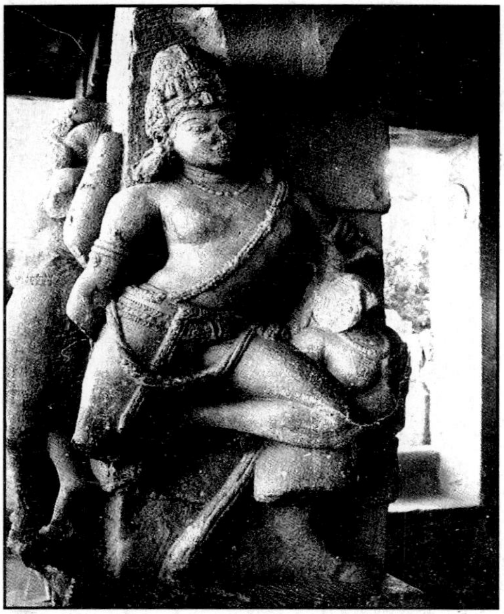

Pl. 22.14 Durgā Temple, Aihoḷe: Chastisement of Chhāyā at position 10 on plan.

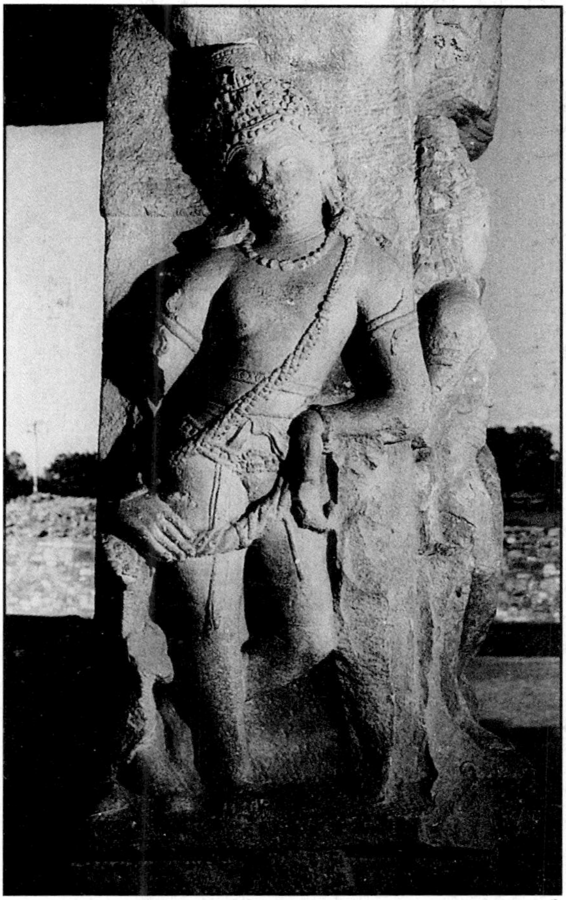

Pl. 22.13 Durgā Temple, Aihoḷe: Dvārapāla at position 11 on plan.

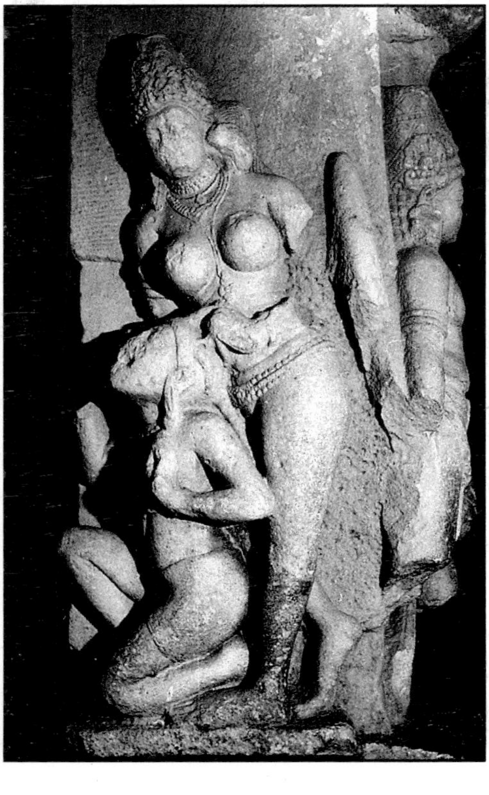

Pl. 22.15 Durgā Temple, Aihoḷe: *Yakṣī* seducing *Brahmachāri* at position 9 on plan.

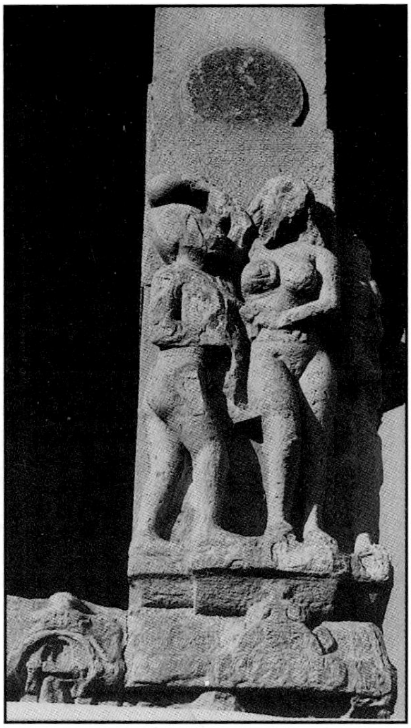

Pl. 22.16 Durgā Temple, Aihoḷe: *Aśvamukhī* haunting *Brahmachārī* at position 7 on plan.

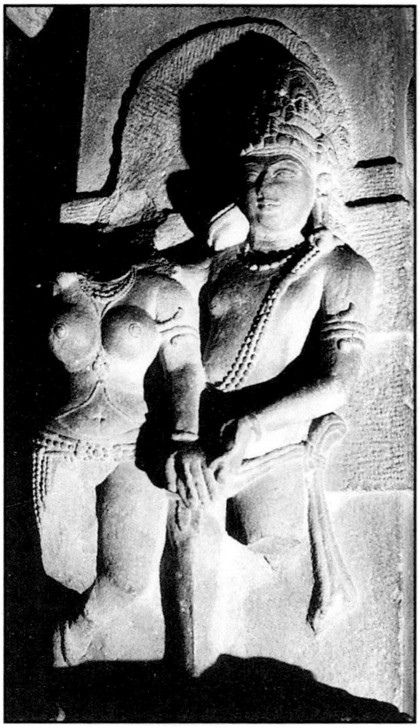

Pl. 22.18 Durgā Temple, Aihoḷe: *Daṁpatis* as *āsakta-mithuna* at position 21 on plan.

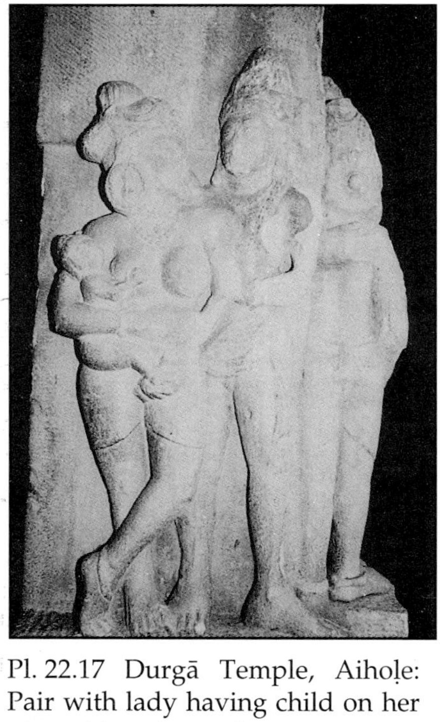

Pl. 22.17 Durgā Temple, Aihoḷe: Pair with lady having child on her at position 4 on plan.

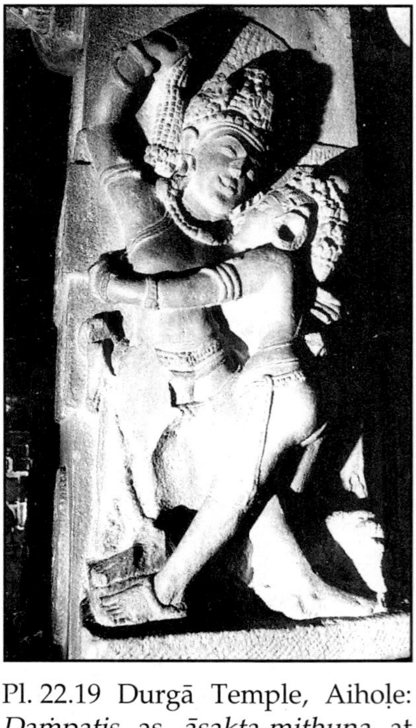

Pl. 22.19 Durgā Temple, Aihoḷe: *Daṁpatis* as *āsakta-mithuna* at position 26 on plan.